The Spiritual Awakeners

The Spiritual Awakeners

American Revivalists from Solomon Stoddard to D. L. Moody

by

Keith J. Hardman

MOODY PRESS
CHICAGO

© 1983 by
THE MOODY BIBLE INSTITUTE
OF CHICAGO

Library of Congress Cataloging in Publication Data

Hardman, Keith.
  The spiritual awakeners.

  Bibliography: p. 219
  1. Evangelists—United States—Biography.
2. Revivals—United States—History. I. Title.
BV3780.H37 1983   269'.2'0922 [B]   83-934
ISBN: 0-8024-0177-5

1 2 3 4 5 6 7 Printing/EB/Year 87 86 85 84 83

Printed in the United States of America

To Jean

Contents

Preface

The last two hundred years have witnessed history's most massive intellectual assaults against Christianity. Repeatedly, its enemies have accompanied their assaults with predictions that Christianity was an anachronism needing any little blast at all to collapse ignominiously. But under those many attacks, instead of collapsing, Christianity responded with impressive resiliency and adaptability.

Much of this resilience has been in the form of awakenings in various lands: Indonesia, Korea, India, Africa, the United States, Norway, the British Isles, Germany, Manchuria, the Ukraine, Hawaii, and elsewhere. But history has not dealt fairly with the awakenings of Christianity. For the most part secular historians have been unmindful of them, except in general terms. The long-term influences stemming from awakenings also have generally gone unnoticed.

Such secular neglect has been particularly true of awakenings in American history. From revivals a large number of beneficial by-products have flowed into the country's life: the founding of educational institutions, impulses toward reform on a dozen fronts, the bolstering of morality, the evangelizing of a wild frontier, and so on. Yet when attention was given by secular historians or reporters, they all too often seized upon a few eccentrics and from them projected a totally false stereotype of the revivalist. Many people, including great numbers within the churches, smile with bemused toleration when the subject of awakenings is mentioned today. Most people have no desire for accurate information or an unbiased portrayal. Nevertheless, there has always been a curiosity and fascination about awakenings, something of a grudging admiration for a venerable phenomenon.

That which follows is an attempt to set forth a survey of the great sweep of awakenings that occurred in America until 1900 and to alert contemporary Christians to the great heritage the church possesses in those movements. The difficulties of covering several centuries and many leaders in one volume are great, and this is certainly the reason a survey of America's awakenings has seldom been attempted. For instance, one might question the wisdom of giving Solomon Stoddard an entire chapter when the numerical results of his "harvests" were relatively few, whereas the mighty Third Awakening of 1858 is covered more briefly, despite its bringing over one million converts into the churches. But if Stoddard had not pressed his methodology in the cause of revival on the churches of that day, the entire future of awakenings might have been quite different. Who, other than the omniscient Lord, can say? And yet there was arguably that possibility. Jonathan Edwards was greatly influenced by his grandfather Stoddard's theories and success. Seventy years later, when New England was again losing many church members, Timothy Dwight was greatly influenced by *his* grandfather's (Jonathan Edwards) theories and success. Thus, several of Stoddard's descendants played monumental roles in the history of awakenings. So, beyond raw statistics and mere historical recounting, there is the intriguing account of significant awakeners' works and influences and, preeminently, of God's mysterious ways. Within the limitations of space, I have tried to convey each of these aspects.

This work has grown out of doctoral dissertation research done at the University of Pennsylvania. Since those pleasant days, my interest in the whole field of awakenings has continued to grow. Without attempting to name all those to whom I am indebted for encouragement and assistance, I must thank Dr. J. Edwin Orr, a foremost authority on awakenings, whose seminars on the subject at Oxford University I have attended with much profit. I also appreciate the supportive and expert editing I have received from Moody Press. Mr. Philip Rawley is an editor of sensitivity, skill, and graciousness, and the manuscript has profited much from his aid. Many colleagues in the academic world have been helpful, as well as librarians at Princeton University, Haverford College, Yale University, Oberlin College, the University of Pennsylvania, Williams College, Princeton Theological Seminary, Ursinus College, the Presbyterian Historical Society, Columbia University, and the Historical Society of Pennsylvania. For some years the interest of numerous of my students has heightened my own interest in prominent leaders and awakenings. I have appreciated their lively curiosity. Thanks are also due to Mr. and Mrs. Charles E. Sharpe for much encouragement, skillful typing, and sage advice.

In dedicating this volume to my wife, Jean, I have tried to express a small measure of my gratitude to her. She has been of incalculable help in many ways.

Introduction

In the last century historians have advanced several notable methods of interpreting history to explain trends and reactions in Europe and America. In 1913 a Frenchman, Elie Halévy, wrote his classic work *England in 1815*. In it he considered the stability and permanence of English society and institutions during the period 1750-1815, as contrasted with the turmoil and instability of his native France before and after its Revolution. After years of studying the subject Halévy advanced his famous Halévy Thesis that between 1789 and 1815, when the demons of revolution and bloodshed tormented the Continent, England was spared the revolution toward which many factors seemed to be bringing her. The stabilizing influences of the Evangelical Awakening,[1] a massive revival of English Protestantism, was a major factor in preventing a French-style revolution. With the conversion of souls effects of the revival merely began, Halévy argued; it was the social concern of the new Christians, putting into practice Christ's compassion for the poor and needy, that in large measure raised English society from the low and depraved state of earlier years, and kept revolution at bay.

Why was it that of all the countries of Europe, England has been the most free from revolutions, violent crises, and sudden changes? We have sought in vain to find the explanation by an analysis of her political institutions and economic organization. Her political institutions were

---

1. Elie Halévy, *The Birth of Methodism in England,* ed. Bernard Semmel (Chicago: U. of Chicago, 1971), p. 1. See also Wellman J. Warner, *The Wesleyan Movement in the Industrial Revolution* (New York: Russell, 1967), pp. 61-72, 281.

such that society might easily have lapsed into anarchy had there existed in England a bourgeoisie animated by the spirit of revolution. . . . . But the elite of the working class, the hard-working and capable bourgeois, had been imbued by the evangelical movement with a spirit from which the established order had nothing to fear. . . . In the vast work of social organization which is one of the dominant characteristics of nineteenth-century England, it would be difficult to overestimate the part played by the Wesleyan revival.[2]

The early Methodists' success in ministering to the poverty-stricken of England and organizing many of them into decent, law-abiding communities was only one of their achievements. In addition, the revival was instrumental in sensitizing the consciences of a number of prominent political figures who then worked for many reforms. "Among all the reforms of which the Evangelical party were justly proud," Halévy stated, "the most glorious was the abolition of the slave trade."[3] Christian laymen such as the brilliant William Wilberforce (1759-1833), who led the forces of the abolition party in Parliament for twenty years, thus carried their spiritual convictions into every realm of life, working for the cause of human betterment.

Have theories similar to Halévy's been advanced for the awakenings in American history? When we come to America, the problem is more complex. From America's beginnings, there was a general adherence to Christian ideals, which were never put in such jeopardy as was experienced during the crisis in eighteenth-century England. Still, there are scholars who have argued that many of the finest impulses of social reform and action in American history have flowed from times of awakening.

The first of these, the Great Awakening of 1740-1745, provides sufficient examples. Most scholars would agree with Richard Bushman that "A psychological earthquake had reshaped the human landscape"[4] in those years. It was probably inevitable. Perry Miller, the leading intellectual historian of America, saw the Great Awakening as "the end of the reign over the New England and American mind of a European and scholastical conception of an authority put over men because men were incapable of recognizing their own welfare. . . . What was awakened in 1740," Miller observed, "was the

2. Elie Halévy, *England in 1815* (New York: Peter Smith, 1949), pp. 424-25.
3. Ibid., p. 455.
4. Richard L. Bushman, *From Puritan to Yankee: Character and Social Order in Connecticut, 1690-1775* (Cambridge, Mass.: Harvard U., 1967), p. 187.

spirit of American democracy."[5] Winthrop Hudson in *Religion in America* has agreed.

> And because the Awakening was general, it played an important role in forming a national consciousness among people of different colonies whose primary ties were with Europe rather than with one another. As a spontaneous movement which swept across all colonial boundaries, generated a common interest and a common loyalty, bound people together in a common cause, and reinforced the conviction that God had a special destiny in store for America, the Awakening contributed greatly to the development of a sense of cohesiveness among the American people. It was more influential in this respect than all the colonial wars the colonists were called upon to fight, more influential in fact than many of the political squabbles they had had with the mother country since the latter as often served to separate as to unite them. Whitefield, Tennent, and Edwards were rallying names for Americans a full three decades before Washington, Jefferson, Franklin, and Samuel Adams became familiar household names.[6]

Hudson then goes on to give other beneficial effects of the Great Awakening, apart from church growth and membership increases: institutional consequences, such as the rejuvenation of higher education and the founding of colleges; the birth of the missionary spirit, especially to the Indians; and the heightened roles of both clergy and laity.[7]

When we come to the Second Great Awakening (1790-1840), a different and much more massive social concern is seen to arise. As Donald G. Mathews has said, the Second Awakening brought forth "a general social movement that organized thousands of people into small groups. . . . Its expansion was in large part the work of a dedicated corps of charismatic leaders who proposed to change the moral character of America. . . . Mobilizing Americans in unprecedented numbers, it had the power to shape part of our history."[8] Now largely unknown even to Christians, this united crusade to respond to numerous needs of society has been called the "Benevolence Empire." It was awe-inspiring in its scope. Antislavery, wom-

5. Alan Heimert and Perry Miller, eds., *The Great Awakening: Documents Illustrating the Crisis and Its Consequences* (Indianapolis: Bobbs-Merrill, 1967), p. lxi.
6. Winthrop S. Hudson, *Religion in America,* 3d ed. (New York: Scribner's, 1981), pp. 76-77. Reprinted with the permission of Charles Scribner's Sons.
7. Ibid., pp. 77-82. See also Sydney E. Ahlstrom, *A Religious History of the American People* (New Haven, Conn.: Yale U., 1972), pp. 287-94.
8. Donald G. Mathews, "The Second Great Awakening as an Organizing Process, 1780-1830: An Hypothesis," *American Quarterly* 21, no. 1 (Spring 1969):30-31.

en's rights, temperance, prison reform, Scripture distribution, missions, tract distribution, and pacifism were but a few of the concerns. In the first three decades of the nineteenth century thousands of Christian societies were organized, and innumerable Americans set themselves to the tasks of erecting what they were convinced would become an empire of benevolence in which Christ would rule His obedient people for a thousand years of peace. The financial giving that supported such causes was enormous when we calculate the giving in terms of today's currency.[9] By 1834 the annual income of the fourteen leading societies had risen to nearly 9 million dollars per year, or an equivalent of 135 million dollars in today's currency. And this was for a nation with a total population of fourteen million.

In Timothy L. Smith's award-winning study, *Revivalism and Social Reform: American Protestantism on the Eve of the Civil War,* he argues forcefully that "If God seemed near in nineteenth-century America, it was not because an elite circle of theologians read Darwin's book on *The Descent of Man.* It was rather due to the fact that in countless revivals the 'tongue of fire' had descended on the disciples, freeing them from the bondage of sin and selfishness, and dedicating them to the task of making over the world."[10] With solid documentation, Smith demonstrates that direct links connected the social gospel, which appeared later in the century, with the evangelical reform movements stemming from the revivalist Charles G. Finney (1792-1875) and the other reformers who preceded or were converted by Finney.

> It is incorrect, of course, to suppose that liberal Christians and rational men who rejected religious sentiments were in all cases less interested in the plight of the poor. . . . But the preponderance of wealth and numbers was on the side of the evangelicals. The power which earliest opposed the organized evils of urban society and stretched out hands of mercy to help the poor was sanctified compassion. Glowing hopes for the establishment of the kingdom of Christ on earth lighted its way. "Infidelity makes a great outcry about its philanthropy," growled the conservative *New York Observer* in 1855, "but religion does the work."[11]

The preceding is but a sampling of scholarly opinion regarding the

---

9. A multiplication by fifteen will yield estimated equivalents of the contemporary value.

10. Timothy L. Smith, *Revivalism and Social Reform; American Protestantism on the Eve of the Civil War* (New York: Harper & Row, 1965), p. 162.

11. Ibid., p. 176.

connections between awakenings and social reform from 1740 to 1860. Many revivalists during those years and later saw their role to be primarily in preaching the gospel and overseeing the conversion of the lost, and they believed that if they became reformers as well, no matter how desperate the needs of society, they would dilute their mission and wander off into secondary imperatives. They assumed, and often preached, that converted and enlightened laymen would take up the sanctified causes of their times. Finney, for example, saw his mission principally as an evangelist, not as a reformer,[12] but throughout his *Lectures on Revivals of Religion* he demanded that all Christians be involved in the warfare against all forms of evil.

> Young converts should be *trained to labor* just as carefully as young recruits in an army are trained for war. Suppose a captain in the army should get his company enlisted, and then take no more pains to teach and train, and discipline them, than are taken by many pastors to train and lead forward their young converts. Why, the enemy would laugh at such an army. Call them soldiers! . . . Take the subject of tracts, or missions, or Sabbath Schools, or temperance, for instance—what cavils, and objections, and resistance, and opposition, have been encountered from members of the churches in different places. Go through the churches, and where you find young converts have been well taught, you never find *them* making difficulty, or raising objections, or putting forth cavils. . . . It is curious to see how ready young converts are to take right ground on any subject that may be proposed. See what they are willing to do for the education of ministers, for missions, moral reform, or for the slaves![13]

Interestingly, Finney's passion for the salvation of souls coupled with his intense moral zeal enabled him to be enormously successful in both evangelism and reform. "Finney probably won as many converts to the cause [of abolition] as William Lloyd Garrison, even though he shunned the role of political agitator for that of a winner of souls."[14]

Others involved with past awakenings were in their minds unable to separate the compulsion to preach the gospel to every creature from their determination to alleviate human misery in its many forms. Samuel J. Mills (1783-1818) is an excellent example of this broad approach to mankind's needs, for in his brief lifetime he made

---

12. Ibid., p. 149.
13. Charles G. Finney, *Revivals of Religion* (Westwood, N.J.: Revell, 1951), pp. 484-85, 487.
14. Smith, p. 180.

great contributions to the evangelization of the American West and to the furtherance of world missions, and then turned to temporal concerns in helping to found Liberia, the African colony for freed slaves.

Still other revivalists were silent on the ills of society, concentrating their efforts almost entirely on evangelism. George Whitefield (1714-1770), for example, accepted slavery and did not preach or work against it, although he did attack the cruelty of some slave owners as "masters of Barbarity."[15]

What has been surveyed above are some of the measurable results of the revivals of recent times. For Christians, many of the accomplishments will be known only in the next life. But these are the results, and not the thing itself. We now turn to the definition of revival.

Revival, the periodic restoration of God's people after a time of indifference and decline, is a principle firmly taught in the Word of God (see, for example, Psalm 85:6; 138:7; Isaiah 57:15; Habakkuk 3:2). In the Scriptures, revival came to the Israelites under King Asa (2 Chronicles 15), under King Jehoash (2 Kings 11-12), under King Hezekiah (2 Kings 18), and especially under King Josiah (2 Kings 22-23), at the time of Zerubbabel (Ezra 5-6), and under Nehemiah (Nehemiah 8-9, 13). In the New Testament, revival came upon God's people at Pentecost (Acts 2), which was to be the paradigm for all awakenings, and again in Acts 4:23-37, which prepared the infant church for the fierce persecutions to come.

In the face of these examples, it is difficult to deny that Scripture holds forth on the one hand a state of awakened zeal and spiritual growth for God's people as the ideal to pray toward, while at the same time teaching by implication that a cyclical alternation between decline and new life is to be expected. It is not that the Holy Spirit cannot sustain the higher life for Christians; it is rather that the Spirit allows times of declension to cause His people to pray for renewal.

Awakenings for the universal church of Christ are therefore not isolated phenomena or chance happenings in the convulsions of various societies, admitting no laws and each isolated in cause and effect from the rest. Although sociology and the study of history do

---

15. An excellent description of the attitudes of Christians to social problems is found in John D. Woodbridge, Mark A. Noll, and Nathan O. Hatch, *The Gospel in America* (Grand Rapids: Zondervan, 1979), pp. 225-47.

not normally consider the workings of God, it is interesting to note that some contemporary theories in these fields substantiate and are compatible with Christian ideas depicting the workings of the Divine among men. In his book *Revivals: Their Laws and Leaders,* James Burns declares that awakenings "reveal the operations of God's laws in the realm of spiritual experience, and in the guidance of His Church. They declare that God does not sit unmindful of His creation, but that through His laws He is ceaselessly operating for the world's good, and for the salvation of His people."[16]

Kenneth S. Latourette, the eminent church historian, has demonstrated that the progress of Christianity, both as a faith and as an influence over men, has been by marked stages of advancement followed by marked periods of decline, followed again by periods of advance.[17] Latourette has compared this pattern to the incoming ocean as it moves toward high tide; there is constant movement, even retreat and fluctuation, but the advance is greater than the retreat. The great awakenings over the centuries—the amazing spread of the early church despite persecutions, the Franciscan movement, the Reformation, the Puritan awakening in England, the great awakenings in America and Britain, the worldwide missionary movement of the nineteenth century, and the Welsh revival—are all examples of the periodic nature of Christian advance.

In a recent work, *Revivals, Awakenings, and Reform,* William G. McLoughlin has adapted a formulation of cultural change described by the anthropologist Anthony F. C. Wallace and entitled a "revitalization movement." Wallace derived his theory from studies of primitive peoples, and although it is not completely applicable to the concept of awakening in Christianity, Professor McLoughlin finds that the general configurations are sufficiently similar for the theory to be helpful in understanding awakenings. He states that this "will not necessarily contradict the faith system of either the behavioral psychologist or the Judeo-Christian theologian," but that his concern "is with the social function of religious systems and with achieving a historical perspective on their periodic transformations."[18]

Using this anthropological approach, McLoughlin finds that preju-

16. James Burns, *Revivals: Their Laws and Leaders* (London: Hodder and Stoughton, 1909), p. 2.
17. Kenneth S. Latourette, *The Unquenchable Light* (London: Eyre and Spottiswoode, 1945).
18. William G. McLoughlin, *Revivals, Awakenings, and Reform* (Chicago: U. of Chicago, 1978), p. 8.

dices and misconceptions of awakenings that consider them to be "brief outbursts of mass emotionalism" or "periods of social neurosis" are wrong. Rather,

> Awakenings begin in periods of cultural distortion and grave personal stress, when we lose faith in the legitimacy of our norms, the viability of our institutions, and the authority of our leaders in church and state. . . . They are times of revitalization. They are therapeutic and cathartic, not pathological. They restore our cultural verve and our self-confidence, helping us to maintain faith in ourselves, our ideals, and our "covenant with God" even while they compel us to reinterpret that covenant in the light of new experience. . . .
> I shall treat each of the five awakenings as a period of fundamental social and intellectual reorientation of the American belief-value system, behavior patterns, and institutional structure. But I shall also contend that these reorientations have revolved around a constant culture core of rather broadly stated beliefs. These beliefs (though radically altered in definition during each awakening) have provided the continuity that sustains the culture. In short, great awakenings are periods when the culture system has had to be revitalized in order to overcome jarring disjunctions between norms and experience, old beliefs and new realities, dying patterns and emerging patterns of behavior.[19]

The full theory, and the stages within it, are complex—McLoughlin's book should be consulted for a full understanding of it. There are problems in applying the theory to recent awakenings. McLoughlin notes, "America's revitalistic movements consequently fall outside Wallace's model, and it is useful to cite Peter Worsley's work *The Trumpet Shall Sound* (1968) to supplement it."[20] Even after studying the theory, many Christians would probably view it as deficient, arguing that while such tracings of the sociopsychological dynamics of "revitalization movements" bear many external resemblances to awakenings within Christianity, there are still some significant differences. However that may be, it should not blind Christians to the recognition that such an approach can be very advantageous in removing awakenings from the pale of neurotic or pathological behavior (as they were uniformly considered by secular scholars until quite recently) and placing them within the realm of salutary, creative wellsprings of cultural life. Indeed, if Christian awakenings have been

---

19. Ibid., pp. 2, 10.
20. Ibid., p. 17.

among the most massive and enduring for two thousand years, then by Wallace's theory they have been not the wild excesses and emotionalism of fanatics, but crucially necessary, therapeutic, cathartic, and enormously beneficial.

The phenomena of spiritual awakening, whether in the Scriptures or in more recent history, manifest patterns that are generally similar, often strikingly so. Although all the following elements may not be present in each instance, for the most part revivals progress through a cycle whose phases include component parts of God's working. *First,* revival is usually preceded by a time of spiritual depression, apathy, and gross sin, in which the great majority of nominal Christians are hardly different in any substantive way from the members of secular society, and the churches are moribund. The causes of each decline differ widely, but when the prophetic voice and moral leadership of the church has been stilled for some time, social evils are usually rampant. Eighteenth-century England is an excellent example, as the Halévy Thesis demonstrates. Alcoholism was at an all-time high, capital punishment was meted out routinely for unbelievably trivial crimes, slavery was practiced throughout the British Empire, and the churches were practically moribund. The Evangelical Awakening, by the sensitizing of the English conscience and by direct political pressure and action, cured these and many other ills.

Second, an individual or a small group of God's people becomes conscious of its sins and backslidden condition, and vows to forsake all that is displeasing to God. People recall past outpourings of God's grace and power, and long for them to be manifest again. When histories of revivals have been written in later years, it has been occasionally discovered that individuals at great distances and completely unknown to each other had, prior to the awakening, been praying simultaneously to the same end.

Third, as occasional Christians begin to yearn for a manifestation of God's power, one or more leaders arise with prophetic insights into the causes and remedies of the problems. A new revelation of the holy and pure character of the Lord is given. This standard of holiness exposes the degeneracy of the age and stimulates a striving after holiness by God's people. The leaders find that their eagerness for God's moving is shared by many who have been waiting for God to act, and who will rise to follow.

Fourth, the awakening of Christians occurs. An understanding and an appropriation of the higher spiritual life is made possible for many. The evangelism of the unsaved may or may not be concurrent with this renewal of Christians. In the great revival of the Reformation, the bringing of salvation to those outside the church was not a paramount issue, whereas the dissemination of scriptural doctrine was (along with the establishment of ecclesiastical structures that might be true to that doctrine). This is but another reason it is wrong to make the term *revivalism* synonymous with *evangelism*. One writer, giving a humanistic interpretation to the quickening of the church by the Holy Spirit, has defined revivalism as "professional mass evangelism," and has confused this with the general awakenings.

Certainly in all genuine movements of God's Spirit unsaved people will come to accept Christ as Savior. But if a society has been bathed in the truths of the gospel for a long period, evangelism may not be the central thrust. This was the case in the Welsh revival of 1905, in which most of the people of Wales considered themselves regenerate. In examining the paradigm of Pentecost (Acts 2), we see that revival of Christ's redeemed people and the bestowal of the Holy Spirit at the birthday of the church (2:1-4) *was* followed by evangelism of the unsaved witnesses (2:5-12, 37-41). So the paradigm illustrates the two aspects of the Holy Spirit's work in the awakening of the church, but keeps them separate. As a norm, it may be stated that a revival is a widespread awakening that includes the simultaneous conversion of many people to Christ.

Fifth, the awakening may be God's preparation to strengthen His people for future challenges or trials. Throughout church history, renewal has often been antecedent to persecutions and severe tests, as yet unseen, that were to come and winnow God's people.

Because awakenings have been such powerful agencies for conversion and for the dissemination of God's truth, it is not surprising that they have been the object of ridicule for unbelievers. Since the long-term results of awakenings have been so beneficial, those who would ridicule have had to look elsewhere to find something they could exaggerate, distort, or caricature. They have found a ready target in the excesses of enthusiasm.

Every earnest student of Scripture is aware that Satan is determined to produce counterfeits to every part of God's program, in order to confuse and deceive. Among his most hated objects to attack, we may expect that awakenings would be singled out for special attention. Predictably, Satan over the centuries has effectively mimicked and derided genuine revivals with counterfeit excitements. An excellent example of this is what happened during the greatest revival since Pentecost, the Reformation. For years Martin Luther was plagued by enthusiasts (*Schwärmer*), who claimed they were led directly in their antinomian acts by the Spirit and were therefore above the Scriptures, which they disdained. Claiming to be "protestant," they brought disrepute and confusion to those seeking God's truth. Luther pointed out in the Smalcald Articles of 1537 that those enthusiasts were utterly unreasonable and inconsistent.

> All this is the old devil and old serpent, who even turned Adam and Eve into enthusiasts and led them from the external Word of God to spiritualizing and self-conceit and yet accomplished this, too, through other external words. Just so our enthusiasts are condemning the external Word and yet are not silent themselves but are filling the world with prating and writing, just as though the Spirit could not come through the writing or the spoken Word of the Apostles but must come through their own writing and word.[21]

Two centuries later, the brilliant theologian Jonathan Edwards detected the same tendencies at work. He watched as enthusiasts brought discredit upon the Great Awakening, and with his masterful insight Edwards surveyed the damage done over the centuries by these human tendencies.

> If we look back into the history of the Church of God in past ages, we may observe that it has been a common device of the devil, to overset a revival of religion, when he finds he can keep men quiet and secure no longer, then to drive them into excesses and extravagances. He holds them back as long as he can; but when he can do it no longer, then he will push them on, and if possible, run them upon their heads. And it has been by this means chiefly that he has been successful in several instances to overthrow most hopeful and promising beginnings; yea, the principal means by which the devil was successful, by degrees, to overset that great religious revival of the world, that was in the primitive ages of Christianity; and, in a manner to overthrow the Christian Church through the earth, and to make way for, and bring on the grand anti-Christian apostasy, that masterpiece of all the devil's work, was to improve the indiscrete zeal of Christians, to drive them into those three extremes of enthusiasm, superstition, and severity towards opposers, which should be enough for an everlasting warning to the Christian

---

21. E. M. Plass, ed., *What Luther Says: An Anthology* (St. Louis: Concordia, 1959), 2:917.

Church. And though the devil will do his diligence to stir up the open enemies of religion, yet he knows what is his interest so well, that in a time of revival of religion, his main strength shall be tried with the friends of it, and he will chiefly exert himself in his attempts upon them to mislead them. One truly zealous person, in the time of such an event, that seems to have a great hand in the affair, and draws the eye of many upon him, may do more (through Satan's being too subtle for him) to hinder the work, than a hundred great, and strong, and open opposers.[22]

In spite of the fanaticism that tries to legitimize itself at the time of an awakening, it is surprising how many revivals have *not* been accompanied by emotional excesses. One of the fascinating observations that may be made from a careful study of American revivals is how many of them have been accompanied with great orderliness and a majestic sincerity too profound and genuine for transitory emotionalism. This orderliness the humanist historians of revivals have been careful to minimize or ignore. In his own volume on revivals, Dr. William W. Sweet declared,

No phase of the religious development of America has been more misunderstood and as a consequence more maligned than has revivalism. It has been the victim of much cheap debunking and has suffered at the hands of writers who have been interested only in its excesses. . . . Rather revivalism might well be compared to the new cascade [of a stream] which recreates, even though at times its waters may have been difficult to control.

Strange as it may seem to those who think of revivalism only in terms of ignorance, superstition, and an exaggerated emotionalism, there is a very close relationship between the history of higher education in America and revivalism. Of the nine colonial colleges, the six established between 1740 and 1769—Pennsylvania, Princeton, Columbia, Rutgers, Brown, and Dartmouth—had some relationship either directly or indirectly to the great colonial awakenings. . . . The influence of the Second Great Awakening upon the establishment of colleges is also easily discernible.[23]

It is certainly true that the Great Awakening ran into its disorders, and the Second Awakening *in the West* has been the perennial source of illustrations of primitive agitation. On the other hand, the spiritu-

22. Jonathan Edwards, *Some Thoughts Concerning the Present Revival of Religion in New-England* (Boston: J. Draper, 1742), p. 190.
23. William Warren Sweet, *Revivalism in America: Its Origin, Growth, and Decline* (New York: Scribner's, 1944), pp. xiv-xv, 147-48. Reprinted with the permission of Charles Scribner's Sons.

al harvests of Solomon Stoddard were completely orderly, as was the 1734 revival at Northampton under Jonathan Edwards. The Second Awakening *in the East* was universally known for its dignity and decorum as well as its longevity over three decades, which could certainly not have been maintained if it had brought disgrace upon itself. From the beginning of his ministry in 1824, Charles G. Finney always insisted on order and dignity, and the thousands of converts who flowed from his meetings attested to the power that attended them, and the absence of fanaticism. Describing Finney's Rochester, New York revival of 1830-1831, Whitney R. Cross declared, "No more impressive revival has occurred in American history. . . . But the exceptional feature was the phenomenal dignity of this awakening."[24] The "laymen's" awakening of 1857-58 was commended by the secular press for its quietness and restraint everywhere, while because of its effect more than a million converts were added to the membership of the major denominations. Then, when Dwight L. Moody began his ministry as a world evangelist in 1873, it was with the same determination to avoid emotionalism in his audiences. For this, "the common people heard him gladly," even as they thronged to hear Moody's Lord. In addition, his great meetings drew the rich, the powerful, and the important.

The advice given by William B. Sprague in 1832, in his influential *Lectures on Revivals of Religion,* is as true today as then.

> It is no certain indication of a genuine revival that there is great excitement. It is admitted indeed that great excitement may attend a true revival; but it is not the necessary accompaniment of one, and it may exist where the work is entirely spurious. It may be an excitement produced not by the power of divine truth, but by artificial stimulus applied to the imagination and the passions, for the very purpose of producing commotion both within and without.[25]

---

24. Whitney R. Cross, *The Burned-over District: The Social and Intellectual History of Enthusiastic Religion in Western New York, 1800-1850* (New York: Harper & Row, 1965), p. 155.
25. William B. Sprague, *Lectures on Revivals of Religion* (Edinburgh: Banner of Truth, 1958), p. 13.

1

The Beginnings of Revivalist Ecclesiology— Solomon Stoddard

The Puritans who founded New England stood firmly in the tradition of John Calvin and entertained no illusions about the true nature of man. Human nature was at its core thoroughly sinful and fallen, and only the love and grace of God manifested in the vicarious atonement of Christ on the cross could redeem men. Utopian society was impossible on this earth, and all the good hopes of John Winthrop, William Bradford, and William Brewster could not make a paradise in the wilderness.

> But hear I cannot but stay and make a pause, and stand half amased at this poore peoples presente condition; and so I thinke will the reader too, when he well considers the same. Being thus passed the vast ocean, and a sea of troubles before in their preparation (as may be remembered by that which wente before), they had now no freinds to wellcome them, nor inns to entertaine or refresh their weatherbeaten bodys, no houses or much less townes to repaire too, to seeke for succoure.... These savage barbarians, when they mette with them (as after will appeare) were readier to fill their sids full of arrows then otherwise. And for the season it was winter, and they that know the winters of that cuntrie know them to be sharp and violent, and subjecte to cruell and fierce stormes, deangerous to travill to known places, much more to serch an unknown coast. Besides, what could they see but a hidious and desolate wildernes, full of wild beasts and willd men? and what multituds ther might be of them they knew not.... What could now sustaine them but the spirite of God and his grace? May not and ought not the children of these fathers rightly say: Our faithers were Englishmen which came over this great ocean,

and were ready to perish in this willdernes; but they cried unto the Lord, and he heard their voyce, and looked on their adversitie, etc. Let them therefore praise the Lord, because he is good, and his mercies endure for ever.[1]

This being the case, the Puritans reasoned that Satan would be on the attack in New England as he was in the Old World. There were those who were not regenerate, and the first formal statement of faith adopted in New England, the Cambridge Platform (1648), emphasized that conversion preceded church membership.

> The Doors of the Churches of Christ upon Earth, do not by God's appointment stand so wide open, that all sorts of People, good or bad, may freely enter therein at their pleasure, but such as are admitted thereto, as Members, ought to be examined and tried first, whether they be fit and meet to be received into Church Society, or not. . . . The

Figure 1.1 Landing of the Puritans in Massachusetts (from an old engraving)

1. William Bradford, "History of Plimoth Plantation," cited in Perry Miller and Thomas H. Johnson, *The Puritans* (New York: Harper & Row, 1963), 1:100-101.

Officers are charged with the keeping of the Doors of the Church, and therefore are in a special manner to make Tryal of the fitness of such who enter. . . .

The things which are requisite to be found in all Church Members, are repentance from Sin, and Faith in Jesus Christ. . . .

The weakest measure of Faith is to be accepted in those that desire to be admitted into the Church, because weak Christians, if sincere, have the substance of that Faith, Repentance and Holiness which is required in Church-Members, and such have most need of the Ordinances for their Confirmation and growth in Grace.[2]

With this strict insistence upon conversion and the constant reminders in the Puritan society of Christian sacraments and symbolism, it was inevitable that the second and third generations would present problems. If they were unable to fulfill such requirements of membership, could their children, at least, be baptized? The problem grew out of the federal or covenant theology of the Puritans, according to which church membership included both the covenanting adult and his children. However, on reaching the age of discretion, the children were required to make their own confession of personal conversion, if they were to attain full communicant status. With the decline of religious zeal in the second and third generations, an increasing number of adults could not qualify for communicant status, and were termed "half-way covenanters." But if they had never made a profession of faith, could their children receive baptism? The synod of 1646-1648, which produced the Cambridge Platform, postponed decisive action on the question, and controversy continued at a high pitch until 1662, when another synod decided that the children of half-way covenanters should be baptized. Many feared that this would lead to further laxity, and such was the result as the clergy continued to lose prestige and power despite the enlarged congregations.

From the 1660s the clergy of New England had frequently arraigned the laity for "declension" from the earnestness of their fathers. As embodied in the formula of the jeremiad, New England's lamentations for its departed glory were accompanied by warnings of God's judgments on a backslidden people. Since the jeremiad is so frequent in the pulpit arsenal of Puritan preachers from this time

---

2. Quoted in H. Shelton Smith, et al., *American Christianity: An Historical Interpretation with Representative Documents* (New York: Scribner's, 1960-1963), 1:136.

through to the Great Awakening, it is certain that the pastors were genuinely frightened and were not merely demonstrating ability in verbal pyrotechnics. Samuel Torrey, pastor of the church in Weymouth, in 1683 bewailed the evils of the day before the general court of the Massachusetts colony.

> That there hath been a vital Decay, a Decay upon the very Vitals of Religion, by a deep Declension in the Life, & Power of it; that there is already a great Death upon Religion, little more left than a Name to live; that the Things which remain are ready to die; and that we are in great Danger of dying together with it: This is one of the most awakening, and humbling Considerations of our present State and Condition. . . . Consider we then how much it is dying respecting the very Being of it, by the general Failure of the Work of Conversion; whereby only it is that Religion is propagated, continued, and upheld in Being among any People. As Converting-Work doth cease, so Religion doth die away; though more insensibly, yet most irrecoverably. How much Religion is dying in the very Hearts of sincere Christians, by their Declensions in Grace, Holiness, and the Power of Godliness![3]

Increase Mather (1639-1723), pastor of the Second Church of Boston, declared in 1677, "There never was a generation that did so perfectly shake off the dust of Babylon . . . as the first generation of Christians that came to this land for the Gospel's sake."[4] Against that claim, any posterity would be hard pressed to excel, and in the next year Mather addressed his contemporaries' failures, as he saw them:

> Prayer is needful on this Account, in that Conversions are become rare in this Age of the World. . . . In the last Age, in the Days of our Fathers, in other Parts of the World, scarce a Sermon preached but some evidently converted, and sometimes Hundreds in a Sermon. Which of us can say we have seen the like? Clear, sound Conversions are not frequent in some Congregations. The Body of the rising Generation is a poor, perishing, unconverted and (except the Lord pour down his Spirit) an undone Generation. Many that are Profane, Drunkards, Swearers, Lascivious, Scoffers at the Power of Godliness, Despisers of those that are good, Disobedient. Others that are only

---

3. Samuel Torrey, *A Plea for the Life of Dying Religion*, cited in Thomas Prince, Jr., ed., *The Christian History, Containing Accounts of the Revival and Propagation of Religion in Great Britain, America, &c.* (Boston: S. Kneeland and T. Green), no. 13, May 28, 1743.
4. Cited in W. W. Sweet, *The Story of Religion in America* (New York: Harper and Brothers, 1950), p. 2.

civil, and outwardly conformed to good Order, by Reason of their Education, but never knew what the New Birth means.[5]

In 1679 the decline in spirituality was sufficiently pronounced to warrant calling a "Reforming Synod." A series of calamities, including King Philip's War, the outbreak of smallpox, a major fire in Boston, and the enmity of King James II, persuaded Increase Mather and other prominent ministers that "God hath a Controversy with his New-England People." Addressing itself to the "necessity of reformation," the synod produced a gigantic jeremiad in thirteen major sections, giving a detailed indictment of the sins of the "Holy Commonwealth": (1) the visible decay of godliness among Christians; (2) a proud spirit, in spiritual matters and in dress; (3) neglect of the church and its ordinances; (4) profanity and irreverent behavior; (5) sabbath-breaking; (6) the decline of spirituality in the family; (7) "Sinful Heats and Hatreds," "unrighteous Censures, Backbitings, hearing and telling Tales"; (8) intemperance and drunkenness; (9) "want of Truth"; (10) worldliness and idolatry; (11) obstinance to reformation; (12) selfishness and lack of concern for others and the colony; and (13) impenitence and unbelief.

Despite this massive condemnation and diagnosis of societal ills, the decline continued, and Increase Mather spent the rest of his long life seeing no improvement among the populace, as he bemoaned in 1721:

> I am now in the eighty third Year of my Age: and having had an Opportunity to converse with the first Planters of this Country, and having been for sixty five Years a Preacher of the Gospel; I cannot but be in the Disposition of those ancient Men who had seen the Foundation of the first House, and wept with a loud Voice to see what a Change the Work of the Temple had upon it. . . . I complain there is a grievous Decay of Piety in the Land . . . and the very Interest of New-England seems to be changed from a religious to a worldly one. Oh! that my Head were Waters, and mine Eyes a Fountain of Tears.[6]

Solomon Stoddard (1643-1729), pastor of the church at Northampton from 1672 until his death, would not accept defeat at the hands of increasing worldliness. The measures he proposed to re-cultivate a vital spiritual tone became normative for much of American Protestantism. Because he was the dominant pastor in

---

5. Cited in Prince, no. 13, May 28, 1743.
6. Ibid.

the Connecticut River Valley, and an imperious figure among both clergy and laity, he was able to impose his hopes and methods on that frontier, where an evangelistic approach might be more successful than in sophisticated Boston.

As he often reaffirmed in his own writings, Stoddard was an evangelical, a soul-winner, and had an intense desire to reach the unconverted. His labors were crowned with much success, as his grandson, Jonathan Edwards, relates: "And as he was eminent and renowned for his gifts and grace: so he was blessed, from the beginning, with extraordinary success in his ministry, in the conversion of many souls. He had five harvests, as he called them . . . in each of them, I have heard my grandfather say, the greater part of the young people in the town seemed to be mainly concerned for their eternal salvation."[7]

Where did Stoddard get the idea of "harvests," or revivals? He derived it from the history of the Christian church, which had frequently experienced awakenings over the centuries. The Puritans, ever zealous students of Scripture, looked to sections such as Psalm 85:6, "Wilt thou not revive us again, that thy people may rejoice in thee?", as injunctions to pray for the renewing of believers. The absence of revivals, as in Increase Mather's experience, was cause for great distress and searching of the soul. Along with other Christians, Puritans looked to the outpouring of the Holy Spirit at Pentecost (Acts 2:1-47) as the paradigm to be emulated in successive eras. John Calvin had written out of the Reformation background (which was regarded as one of the church's great revival periods) concerning Peter's sermon at Pentecost, based on Joel 2:28-32.

> Wherefore, that which Peter bringeth . . . [was] that the Jews might know that the Church could by no other means be restored, which was then decayed, but by being renewed by the Spirit of God. Again, because the repairing of the Church should be like unto a new world, therefore Peter saith that it shall be in the last days. And surely this was a common and familiar thing among the Jews, that all those great promises concerning the blessed and well-ordered state of the Church should not be fulfilled until Christ, by his coming, should restore all things. [8]

---

7. Jonathan Edwards, *A Faithful Narrative of a Surprising Work of God in the Conversion of Many Hundred Souls in Northampton and the Neighboring Towns and Villages* (Boston: S. Kneeland and T. Green, 1737), p. 12.
8. John Calvin, *Commentary upon the Acts of the Apostles* (Edinburgh: Teesdale and Son, 1844), 2:84.

In addition, the Puritans were mindful that specific revivals had occurred since the Reformation, particularly in the British Isles. There had been an awakening at the Scottish General Assembly of 1596 under the preaching of Bruce of Edinburgh. Among the best known of the awakenings was the "Stewarton Sickness," which lasted for several years, beginning in 1625. David Dickson, the son of a wealthy merchant of Glasgow, was born about 1583. After receiving the degree of master of arts from the University of Glasgow, he became the professor of philosophy at that school for eight years. In 1618 he was ordained minister to the town of Irvine, where he labored until 1642. His ministry was one of the most successful in Scotland at that time.

> Crowds, under spiritual concern, came from all the parishes round about Irvine, and many settled in the neighborhood, to enjoy his ministrations. Thus encouraged, Mr. Dickson began a weekly lecture on the Mondays, being the market-day in Irvine, when the town was thronged with people from the country. The people from the parish of Stewarton, especially, availed themselves of this privilege, to which they were strongly encouraged by their own minister. The impression produced upon them was very extraordinary. In a large hall within the manse there would often be assembled upwards of a hundred persons, under deep impressions of religion, waiting to converse with the minister, whose public discourses had led them to discover the exceeding sinfulness of sin, and to cry, "What shall I do to be saved?" And it was by means of these week-day discourses and meetings that the famous Stewarton revival, or the "Stewarton sickness," as it was derisively called, began, and spread afterwards from house to house for many miles along the valley in Ayrshire. . . .
>
> The impulse given by this revival continued from 1625 to 1630, when it was followed by a similar effusion of the influences of the Spirit in another part of the country. This took place at the Kirk of Shotts. And here also it is observable that the honour of originating the revival was reserved not to the minister of the parish, but to one of those faithful servants who suffered for their nonconformity to the innovations of the time. . . . An immense concourse of people gathered from all parts to attend the dispensation of the ordinance, which was fixed for Sabbath the 20th of June 1630. Among the ministers invited on this occasion . . . were the noble and venerable champion, Robert Bruce of Kinnard, who was still able to preach with his wonted majesty and authority, and John Livingstone, chaplain to the countess of Wigton.[9]

---

9. Thomas McCrie, *Sketches of Scottish Church History* (London: Blanchard and Ott, 1846), 1:190-93.

Livingstone was twenty-seven at that time and left this record of the occasion:

> The only day in all my life wherein I found most of the presence of God in preaching was on a Monday after the communion, preaching in the church-yard of Shotts, June 21, 1630. The night before I had been with some Christians, who spent the night in prayer and conference. When I was alone in the fields, about eight or nine of the clock in the morning, before we were to go to sermon, there came such a misgiving of spirit upon me, considering my unworthiness and weakness, and the multitude and expectation of the people, that I was consulting with myself to have stolen away somewhere and declined that day's preaching, but that I thought I durst not so far distrust God, and so went to sermon, and got good assistance about an hour and a half upon the points which I had meditated upon. . . . And in the end, offering to close with some words of exhortation, I was led on about an hour's time, in a strain of exhortation and warning, with such liberty and melting of heart, as I never had the like in public all my lifetime.[10]

In gratitude, the Church of Scotland for over two centuries devoted the day after that communion to a day of public thanksgiving. "To this sermon, under the blessing of God, no less than five hundred people ascribed their conversion. . . . From this, and other well-attested instances, it appears that the revival on this occasion was not characterized by those excesses which have brought discredit on similar scenes in our own country and elsewhere."[11]

Puritans everywhere were mindful that the church since its founding experienced periods of awakening such as these, and their ecclesiology demanded that revivals recur periodically if the church was to prosper. But it was Stoddard who first brought awakenings to the colonial churches.

The First Church of Northampton, Massachusetts, scene of Stoddard's ministrations, was founded in 1661. Its first pastor was Eleazer Mather, brother of Increase, who by 1669 found that he needed assistance. Stoddard, the son of a wealthy Boston merchant and a 1662 graduate from Harvard, accepted the call to be Mather's assistant. Soon Mather died. Stoddard then followed the frequent practice of marrying his predecessor's widow (making him Increase Mather's brother-in-law), and began an extremely influential pastorate lasting nearly sixty years. Following the views of J. R. Trum-

---

10. Ibid., pp. 193-94.
11. Ibid., pp. 194, 196.

bull[12] and Perry Miller,[13] many scholars have accepted the idea that "after 1700 [Stoddard] dominated the Connecticut Valley down to New Haven,"[14] and his wishes and practices generally prevailed in these churches. One practice of Stoddard's was open Communion, based on his view that any person over the age of fourteen could be admitted to church membership and the Lord's Supper, if morally respectable and possessed of sound understanding of Christian doctrine. However, several other churches in the area had practiced open communion before Stoddard came to Northampton. Therefore, on the evidence of the Connecticut Valley's ecclesiastical records that indicate the opposition of many of the clergy and laity,[15] Paul R. Lucas has cautioned against the assumption that Stoddard's domination was complete.

Stoddard's power over his own church, however, was undeniable. At first his congregation balked at the autocracy and gave him the nickname "Pope Stoddard" in resentment. Later the same nickname was used increasingly in love—"in his last years they were with him to a man."[16] He began by abandoning the Half-Way Covenant at Northampton and opening the sacrament to all who would partake. Although other churches had open communion, particularly in Connecticut, this was still viewed as a controversion of the "New England way," and a startling departure, especially in Boston. Stoddard defended the change by saying that only God knew who was truly regenerate, and that taking the communion was a "converting ordinance." Clearly his reasoning was that an influential pastor (such as himself) could thereby have some sway over the half-way covenanters and in time bring about their conversion. Such a control over the consciences of many in the area might conceivably bring about, through the instrumentality of powerful preaching, mass conversions and thus revivals. According to Stoddard, all "visible saints" who were "not scandalous," and who "have knowledge to examine themselves and discern the Lord's Body" should be encouraged to attend preaching and partake of the Com-

---

12. J. R. Trumbull, *A History of Northampton* (Northampton, Mass.: Ives, 1898).
13. Perry Miller, "Solomon Stoddard," *Harvard Theological Review* 34 (1941):277-320.
14. Perry Miller, *The New England Mind: From Colony to Province* (Boston: Harvard U., 1953), p. 228.
15. Paul R. Lucas, "An Appeal to the Learned: The Mind of Solomon Stoddard," *William and Mary Quarterly* 30 (1943):257-92.
16. Miller, *New England Mind,* p. 228.

munion, even though they could not profess a definite experience of saving grace. To Stoddard, the concept of "visible saints" meant all persons who make "a serious profession of the true Religion, together with those that do descend from them, till rejected by God."[17]

Perry Miller has remarked that, by this action of throwing open the communion to all who were not scandalous, Stoddard "identified the visible church no longer with the communion of the saints, but with the town meeting."[18] In response to the strong preaching and pastoral methods of Stoddard, five awakenings (or "harvests" as he called them) in 1679, 1683, 1696, 1712, and 1718, converted souls in numbers probably unequaled anywhere else in New England before the Great Awakening. Thus he could claim to speak with authority about the ways of divine grace, and particularly about the ways in which the clergy could assist the Almighty in bringing revivals.

In cosmopolitan Boston, however, awakenings eluded the clergy and their jeremiads mounted in intensity. In 1687 Stoddard completed his first book, the massive *Safety of Appearing at the Day of Judgment*, and asked his brother-in-law Increase Mather to write a preface for it ("it may be a few words from your selfe may gain it the greater acceptance"), but Mather had been so nettled for years by Stoddard's independence of Boston's leadership and his successes in contrast to Mather's problems, that he refused to write such a preface. Mather had originally opposed the Half-Way Covenant, but he became one of its supporters by the late 1670s, and from his anger at Stoddard's innovations he engaged in a pamphlet controversy with the "Pope" of Northampton for the next thirty years, as in the following example.

> In Mr. Stoddard's Sermon on Exodus xii. 47, 48. lately published, there are many Passages which have given Offence to the Churches in New England, as being contrary to the Doctrine which they have learned from the Scriptures, and from those blessed Servants of the Lord, who were the Instruments in the Hand of Christ in building Sanctuaries for His Name, in this part of the Earth. But there are Especially two Heterodox Assertions therein; One is, That Sanctification is not a necessary qualification to Partaking in the Lord's Supper. The other is, That the Lord's Supper is a Converting Ordinance;

---

17. Solomon Stoddard, *The Doctrine of Instituted Churches Explained, and Proved from the Word of God* (London: Spottiswoode, 1700), p. 6.
18. Miller, "Solomon Stoddard," p. 298.

> Consequently, That Persons who know themselves to be in an Unregenerate Estate, may & ought to approach unto the Holy Table of the Lord, whilest they remain in their Sins. . . .
>
> But Mr. S. has the strangest Notion that ever was heard of in the World. For his assertion is, The Saints by calling are to be accepted of the Church, whether they be converted or no. But did you ever hear of Unconverted Saints by calling before? Had he said, Visible Saints, and Seemingly Called, but not Really and Inwardly such in the sight of God, may be acceptable by the Church, he would have affirmed, that which no body will contradict; but as he expresseth it, his Notion is *Contradictio in adjecto*, a notorious Contradiction of itself. Certainly, so far as men are Sanctified, they are Converted. If they are called to be Saints, they are called out of their Worldly, and so out of their Natural Unconverted Estate, John 15.19.[19]

Whatever might have been the tendencies of these practices in Increase Mather's eyes, Stoddard did not mean to play down conversion, nor did he mean to deprecate the founders and their theology. "Men are wont to make a great noise," Stoddard complained obviously of Increase's attacks, "that we are bringing in of Innovations, and depart from the Old Way: But it is beyond me to find out wherein the iniquity does lye. We may see cause to alter some practices of our Fathers, without despising of them, without priding our selves in our own Wisdom, without Apostacy."[20] How could he be the one, with his stalwart evangelism, who was open to the charge of bringing declension? Rather it was the clergy of eastern Massachusetts—those who looked only to the defense of traditionalism and had no answers for the dilemmas of the day—who had allowed their area to backslide with few conversions and many problems. Stoddard advocated more powerful attacks on the false security of the people, but how could such assaults on the consciences be made if the people were neglecting the churches, rather than being brought in to hear powerful and convicting preaching?

Stoddard emerged from his debates with the Mathers and others as a man of great power and confidence who was so convinced of the rightness of his cause that he held off all attackers for decades; Perry Miller has called him "a magnificent individual."

---

19. Increase Mather, *A Dissertation Concerning the Strange Doctrine of Mr. Stoddard* (Boston: D. Henchman, 1708), pp. 1, 20-21.
20. Solomon Stoddard, *The Inexcusableness of Neglecting the Worship of God, Under A Pretense of Being in an Unconverted Condition* (Boston: B. Green, 1708), preface.

He appears to our eyes as the herald of a new century and a new land, the eighteenth against the seventeenth, the West against the East. He was the first great "revivalist" in New England. . . . His sermons were outstanding in his day for the decision with which he swept away the paraphernalia of theology and logic, to arouse men to becoming partakers of the divine nature, and he was the first minister in New England openly to advocate the preaching of Hell-fire and brimstone in order to frighten men into conversion.[21]

The method that Stoddard advocated for other pastors to copy in their own ministries was a carefully worked out elaboration of skeletal concepts first presented in *The Safety of Appearing*. First, the gospel of Christ's love and forgiveness was the only means to conversion. Before conversion every sinner had to undergo certain preparatory stages, although those stages had no salvific power in themselves. Those preparations were similar to the Puritan idea of "convictions," in which a "law work" based on the paradigm of the Old Testament legal dispensation was effected in the person's life. He had to be shown his utter helplessness and need of forgiveness before he could be introduced to the saving grace of Christ. Preparations, said Stoddard, were in two stages, humiliation and contrition, and if the person was in attendance at the ordinances of the church—communion, preaching, the Word—he would be helped toward the moment when grace would enter.

Since the faithful pastor played such a large part in the conversion of sinners, Stoddard frequently warned his colleagues that theirs was an awesome responsibility, publicly and privately, as they dealt with people.

Men should be solemnly Warned against all evil Carriages; and if this be omitted, it gives great increase of Sin in the Land. . . . Faithful Preaching would be beneficial in two ways; one way as it would cut off occasions of anger, and prevent those sins, that bring down the Wrath of God on the Land; we should enjoy much more Publick Prosperity: The other is, that it would deliver men from those Vicious Practises that are a great hindrance to Conversion.[22]

He would deal plainly with his colleagues in the ministry, said Stoddard. It was *their* fault that conversions were so few. Some preaching actually hardens men in their sins, because it does not

21. Miller, "Solomon Stoddard," pp. 316-17.
22. Solomon Stoddard, *The Defects of Preachers Reproved in a Sermon Preached at Northampton, May 19, 1723* (New London, Conn.: T. Green, 1724), pp. 20-21.

make the way of salvation clear, and therefore sinners do not strive for salvation, thinking it very difficult or uncertain. "In some Towns godly men are very thin sown. Most of the People are in as bad a condition as if they had never heard the Gospel."[23] The preacher's job is not easy or popular, and men will initially hate the proclamation of the gospel, as it condemns their sins; but after conversion, they will be greatly blessed, and thankful. "Hence many men that make an high Profession, lead Unsanctified Lives . . . They are not dealt Roundly with; and they believe they are in a good Estate, and Conscience suffers them to Live after a Corrupt Manner. . . . If they were rebuked Sharply, that might be a means to make them Sound in the Faith, Tit.1.13. It might make them not only to Reform, but lay a better Foundation for Eternal Life."[24]

How was this preaching to be done? It was to be done without notes, the method Stoddard used and was famous for. Now, this did not mean that a message might be given extemporaneously. Stoddard's well organized sermons show the marks of very great preparation—he had developed the practice of mastering the manuscript before entering the pulpit, and then delivering it from memory, or at least giving a close approximation to the original.

> The reading of Sermons is a dull way of Preaching. Sermons when Read are not delivered with Authority and in an affecting way. It is Prophecied of Christ, Mic. 5.4. He shall stand and feed in the Strength of the Lord, in the Majesty of the Name of the Lord his God. When Sermons are delivered without Notes, the looks and gesture of the Minister, is a great means to command Attention and stir up Affection. Men are apt to be Drowsy in hearing the Word, and the Liveliness of the Preacher is a means to stir up the Attention of the Hearers, and beget suitable Affection in them. Sermons that are Read are not delivered with Authority, they favour of the Sermons of the Scribes, Mat. 7.29. Experience shows that Sermons Read are not so Profitable as others. It may be Argued, that it is harder to remember Rhetorical Sermons, than meer Rational Discourses; but it may be Answered, that it is far more Profitable to Preach in the Demonstration of the Spirit, than with the enticing Words of mans wisdom.[25]

And what should be the content of these closely-reasoned, well-prepared, and actively presented discourses? Stoddard was very pre-

---

23. Ibid., p. 26.
24. Ibid., p. 27.
25. Ibid., p. 18.

cise at this point; it is little wonder that conversions were so few, with the mass of unsound doctrine that was coming over the pulpits. That, combined with the dull, listless homilies that concurrently afflicted New England, was a sure recipe for sinners to grow colder and farther from God. "If any be taught that frequently men are ignorant of the Time of their Conversion, that is not good Preaching. . . . Men are frequently at a loss whether their Conversion were true or not; but surely men that are Converted must take some notice of the Time when God made a Change in them: Conversion is a great change, from darkness to light, from death to life. . . . Conversion is the greatest change that men undergo in this world, surely it falls under Observation."[26] Here was another result of weak and faulty preaching, that there had not been sufficient stress put upon sanctification, so that New Englanders might know that there is always a decisive alteration in a person's life after conversion. Some preachers put so little emphasis upon this companion doctrine to justification, that many congregations did not even understand the importance of the changed life.

In addition, "If any be taught that Humiliation is not necessary before Faith, that is not good Preaching. Such Doctrine has been taught privately and publickly, and is a means to make some men mistake their condition, and think themselves happy when they are miserable. . . . Men must be led into the Understanding of the badness of their Hearts and the strictness of the Law, before they will be convinced of the Preciousness of Christ."[27] This humbling is standard Puritan doctrine, the idea that the humbled man is the prepared man. This work of illumination is strictly an operation of the Spirit, whereby the truth in Christ of the soul's lost condition and its great need is presented so that pride is crushed and the riches of Christ's salvation is elevated to its proper place in the soul. Stoddard also called this spiritual light by the terms *spiritual conviction, spiritual knowledge,* and *spiritual sight.* It must be contrasted to the "common illumination" that the natural man's reason may receive.

And what of damnation? Stoddard continued,

> When Men don't Preach much about the danger of Damnation, there is want of good Preaching. Some Ministers preach much about Moral Duties and the blessed Estate of godly Men, but don't seek to awaken

26. Ibid., p. 20.
27. Ibid., pp. 11-12.

Sinners and make them sensible of their Danger; they cry for Reformation: These things are very needful in their places to be spoken unto; but if Sinners don't hear often of Judgment and Damnation, few will be Converted. Many men are in a deep Sleep and flatter themselves as if there were no Hell, or at least that God will not deal so harshly with them as to Damn them. Psal. 36.2. . . . Ministers must give them no rest in such a condition: They must pull them as Brands out of the burnings. . . . Ministers are faulty when they speak to them with gentleness, as Eli rebuked his Sons. Christ Jesus often warned them of the danger of Damnation: Mat. 5.29.30.[28]

Stoddard thus inaugurated the era of evangelism. Proper preaching for him was not the delicate homilies of some, which were calculated not to offend any sensitive souls, nor was proper preaching even the jeremiads of many of New England's clergy. Such tirades were general threats and whimperings and cajolings that did little good, for they were not poised as a dart aimed at the foul and dissimulating human heart. Stoddard's formula for keeping the church voluntaristic and full was to preach the terrors of the law, to offer to the populace open communion, to preach in the plain style, to balance the law's terrors with the love of the new birth, and then to combine all this with strict church discipline. He admitted that people were more concerned with their salvation at certain seasons than at others, that "piety is not natural to a people, and so they do not hold it long," but he held forth to other pastors this proper combination of fear and hope as the method for bringing new concern for salvation.

Good preaching is doctrinal preaching, Stoddard insisted, and the proper beginning is with the sovereignty of God and the lostness of man. "If men be thoroughly scared with the danger of Damnation, they will readily improve their possibility, and not stand for assurance of Success."[29] Preaching must be modified accordingly, to aim at conviction and decision. Currently, many are asleep in a perishing state, and the general run of preaching is entirely ineffective to alert them to their danger.

They are so hardnd, that talking moderately to them . . . takes no more impression on them, than on the Seats of the Meeting house. . . . Gods way is to bless suitable Means. . . . Some Ministers affect Rhetorical strains of Speech, as if they were making an Oration in the

---

28. Ibid., pp. 13-14.
29. Solomon Stoddard, *A Guide to Christ* (Boston: B. Green, 1714), p. 39.

Schools; this may tickle the Fancies of Men, and scratch Itching Ears; but we have Mens Consciences to deal with: . . . We are not sent into the Pulpit to shew our Wit and Eloquence, but to set the Consciences of Men on fire; not to nourish the vain humours of People, but to lance and wound the Consciences of Men. [30]

This brought Stoddard to his theology of revival. It is actually developed in numerous works and, with the exception of his first published book, the massive *Safety of Appearing at the Day of Judgment*, those are later writings giving the more mature reflections of his last years. Perry Miller has called those works, including *The Presence of Christ with the Ministers of the Gospel* (1718), *A Treatise Concerning Conversion* (1719), and *The Defects of Preachers Revealed* (1724), "as searching investigations of the religious psychology as any published in New England."[31]

In his magnum opus, *The Safety of Appearing*, Stoddard began by stating that God's wisdom is always inscrutable; He deals with mankind in ways unknown to any mortal. Men are generally hardened in this day, and "God does sometimes withdraw from his own children the sensible quickenings of his Spirit."[32] Although the Spirit of God is never wholly withdrawn in times when His dealings with men are less than at others, men at such times are dull and senseless, and a stoniness takes over their hearts. We must learn from this that the church of God is subject to great fluctuations. It is the same with individuals. At times they are greatly concerned with the progress of the gospel. "And at other times they are in a slumbering Condition; they are like sick Men that are unfit for Service, like Trees in Winter."[33] But in times of diligence to spiritual things, men try to take the Kingdom of Heaven with violence, honoring God and their religious profession, their lights shining before men. Therefore, when the church is in a withering condition we must not conclude that it will always be so. These things are in God's hand, and flourishing times will indeed return.[34]

---

30. Solomon Stoddard, *The Presence of Christ with the Ministers of the Gospel* (Boston: B. Green, 1718), pp. 27-28.
31. Miller, *New England Mind,* p. 282.
32. Solomon Stoddard, *The Safety of Appearing at the Day of Judgment, in the Righteousness of Christ* (Boston: Little and Day, 1689), p. 277.
33. Solomon Stoddard, *The Efficacy of the Fear of Hell* (Boston: B. Green, 1713), p. 194. This is the seventh sermon, with no title, on the doctrine "There are some special seasons wherein God doth in a remarkable manner revive religion among His people." It had been preached in 1712.
34. Ibid.

During flourishing times and languishing times, both ministers and church people have responsibilities. It is the pastor's duty at all times to remind his flock of the dangers of being outside Christ, of sudden death, the great span of eternity, and the awful misery of hell.

The people's responsibility is always to be faithful. God constantly builds up His people to live a life of faith, to depend upon Him according to His Word. "He does in his Providences put them upon that; he takes away other Props that they may lean upon the Promise more."[35] The people of God are to live by faith, and not to depend upon signs. At times God's people have put more trust in signs than in their faith in the infallible testimony of God. Signs are occasionally given by God, but often no signs are given; "when God denies signs there is a sufficient foundation for Faith."[36] This is what God delights at, to see His people resting firmly upon acts of faith.

Then, when both preachers and laity are faithful to their duties, revival will eventually come. Here Stoddard explained what an awakening would be like, in his experience.

Q: How is it with a People when Religion is revived?

A: 1. *Saints are quickened*. It contributes much to the flourishing of Religion, when Righteous men flourish in Holiness, as it is foretold, Psal. 92.12. . . . There be times of Temptation, when godly Men are in a flourishing Condition, Math. 25.5. While the Bridegroom tarried, they all slumbered and slept. They grew worldly, and Proud, and Formal, and don't maintain much of the Life of Godliness. And there be times when their Hearts are lifted up in the ways of God. . . . When their Souls are in a prosperous Condition, and they are in gracious Frames of Spirit, going on from Strength to Strength. Sometimes they run the Ways of God's Commandments, because God enlarges their Hearts. . . . This mightily increaseth Holiness among a People.

2. *Sinners are Converted*. God makes the Gospel at times to be very Powerful. So it was in the Primitive times, Rom. 15.29. . . . The Gospel was written to the End that Men might believe and be saved. Joh. 20.21. And it is preached for that End; and sometimes God gives great Success to it. . . . There is a mighty Change wrought in a little Time: They that were Dead, are made Alive, and they that were Lost are Found. The Gospel is made a savour of Life to many. Some times there is a great Complaint for want of this. Psal. 12.1. . . . At other Times the Number of Saints is greatly multiplied. Acts 9.31. . . .

35. Ibid., p. 279.
36. Ibid., p. 343.

3. *Many that are not Converted, do become more Religious.* When Israel went out of Egypt, there was a mixt Multitude that went with them. So when God is pleased to Convert a Number, there be many others that have a common Work of the Spirit on their Hearts: they are affected with their Condition, Reform their evil Manners, and engage in Religious Duties, and attain to considerable Zeal, and are full of Religious Affections. When God works savingly upon some, it is frequent that others have common Illuminations, whereby great Reformation is wrought, and the Reputation of Religion advanced, and People are disposed to keep the external Covenant.[37]

Solomon Stoddard is important because he confronted the theological problems of America with new answers that were effective in bringing revival. He also strikingly introduced what was to become the paramount question in the theology of revivals, namely, To what extent can clergy and laity be partners with the Almighty in the bringing of awakenings? During Stoddard's lifetime, while he explored the possibilities of his theology, the clergy of eastern Massachusetts despaired over declining church membership and relied on a sterile ecclesiology that had nothing new to contribute. They were committed to the ideology of the jeremiad and the system of covenants, in the context of which they lamented declension, deplored the scarcity of converts, threatened divine wrath, attempted to improve the baptismal covenant, and urged owning of the covenant in order to baptize a few more. But the decline continued.

The old-world theology of revivals, and also the one of eastern Massachusetts, was that awakenings would come only in the Lord's good time. Although Stoddard gave lip service to this ("There are some special Seasons wherein God doth in a remarkable Manner revive Religion among his People"[38]), his entire approach assumed that clergy and laity could indeed assist in the bringing of revival, and his methodology was the first to delineate the steps necessary to cooperate with God in this. He urged the acceptance of the following as a proven methodology of revival: the preaching of damnation; the teaching that only God knows who is regenerate anyway, so that all should respond to the gospel invitation; the requirement of humbling as the sinner examines his life and passes through the successive stages of preparation; the preaching of spiritual illumination and the germ of faith implanted by the Holy Spirit; the subse-

---

37. Stoddard, *Efficacy of the Fear of Hell*, pp. 187-89.
38. Ibid., p. 186.

quent ability of the sinner to respond in faith to the gospel, and the shattering experience of conversion as a dateable event upon which some assurance of salvation could be erected.[39] Although later revivalists in America would differ from Stoddard at points, generally this pattern would be adhered to.

Stoddard would have made a large contribution had he done no more than assail the despair many felt in their assumption that they were not of the elect. He taught that election cannot be known for sure in this life and therefore everyone should respond to the gospel as if he were elect. Stoddard's modification required that men have more scope in working out their salvation than Calvinism had traditionally allowed. Previously it was thought absurd to persuade people to seek salvation if they were as lost and helpless as Calvinism seemed to decree. The resulting contradiction between Calvinistic theory and Stoddard's revivalistic practice he hoped to resolve by his insistence on the unknowability of it all. He clung tenaciously to the scriptural picture of total inability before God, but at the same time Stoddard developed concepts of "undertaking," "holy violence," "coming," and "choosing," by explaining in great detail exactly what his hearers and readers could do in the stages leading to regeneration. He rationalized this "contradiction" between theology and practice by arguing that men are free only to prepare themselves to receive God's grace, but that the actual granting of grace is entirely in God's power. This was precisely the breakthrough that was needed, and was to be followed by his grandson Jonathan Edwards, by Jonathan Dickinson, and every other revivalist of consequence in the Great Awakening.

---

39. See Thomas A. Schafer, "Solomon Stoddard and the Theology of the Revival," in *A Miscellany of American Christianity,* edited by Stuart C. Henry (Durham, N.C.: U. of North Carolina, 1963), pp. 328-61.

2

The Origins of the Great Awakening— Theodore Frelinghuysen and the Tennents

As the Rev. Bernard Freeman opened his parsonage door on the cold morning of March 12, 1723, three men bundled in large coats confronted him. By the looks of their horses which they had tied to a tree by the road, they had come a long distance to see this pastor of the Dutch Reformed church on Long Island, New York.

"Yes, may I help you?" the pastor asked.

"Good day, pastor. I am Pieter DuMont, and this is Simon Wyckoff and Hendrick Vroom. We have come from the Dutch congregations of Raritan in New Jersey. May we see you?"

"Of course. Please come in, and let me have your coats."

After the three had been seated in Freeman's study, he asked in what way he might serve them, although he suspected the answer to that.

"Pastor, we have come to you as a faithful domine of the Dutch Reformed church, to lay against our pastor at Raritan, Rev. Frelinghuysen, the charge that he does not teach correct doctrine."

"Hmmm. That is a very serious charge, brethren. Of course I know Reverend Frelinghuysen quite well. He has been among us over three years now."

"Yes, Pastor Freeman, and in that time since he came to our little churches from Holland we have had nothing but difficulties!"

"Well," said Freeman, "be careful that you do not unjustly accuse your pastor, for he has been abundantly certified by the Synod of Emberland in Holland, and also by the Classis of Amsterdam, which declared him to be orthodox and sent him to you."

DuMont and the others bristled. As the spokesman for the trio, DuMont gathered his thoughts together that he might be as persuasive as possible. His brows knit. "That may be so, but have you heard that he teaches from his pulpit that no one in the congregation has exhibited true sorrow for sin? And after one communion service, Frelinghuysen told us that we had just eaten judgment to ourselves at the Lord's table! And he has been refusing to baptize children!"

"But DuMont, that is not heresy, nor soul-destroying doctrine. You are separating his utterances from their foundations, the text from the context. If you come to accuse him of errors in the foundations of the faith, *you* are under obligation to furnish the proof."

Unable to restrain himself any longer, Wyckoff took the lead from DuMont. When he finally broke his silence, he almost shouted at Freeman, "But, Pastor Freeman, what *are* the foundational teachings of the faith?" He had no sooner said that, when all realized Wyckoff had made a very damaging statement of ignorance.

Rising to his feet with obvious anger, Freeman strode to Wyckoff. "What kind of a question is that? Don't you *know* what are the foundations of our church and faith? How then can you so boldly accuse your pastor of teaching false doctrine?!" Then Freeman, realizing the type of people he was dealing with, went through the cardinal doctrines of Christianity rapidly.

"Well," said DuMont, "although we could not prove anything against Frelinghuysen in reference to these doctrines, yet we believe he is untrue, and such a man is a teacher of false doctrine."

"Mr. DuMont," Freeman replied, "now I see that you are all affected by the spirit of hatred and revenge. Because he sharply exposes sin, you try to help the devil! You should love your spiritual father, who earnestly reproves you, and accepting it in love, apply it to your improvement."

"Domine Freeman," said Wyckoff, "we desire you to advise us what to do in this affair."

"I can advise you if you are disposed for peace. All that you have brought forward so far are only circumstances. Draw up in writing a list of your grievances; subscribe it with your own hand, and give it to your consistory [church board]. They and they only are obliged, according to their office, to give heed to the doctrine of their pastor, and also to the doctrine and conduct of the congregation. If you should do differently, and come to New York, or to this place, you and all who join with you, will be regarded by all honest people as creators of schism in your church at Raritan." Thus saying, Freeman indicated that the interview was over, and showed the three from his study. He felt that he had done, in difficult circumstances, what was best for all parties in the growing dispute over the dynamic and unusual ministry of Theodore J. Frelinghuysen.*

Who was Frelinghuysen, and what had he done to bring on the split in his New Jersey churches?

In the Middle Colonies of America, the first awakener of great importance was this firebrand preacher over whom few could be neutral. Theodore J. Frelinghuysen was born in Westphalia, Germany in 1692 and had received his early education from his parents. He then went to the University of Lingen in Holland, studying there from 1711 to 1717. At the urging of a professor, he became as proficient in the Dutch language as he was in German.

Throughout his youth Frelinghuysen absorbed the influences of the movement known as pietism, which at that time was revitalizing many of the churches in Germany and Holland. Pietism can best be described as orthodox Christianity with more emphasis on "a heart warm toward God" than on doctrine. It demanded the new birth through faith in Christ and taught that denominational differences should not be overplayed. Rather, the oneness of believers in Christ should be emphasized. True faith, pietism taught, was shown not so much in knowledge as in deeds of love to one's neighbor and avoidance of doctrinal disputes.

In Germany pietism had sprung up within the Lutheran churches from the teachings of Philip Jakob Spener (1635-1705) and August Hermann Francke (1663-1727), who stressed the importance of Bible study, the spiritual life, devotional literature, and practical teaching. But in Holland pietism was influenced more by Calvinism or Reformed theology, as the pietism found in English Puritanism. This Reformed pietism was becoming strong in many churches during Frelinghuysen's youth.

All aspects of pietism shared one vastly important expectation—those destined for eternal life went through a definite, palpable

---

*The preceding conversation, starting at the beginning of the chapter, is taken almost verbatim from *Ecclesiastical Records of the State of New York* (Albany, N.Y.: J. B. Lyons, 1902), 3:2197-2200.

Figure 2.1 Theodore Frelinghuysen preparing to depart from Holland to the New World (from an old engraving)

conversion after conviction of and repentance of sin. Formalism in religion, which allowed outward piety and the perfunctory doing of rites, was assailed by the pietists so tellingly that their opponents attempted to show that the pietist ideas were heretical. Clergymen who opposed it were sometimes denounced as unconverted themselves. Those were the influences that Frelinghuysen absorbed during his formative years and reflected the rest of his life.[1]

1. James Tanis, *Dutch Calvinistic Pietism in the Middle Colonies: A Study in the Life of Theodorus Jacobus Frelinghuysen* (The Hague: Martinus Nijhof, 1967), p. 2.

Frelinghuysen was ordained in 1717 and, after holding several posts, was approached by some who were looking for a young minister to go to the demanding field of New Jersey. They were searching for a man of excellent qualifications and great dedication, because work in America was difficult and pastors had to travel much to minister to far-flung congregations. Frelinghuysen expressed a willingness to go, and landed at New York in January 1720. Almost immediately he offended such powerful men as Domine Boel and Domine DuBois, the pastors of the Dutch Reformed church in New York, by his animated preaching and prayers and his omission of the Lord's Prayer.

The stolid Dutch farmers and burghers of Raritan, New Jersey welcomed their new pastor on January 31, 1720. They must have been entirely unprepared for the sermon he preached on his first Sunday in the four small churches he was to serve. To those complacent congregations he declared that a person seeking eternal life must first undergo an agonizing conviction of his sinful condition. Such a person is lost and damned while still in his natural state, and totally unable to achieve his deliverance or redemption by any natural means. The process of regeneration then leads to a period when the sinner falls into great despondency over his spiritual condition, freely confesses his sins, and condemns and abhors himself. Eventually he begins to yearn for the righteousness of Christ, and if the regeneration process is completed, the sinner places his hope on Christ, thus coming out of his spiritual experience in a condition of grace and regeneration.

Frelinghuysen said that only one who has been through such a conversion can possess salvation. Moral and upright people who have not had this experience—but who are often proud and self-righteous—have no hope for eternal life.[2] As he said in an early sermon,

> What think ye my hearers? Are ye poor, contrite in spirit, and those who tremble at the word of God? If you have given your earnest attention, you have been able to learn how it is with you in this respect. Calmly ask yourselves in the presence of the all-seeing God:
> 1. Am I spiritually poor? Have I a sensible knowledge of my sad and condemned state? Do I feel that in myself I am so guilty, impure, and evil—so alienated from God, and the life of God—so wretched, poor, miserable, blind, naked, and unable to deliver myself, or do aught towards my deliverance, that I must perish if I remain thus?

2. T. J. Frelinghuysen, *Sermons* (New York: Moore and Jordan, 1856), pp. 25-36.

2. Have I through a sense of my spiritual need, and desperate state, become distressed, concerned, and at a loss? Do I accuse, condemn, and loathe myself? Am I anxious to know how I may be delivered from so sad a condition? . . .

3. Am I contrite in spirit through a painful sense of sin? Do my sins oppress me? Are they burdensome? Do I experience in my inmost soul sorrow for sin, proceeding from love to God and true excellence, and from hatred and aversion to sin, in its shamefulness, loathsomeness, and deformity; and because committed against so holy, good, and righteous a God; together with a purpose of heart henceforth to live according to the will of God? . . .

I know, indeed, that you will be unwilling to believe that you have no right to come to the Lord's table, although you clearly perceive that you are not of the number of the poor, contrite in spirit, and such as tremble at the word of God; but, I also know, (you may believe it or not,) that according to the word of God, you have no right; and that if you do, you will seal your condemnation. Oh! that you saw how necessary is such frame of mind—that no one can be found in favor with God, unless he be poor, and contrite in spirit.[3]

The Dutch farmers of his congregations did not find such teaching unacceptable in itself. But obviously their new minister regarded many of them as unsaved, pharisaical, and self-righteous. William Demarest, Frelinghuysen's translator, says that ". . . great laxity of manners prevailed through his church, naturally associated with neglect on the part of the rulers, and great tenacity with regard to their abstract church rights on the part of the members—that while horse-racing, gambling, dissipation, and rudeness of various kinds, were common, the sanctuary was attended at convenience, and religion consisted of the mere formal pursuit of the routine of duty."[4]

Some of the Dutch burghers in the churches around Raritan, outraged by Frelinghuysen's considering them unregenerate and his exclusion of some of them from the sacrament, pleaded their case to the New York ministers, Boel and DuBois. Several attempts were made in May 1720 to confer together, but nothing came of it.

Frelinghuysen was as angered by the charges made against him as the burghers were by his actions. When he published three sermons in June 1721, he added this preface defending himself:

---

3. Ibid., pp. 43-47.
4. Ibid., p. 7.

For if you be not a stranger in our New-Netherlands Jerusalem, you are aware that I have been slanderously charged as a schismatic, and a teacher of false doctrines. That I am thus accused is too manifest to require proof. You will allow it that it were the duty of those who thus accuse me, to establish what they say, either by word of mouth or by pen; but since hitherto this has not been done, let no one imagine that it is here my intention to vindicate myself. The trifling stories, the notorious falsehoods, that are circulated concerning me, and are by some so greedily received are not deserving of mention, much less of refutation. It is true, there is much said of my manner in relation to the Lord's Supper, but that I teach nothing else concerning this ordinance, but what has in every age been taught by the Reformed Church, can, in the following discourses, be readily discussed by any impartial person.

. . . I have written nothing that is inconsistant with the rule of faith, and the genuine doctrines of the Reformed Church; for I have followed the steps of numerous orthodox, faithful, and godly men, whose writings I have also employed, since I felt unable to make any improvement upon them.

June 15, 1721.[5]

In 1723, the leaders of the opposition sought advice and encouragement from Bernard Freeman of the Long Island church in the interview given above, but Freeman saw them as troublemakers and rebuked them, telling them to plead their case before the consistory. The opposition then turned for further advice to Boel, stating that Frelinghuysen was unorthodox in his belief in a personal conversion, in his administration of the Communion, and in his criticism of other clergymen. But the members of Frelinghuysen's churches who agreed with their minister challenged those separatists to the church authorities back in Holland:

We . . . lay to heart the evil report which is dogging our minister, that he teaches false doctrine. And although Mr. Boel, and his brother, the lawyer, have not been appointed as Popes and Bishops over us, yet you correspond and consult with the said gentlemen, because they assert that our minister teaches false doctrine; yet they, in three years' time, have not been able to prove this, and, indeed, never will be able. . . . Your course tends only to discord and mutiny in church and civil life. . . . Our pastor has shown himself to be an active and earnest antagonist against the evil lives of many persons. He has exhorted them out of the Word of God and warned them in the name of God,

---

5. Ibid., pp. 23-24.

that the wrath of God and eternal damnation are abiding upon them; and that unless they repent, they are bringing everlasting punishment upon themselves.[6]

The faithful members of Frelinghuysen's congregations felt that the separatists had resisted the straightforward teachings of the Word of God and their lawful pastor, and "hatred, envy, anger, revenge, calumny, falsehood, ignorance, and irreligion prevail among the members of your [seceded] Congregation."[7] The members who opposed Frelinghuysen were ordered by the consistory to present their charges against the pastor, and if they failed to do so they would face charges leading to excommunication.

The opposition refused to come before the consistory, and Frelinghuysen then moved to do what had been threatened, to excommunicate Wyckoff, Hayman, Vroom, and DuMont in September 1723. Many times Frelinghuysen had explained the scriptural discipline allowed to the church, as in this sermon on Matthew 16:19, where Christ speaks of the "keys of the Kingdom."

> Thus Peter employed this key against Simon, the sorcerer (Acts 8:21-23) and Paul in relation to Elymas. And that it may have greater effect, it is associated with a denunciation of the divine curse upon a sinner (I Cor. 16:22). . . .
>
> He sadly mistakes, who regards this opening and shutting of the kingdom of heaven by the preachers of the gospel as vain, and without force, since it is to be recognized as the voice of God, and not merely of man. . . .
>
> In this work of exclusion are comprised four steps:
>
> 1. Admonition, warning, reproof, either in private, or (if this be not regarded) in presence of consistory.
>
> 2. To forbid them the table of the Lord.
>
> 3. To propose to the congregation those who proceed in their erroneous and wicked course; that it may be known that the keys of the kingdom of heaven are used; that the erring may be prayed for, and made ashamed, and turn to the Lord; and this must be done first, with the withholding of the name, and upon continuance in obstinacy, with an announcement of it; that a deeper impression may be made, both upon the offender and the congregation. All this proving ineffectual, we are conducted to the . . .
>
> 4. And last step. The offender is cut off—he is interdicted all fellowship with the Church, and no longer recognized as a brother or sister;

---

6. *Ecclesiastical Records,* 3:2201-2.
7. Ibid., 3:2202.

but regarded as a heathen and publican. This is the Apostle's command, 1 Cor. 5:13: "Put away from among yourselves that wicked person."

. . . The end and object of the ban is not any corporeal infliction, but,

1. To render ashamed, and bring to reflection. (2 Thess. 3:14.)

2. That being led to regard the exercise of authority towards him as an indication of the displeasure of the Lord Jesus, the offender may turn from his evil ways. (1 Cor. 5:5.)

3. To cause others to fear divine inflections.[8]

Still determined to undermine Frelinghuysen, the leaders of the opposition published a *Complaint Against Frelinghuysen* in 1725. This was not only a reply to the consistory's citations of 1723, but also a complaint about Frelinghuysen's assuming the authority to discipline members. This was signed by sixty-nine persons, which gives some idea of the number of opposers in his congregations.

The split in the Raritan congregations continued until 1733, when the articles of peace submitted by the Classis of Amsterdam were received by Frelinghuysen's consistory and the complainants. These articles stipulated that the complainants would return to their congregations and accept Frelinghuysen, and the consistory that had backed him would reinstate those who had been excommunicated and drop the matter.[9] It is interesting that the two New York clergymen, Boel and DuBois, previously united against Frelinghuysen, split at this point. Domine Boel continued his opposition to revivals, whereas Domine DuBois began a movement to join with those gathering around Frelinghuysen in a desire for independence from the Classis of Amsterdam.[10]

Meanwhile, under Frelinghuysen's vibrant preaching and close pastoral care, the members of his four churches were becoming a "very different people." His congregations increased, and there were numerous conversions among people who were new to the Dutch Reformed churches. In some years the number of converts was sufficient to give a foretaste of the time when George Whitefield's preaching would bring in thousands of new Christians. The subjects of Frelinghuysen's revival had all experienced such a conversion as had never before been insisted upon in the Middle Colonies—a

---

8. Frelinghuysen, *Sermons,* pp. 142-43.
9. *Ecclesiastical Records,* 3:2638-39, 3:2652-58.
10. C. H. Maxson, *The Great Awakening in the Middle Colonies* (Chicago: U. of Chicago, 1920), p. 19.

severe spiritual conflict ending in an attachment to Christ as Savior and Lord, followed by a determination to make the attainment of personal sanctification the dominating purpose of life.

Since the Great Awakening, historians have seen the aforementioned background events as a prologue for the evangelism of Frelinghuysen, which converted many in the Raritan area and drove away those who were obstinately unregenerate. This evaluation of Frelinghuysen had the best of credentials. On November 20, 1739, shortly after arriving in the Middle Colonies, George Whitefield preached near Raritan and recorded in his *Journals,*

> Among others who came to hear the Word, were several ministers, whom the Lord has been pleased to honour, in making them instruments of bringing many sons to glory. One was a Dutch Calvinistic minister, named Freeling Housen, pastor of a congregation about four miles from New Brunswick. He is a worthy old soldier of Jesus Christ, and was the beginner of the great work which I trust the Lord is carrying on in these parts. He had been strongly opposed by his carnal brethren.[11]

And Jonathan Edwards gave Frelinghuysen immediate recognition when he included in his *Faithful Narrative of the Surprising Work of God,*

> But this shower of divine blessing has been yet more extensive: there was no small degree of it in some parts of the Jerseys; as I was informed when I was at New York. . . . Especially the Rev. William Tennent, a minister who seemed to have such things much at heart, told me of a very great awakening of many in a place called the Mountains, under the ministry of one Mr. Cross; and of a very considerable revival of religion in another place under the ministry of his brother the Rev. Gilbert Tennent; and also at another place, under the ministry of a very pious young gentleman, a Dutch minister, whose name as I remember was Freelinghousa.[12]

William Tennent, father of Gilbert, was born in 1673, and it is not certain if his birthplace was in Scotland or Ireland. William's family was Scottish and included the American Quaker James Logan, his mother's cousin. His wife, Catherine Kennedy, to whom he was married on May 15, 1702, in County Down, Ireland, was the

---

11. George Whitefield, *Journals* (London: Banner of Truth, 1960), pp. 351-52.
12. C. C. Goen, ed., *The Great Awakening,* "The Works of Jonathan Edwards" (New Haven, Conn.: Yale U., 1972), 4:155-56.

daughter of an eminent Presbyterian minister, the Reverend Gilbert Kennedy.

Gilbert Tennent, the eldest son of William and Catherine, was born on February 5, 1703. Gilbert was baptized by the Reverend Alexander Bruce, Presbyterian minister of Vinnecash, near Gilbert's birthplace in County Armagh, Ireland. With this strong Presbyterian background it is strange that William Tennent entered the Church of Ireland as a deacon in July 1704 and was ordained a priest two years later. The rest of William's children were baptized in the Anglican Church: William, Jr., born in 1705; John in 1706; Eleanor in 1708; and Charles in 1711.

In 1718 William Tennent decided to come to America and was admitted into membership in the Presbyterian Synod of Philadelphia. (He gave a list of scruples for which he felt it necessary to dissent from the Church of Ireland.) After spending several years as minister at Bedford, New York, Tennent in 1727 moved to Neshaminy, Bucks County, Pennsylvania, to minister to that congregation. About that time migrants from Ireland had begun to arrive in large numbers, and many had settled in the rural areas around Philadelphia. Ministers for churches were in great need, and to provide for this, Tennent decided to train men for the ministry. Thus he began his "Log College" at Neshaminy. He was a fine scholar and teacher, without an equal in the Synod. By 1734 four young ministers were admitted into the Presbyterian church, all of whom had been trained by William Tennent. Those were his three sons, Gilbert, John, and William, Jr., and Samuel Blair.

Gilbert Tennent began at an early age to study for the ministry under his father's direction. At one point he became so discouraged about his qualifications that he turned to medicine instead. At the age of fifteen, when crossing the Atlantic, Gilbert was converted; it was, because of this period of "convictions" and "law work," a classic Puritan conversion.

Gilbert's training under his father must have been thorough, because he was licensed by the Presbytery of Philadelphia in 1725 and, having attended Yale College in Connecticut for some time, he received a master of arts degree in the same year.

In 1726 Gilbert Tennent was ordained by the Presbytery of Philadelphia to serve the church at New Brunswick, New Jersey. Almost immediately his relationship with Theodore Frelinghuysen began, and Gilbert learned his methods and preaching well.

Gilbert Tennent has become a valuable source of information about Frelinghuysen's work, as he was an eyewitness of the revival in Raritan from the time of his coming to New Brunswick in 1726. Tennent was always lavish in his praise of Frelinghuysen, as the older man had greatly influenced young Tennent toward a similar evangelistic ministry. Tennent's letter of August 24, 1744 added further to Frelinghuysen's fame by admitting Tennent's dependence on his inspiration and instruction.

> The labors of the Reverend Mr. Frelinghousa, a Dutch Calvinist minister, were much blessed to the people of New Brunswick and places adjacent, especially about the time of his coming among them, which was about twenty-four years ago.
>
> When I came there, which was about seven years after, I had the pleasure of seeing much of the fruits of his ministry; divers of his hearers, with whom I had opportunity of conversing, appeared to be converted persons by their soundness in principle, Christian experience, and pious practice; and these persons declared that the ministrations of the aforesaid gentleman were the means thereof. This, together with a kind letter which he sent me respecting the necessity of dividing the word aright, and giving to every man his portion in due season, through the divine blessing, excited me to greater earnestness in ministerial labors.[13]

The evidence shows that there was an awakening under Frelinghuysen's ministry during the 1720s, although statistically its results were small by comparison with later revivals. Gilbert Tennent remained impressed with Frelinghuysen because there was a spiritual power about the Reformed minister, and Frelinghuysen understood the principles of an evangelical ministry.

In addition to his beginning the revival ministry in the Middle Colonies, several other aspects of Frelinghuysen's ministry may be drawn. One is Frelinghuysen's discovery of some of the answers to the problems that weakened the churches of the colonies. Through his strict techniques and his demand that all in his congregations be soundly converted, he greatly strengthened the authority of the clergy to enforce ecclesiastical discipline. Through these means he developed a responsible membership in his churches, one that did not have the usual indifference of the lay people. Another answer he devised was his development of private devotional meetings, small

---

13. Joseph Tracy, *The Great Awakening. A History of the Revival of Religion in the Time of Edwards and Whitefield* (Boston: Tappan and Dennet, 1842), pp. 33-34.

groups of converted people who met for Bible study, prayer, and mutual encouragement. Again, because clergy were so few in the Middle Colonies, he transformed the lay readers of the Dutch Reformed church into actual lay preachers who could deliver sermons during his attendance at other churches. Some of those lay preachers became quite good and helped greatly to spread his ministry.

Frelinghuysen, therefore, prepared much of New Jersey for the coming of the Great Awakening and led many to expect revival as the proper on-going level of spiritual life for the church. He was a fearless pastor, willing to undergo persecution for what he believed to be the truth in Christ. His doctrine was unremittingly biblical and did not picture conversion as easy, but rather extremely strenuous, as this excerpt from his sermon "A Mirror That Flattereth Not," shows:

> Satan, that revengeful and great Enemy of Man's Happiness and Salvation, keeps the poor Sinner, not only Captive by him at his Will, as Paul said in 2 Timothy 2:26, but he so blinds his Mind, that the Light of the Gospel (which otherwise would have discovered his wretched state) does not shine upon him, as we read in 2 Corinthians 4:6. This the Saviour also teaches, in Luke 8:2. Satan takes the Seed, the Word of God, out of the heart, lest they should believe and be saved. Henceforth the Word of God has no Power on their hearts; it is not unto them as a hammer and fire (Jeremiah 23:29), nor quick and powerful (Hebrews 4:12), but it is to them a dead letter (2 Corinthians 3). For the Word preached does not profit them, not being mixed with faith (Hebrews 4:2). For as Satan through his subtlety deceived Eve, even so he yet deceives and ensnares Men. . . .
>
> This deceit is much encouraged by false teachers who do not faithfully warn the people of this dreadful self-deceit, that do not seek to shew unto them the subtlety of Satan, and the deceitfulness of their hearts, not making known to them the false by-ways. . . . Through default of discovering, convicting, powerful preaching, people continue in a dream that their way is right.[14]

---

14. Frelinghuysen, *Sermons,* pp. 129-31.

3

The Great Awakening in New England— Jonathan Edwards

Brilliant, scholarly, and reflective, Jonathan Edwards knew intuitively that a position as pastor of a small church might be best suited to his desires and abilities in the early years of his career. Yet, he had just received a call to become the assistant minister of the influential and demanding Congregational church of Northampton, Massachusetts (Solomon Stoddard's church). Edwards was both gratified and disturbed by the call—gratified in that the renowned Stoddard, his grandfather, had chosen young Jonathan to come and assist him in his last years, and disturbed in that, should the eighty-four-year-old man be incapacitated or die, the entire responsibility would be thrown upon Jonathan.

Edwards dutifully assumed his tasks in February 1727, and his grandfather lived two more years. From then on Edwards was the sole pastor in Northampton, a town that was the most important in western Massachusetts. Its theological notoriety was due entirely to Stoddard. Through his domineering yet widely-loved personality he had influenced the area greatly over the years. His preaching was powerful and evangelistic, and he had the distinction of having the largest awakenings in New England before the Great Awakening (in 1679, 1683, 1696, 1712, and 1718). Thus Edwards succeeded to one of New England's most important pulpits, where revivals had been an important part of the vitality of the church. In addition, Edwards was born to the evangelical tradition of the Connecticut River Valley and had the blessing of belonging to a family already distinguished for its integrity of life and intellectual attainments.

Jonathan Edwards was born on October 5, 1703, at Windsor, Connecticut. His father, the Reverend Timothy Edwards, was the beloved pastor of the town over a ministry of sixty years. Jonathan, the only son, had ten sisters. From early years he showed great precocity and also much interest in the things of the spiritual life. While still a child he acquired the elements of scriptural knowledge and also underwent several profound spiritual experiences. At fourteen he read John Locke's *Essay Concerning Human Understanding*, a book newly come to America and understood by few adults at the time. He was enrolled at Yale College before he was thirteen and graduated four years later at the head of his class. After two

Figure 3.1 Reverend Jonathan Edwards. Joseph Badger (Yale University Art Gallery, Bequest of Eugene Phelps Edwards, 1938)

unimportant pastorates of short durations, he returned to Yale as a tutor and took his master of arts degree in 1724.

At the Northampton church Edwards secluded himself in his study for thirteen hours a day. In the pulpit he read closely reasoned sermons from a semilegible manuscript, giving him a reputation as a scholar but hardly conforming him to the later image of a revival preacher. He soon became quite distressed by the "licentiousness" of the townspeople, who had lapsed into the degeneracy of the times. "Many of them [were] very much addicted to night-walking, and frequenting the tavern, and lewd practices. . . . It was their manner very frequently to get together in conventions of both sexes, for mirth and jollity, which they called frollics; and they would often spend the greater part of the night in them."[1]

In addition, many of them were "indecent in their carriage at meeting," and "very insensible of the things of religion." Arminian principles, with the doctrine of human ability, were also partly responsible for the spreading complacency of the day, in Edwards's view.

After he became pastor, Jonathan Edwards tried to bring back to his parishioners a concern for their souls; in 1734 he succeeded. The awakening was caused by a series of solidly biblical sermons. No immediate effects became visible, but in December of 1734, as Edwards informs us, "the Spirit of God began extraordinarily to set in, and wonderfully to work among us; and there were, very suddenly, one after another, five or six persons who were to all appearances savingly converted, and some of them wrought upon in a very remarkable manner."[2] His *Faithful Narrative of the Surprising Work of God* made every attempt known to eighteenth-century reporting to be objective and attributed all to the working of the Almighty among the townspeople.

> This work of God, as it was carried on, and the number of true saints multiplied, soon made a glorious alteration in the town; so that in the spring and summer following, anno 1735, the town seemed to be full of the presence of God; it was never so full of love, nor of joy, and yet so full of distress, as it was then. There were remarkable tokens of God's presence in almost every house. It was a time of joy in families on account of salvation being brought unto them.[3]

1. C. C. Goen, ed., *The Great Awakening,* "The Works of Jonathan Edwards" (New Haven, Conn.: Yale U., 1972), 4:146.
2. Ibid., 4:149.
3. Ibid., 4:151.

It must have been to Edwards's great joy and satisfaction when his first "harvest," which lasted well over a year, proved to be the equal of anything that Stoddard had seen over his sixty years of ministry. No available material would indicate that Edwards used any methods that his grandfather had not used and developed in Northampton before him. Perhaps his success was because of the fresh touch of a younger but equally skillful hand. At any rate, the *Narrative* reports that the town was completely enveloped in spiritual concern.

> More than 300 souls were savingly brought home to Christ, in this town, in the space of half a year, and about the same number of males as females. By what I have heard Mr. Stoddard say, this was far from what has been usual in years past; for he observed that in his time, many more women were converted than men. . . . I hope that by far the greater part of persons in this town, above sixteen years of age, are such as have the saving knowledge of Jesus Christ. By what I have heard I suppose it is so in some other places; particularly at Sutherland and South Hadley.[4]

Evidence that Edwards was acceding to Stoddard's kind of leadership of the Valley's churches as well as to his evangelistic style is seen in the revival's spread to quite a few Connecticut towns. Windsor, East Windsor (where Edwards's father was minister), Suffield, Deerfield, Hadfield, and the towns of Lebanon, Coventry, Durham, Mansfield, and others felt the flames of revival.

Eventually the excitement passed, and we may well imagine that the young, thirty-three-year-old revivalist was well pleased with the blessing of God on his ministry. When revival came to the Connecticut Valley in 1735, and then most of New England in 1740, one would think Edwards would have been caught up in the activities usually associated with revivalists who try to spread themselves and their work over impossibly wide areas—but not so. Having thought out the proper theological formulas, he did his duty within his own parish, let other clergy follow suit within theirs if they chose, and let the Spirit guide the movement. Edwards traveled a bit in the Hampshire Valley and as far as Boston defending the cause, but was sedentary when compared to other revivalists. Here again his monumental consistency evokes admiration, willingly or otherwise. If the work be of God, he argued, then God must carry it to its

---

4. Ibid., 4:158.

proper ends. The Almighty needed no puny men to further His designs.

> God has also seemed to have gone out of his usual way, in the quickness of his work, and the swift progress his Spirit has made in his operations on the hearts of many. It is wonderful that persons should be so suddenly, and yet so greatly changed. . . . God's work has also appeared very extraordinary in the degrees of his influences; in the degrees both of awakening and conviction, and also of saving light, love, and joy, that many have experienced. It has also been very extraordinary in the extent of it, and its being so swiftly propagated from town to town. In former times of the pouring out of the Spirit of God on this town, though in some of them it was very remarkable, yet it reached no further than this town: the neighbouring towns all around continuing unmoved.[5]

> It seems, by God's providence, as though God had yet an elect number amongst old sinners in this place, that perhaps he is now about to bring in. It looks as though there were some that long lived under Mr. Stoddard's ministry, that God has not utterly cast off, though they stood it out under such great means as they then enjoyed. It is the more likely that God is now about finishing with them, one way or other, for their having been so long the subjects of such extraordinary means. You have seen former times of the pouring out of God's Spirit upon the town, when others were taken and you left, others were called out of darkness into marvellous light, and were brought into a glorious and happy state, and you saw not good when good came. How dark will your circumstances appear, if you shall also stand it out through this opportunity, and still be left behind![6]

Such cool and studied detachment was typical of Edwards's approach or attitude. His refusal to identify himself as chief source or exponent of revivalistic activities did not so much indicate hesitancy or modesty on his part, as it did a Calvinistic understanding of men being mere means for God's designs. Edwards desired to disclaim the leadership of the Awakening, to take few active measures to further it himself, to publish as accurate an account as he could make (the *Faithful Narrative*) and let God use that if He saw fit. It was only natural that, if he were forced to go with any party during the Awakening in its more spectacular and excessive phases during the early 1740s, he would go with the moderates. It does not seem,

5. Ibid., 4:159.
6. Jonathan Edwards, "Pressing Into the Kingdom of God," in *Puritan Sage,* ed. Vergilius Ferm (New York: Library Publishers, 1953), p. 290.

from all the sources, that extremism was a part of his being. He distrusted human nature too much for that. The moderates who agreed with Edwards were those who looked at the end result of the revival, saw that it was good (i.e., many had, to their mind, been helped or quickened), and therefore accepted it as valid. Although Edwards and the moderates did not condone emotional displays, or ally with enthusiasts, they did not oppose them, either.

The only important thing to Edwards, in the end, was that God was working in the movement. Who is man to judge, if there be evidence that God is deriving glory to Himself from a work? As he was to write in 1742 in *Some Thoughts Concerning the Present Revival Of Religion in New England:*

> Indeed God has not taken that course, nor made use of those means, to begin and carry on this great work, which men in their wisdom would have thought most advisable, if he had asked their counsel; but quite the contrary. But it appears to me that the great God has wrought like himself, in the manner of his carrying on this work; so as very much to shew his own glory, exalt his own sovereignty, power, and all-sufficiency. He has poured contempt on all that human strength, wisdom, prudence, and sufficiency, which men have been wont to trust, and to glory in; so as greatly to cross, rebuke, and chastise the pride and other corruptions of men.[7]

Jonathan Edwards's first work on revivals, *A Divine and Supernatural Light, Immediately Imparted to the Soul by the Spirit of God, Shown to be both a Scriptural, and Rational Doctrine,* was published in Boston in 1734. In some ways it may be regarded as a charter for the Great Awakening it heralded, for it lays down two aspects of a revival that were thereafter adhered to, though in ways Edwards did not foresee.

> I proceed now . . . to show how this Light is immediately given by God, and not obtained by natural means. And here, 'tis not intended that the natural faculties are not made use of in it. . . . They are the subject in such a manner, that they are not merely passive, but active in it; the acts and exercises of man's understanding are concerned and made use of in it. God in letting this Light into the soul, deals with man according to his nature, or as a rational creature, and makes use of his human faculties.[8]

7. Jonathan Edwards, *Some Thoughts Concerning the Present Revival of Religion in New England* (Boston: S. Kneeland and T. Green, 1742), pp. 6-7.
8. Jonathan Edwards, *A Divine and Supernatural Light, Immediately Imparted to the Soul by the Spirit of God, Shown to be both a Scriptural, and Rational Doctrine* (Boston: S. Kneeland and T. Green, 1734), pp. 15-16.

If this statement had been read by those who were to oppose the coming Great Awakening, they would have had to admit that this was the general doctrine of New England and that they had no real quarrel with Edwards. And if it had been read and understood properly by those who were to cause complaints, excesses probably would not have occurred. The movement begun by Edwards in the Connecticut Valley gradually declined, but it did much to prepare for the Awakening in New England, which began in 1740. Its fame became widespread, and both John Wesley and George Whitefield knew of it through *A Faithful Narrative.*

Whitefield made a circuit through the American colonies in 1740, preaching on demand (as was his custom) in cities and towns from Georgia to present-day Maine. His congregations were phenomenal, and in his wake he left results similar to Edwards's 1735 revival. In New England, Whitefield went first to Boston, where after examining Harvard College he was chagrined at its low spiritual tone and the inroads made there by secularism. He stayed three days in Northampton with Edwards, where the two compared their methods. Whitefield at this period was allowing his congregations to display some emotion in response to his preaching, and it was exactly this that Edwards had dealt with in his early work, *A Divine and Supernatural Light.* Estimates of the emotionalism vary greatly, depending upon whether the commentator was friendly or not to the Awakening. One critic, Charles Chauncy, charged Whitefield with inciting praying, singing, exhorting, and so on. Another Boston minister, Benjamin Colman, said, "I do not remember any crying out, or falling down, or fainting, either under Mr. Whitefield's or Mr. Tennent's ministry, all the while they were in Boston, though many were in great concern of soul."[9]

After the encouragement given to each other by Edwards and Whitefield, Edwards renewed his efforts to bring about revival in his area. His most famous sermon, "Sinners in the Hands of an Angry God," was preached at Enfield, Connecticut on July 8, 1741. Although it is a scathing denunciation of sinful humanity, Edwards did not intend for it to frighten his hearers, but rather for them to grasp its arguments and be convinced of them without any show of emotion. Edwards's manner of preaching was far different than Whitefield's. "Mr. Edwards in preaching," remembered one of the townspeople, "used no gestures, but looked straight forward; Gid-

---

9. Luke Tyerman, *Life of George Whitefield* (London: Hodder and Stoughton, 1890), 2:127.

eon Clark said 'he looked on the bell rope until he looked it off.' "[10]
A similar sermon, "The Justice of God in the Damnation of
Sinners," was delivered in the same unemotional way, without any
desire to bring the congregation into hysteria, but rather to make
them *think* and realize the horrors of a future without Christ. But
what congregation, no matter how quiet the delivery, could sit
through such a sermon unmoved? And whenever there was an
emotional outcry—at some points there was so much weeping and
crying to God for mercy that Edwards could not be heard—he
stopped and requested quiet so he could continue. The sermon was
based on the premise of the absolute sovereignty of God.

It is meet that God should order all these things according to his
own pleasure. By reason of his greatness and glory, by which he is
infinitely above all, he is worthy to be sovereign, and that his pleasure
should in all things take place. . . .
In the improvement of this doctrine, I would chiefly direct myself to
sinners who are afraid of damnation, in a use of conviction. This may
be matter of conviction to you, that it would be just and righteous with
God eternally to reject and destroy you. This is what you are in danger
of. You who are a Christless sinner, are a poor condemned creature:
God's wrath still abides upon you; and the sentence of condemnation
lies upon you. You are in God's hands, and it is uncertain what he will
do with you. You are afraid what will become of you. You are afraid
that it will be your portion to suffer eternal burnings, and your fears
are not without grounds; you have reason to tremble every moment.
But be you never so much afraid of it, let eternal damnation be never
so dreadful, yet it is just. God may nevertheless do it, and be righteous,
and holy, and glorious. Though eternal damnation be what you cannot
bear, and how much soever your heart shrinks at the thoughts of it, yet
God's justice may be glorious in it. The dreadfulness of the thing on
your part, and the greatness of your dread of it, do not render it the
less righteous on God's part. If you think otherwise, it is a sign that you
do not see yourself, that you are not sensible what sin is, nor how
much of it you have been guilty of. . . .
Sinners therefore spend their time in foolish arguing and objecting,
making of that which is good for nothing, making those excuses that
are not worth offering. It is in vain to keep making objections. You
stand justly condemned. The blame lies at your door: Thrust it off
from you as often as you will, it will return upon you. Sew fig-leaves as
long as you will, your nakedness will appear. You continue wilfully and
wickedly rejecting Jesus Christ, and will not have him for your Savior,

10. Perry Miller, *Jonathan Edwards* (New York: William Sloane, 1949), p. 51.

and therefore it is sottish madness in you to charge Christ with injustice that he does not save you.

Here is the sin of unbelief! Thus the guilt of that great sin lies upon you! . . .

I will finish what I have to say to natural men in the application of this doctrine, with a *caution* not to improve the doctrine to *discouragement.* For though it would be *righteous* in God forever to cast you off, and destroy you, yet it would also be just in God to save you, in and through Christ, who has made a complete satisfaction for all sin. . . .

Indeed it would not become the glory of God's majesty to show mercy to you, so sinful and vile a creature, for any thing that you have done for such worthless and despicable things as your prayers, and other religious performances. It would be very dishonorable and unworthy of God so to do, and it is in vain to expect it. He will shew mercy only on Christ's account; and that according to his sovereign pleasure, on whom he pleases, when he pleases, and in what manner he pleases. You cannot bring him under *obligation* by your works; do what you will, he will not look on himself obliged. But if it be his pleasure, he can honorably shew mercy through Christ to any sinner of you all, not one in this congregation excepted. Therefore here is encouragement for you still to seek and wait, notwithstanding all your wickedness.[11]

The great spiritual impression produced by Edwards's preaching was the direct result of the Holy Spirit's working. Hence the belief by Edwards's hearers during the Awakening that he was a messenger from God to their souls. When one man heard Edwards deliver a sermon on the day of judgment, he stated that "so vivid and solemn was the impression made on his mind, that he fully supposed that as soon as Mr. Edwards should close his discourse, the judges would descend and the final separation take place." On another occasion, when Edwards was preaching to a listless congregation, a complete change came over the hearers and before the sermon was ended the assembly seemed deeply impressed and convicted of its sin and danger.

In his famous sermon, "Sinners in the Hands of an Angry God," Edwards portrayed hell as vividly as anyone has ever done:

There is nothing that keeps wicked men at any one moment out of hell, but the mere pleasure of God. . . .

---

11. Edwards, "The Justice of God in the Damnation of Sinners," in Ferm, *Puritan Sage,* pp. 298-99, 316, 324.

O sinner, consider the fearful danger you are in! It is a great furnace of wrath, a wide and bottomless pit, full of the fire of wrath that you are held over in the hand of that God whose wrath is provoked and incensed as much against you as against many of the damned in hell. You hang by a slender thread, with the flames of divine wrath flashing about it and ready every moment to singe it, and burn it asunder. . . . And now you have an extraordinary opportunity, a day wherein Christ has thrown the door of mercy wide open, and stands calling, and crying with a loud voice to poor sinners, a day wherein many are flocking to him, and pressing into the kingdom of God; many are daily coming from the east, west, north, and south; many that were very lately in the same miserable condition that you are in are now in a happy state with their hearts filled with love to Him who has loved them, and washed them from their sins in His own blood, and rejoicing in hope of the glory of God.[12]

In actuality, these imprecatory sermons, which are among Edwards's most famous, constitute only a very small proportion of his total number of sermons. Out of the more than one thousand sermons extant, less than a dozen contain such fear-inspiring passages, and those, it should be noted, are for the most part simply Scripture—a collection of what the Bible has to say on the subject.

Until this time those furthering the Awakening had had their way. Many ministers, at first cool to revivals, had been won over—not unlikely because of the hordes of new church members the Awakening was sending to them. But in the pulpit of First Church of Boston, whose occupant had a strategic and authoritative position, was Charles Chauncy, "Old Light," dull, dreary, prosaic and pedantic, and foe of the Great Awakening. He was unquestionably in the vanguard of New England's intellectual life, and it was his influence that in later years would help to bring Arminianism, universalism, and unitarianism into the region. In 1742 he was still, probably intentionally, a Calvinist. By temperament, perhaps more than theologically, he was always of a rationalistic bent, and he firmly believed that everyone else should be the same way.

Chauncy believed that reason worked with revelation and that the Holy Spirit dealt with men as reasonable creatures who could perceive the truth and be persuaded of it. He believed the emotions must be kept under rational control or they would run headlong into fanaticism. In all the occurrences of revival, Chauncy main-

---

12. Jonathan Edwards, *Sinners in the Hands of an Angry God: A Sermon Preached at Enfield, July 8, 1741* (Boston: S. Kneeland and T. Green, 1741), pp. 9, 16, 23.

tained that Edwards and his followers were the innovators. Chauncy called to his support the likes of John Winthrop, Thomas Shepard, Increase and Cotton Mather, all Puritans of unquestionable orthodoxy.

In July 1742 a follower of George Whitefield and Gilbert Tennent, James Davenport, came to Boston to ride the crest of popularity remaining from their visits. Davenport was of unsound mind and judgment and was an exhorter in the worst sense. Immediately upon his arrival he made the rounds of Boston's ministers to inquire if they were converted. Usually he was tolerated, but he made the fatal mistake, with great consequences, of knocking on Chauncy's door with the same errand. Until then Chauncy's opposition had been mild. But at this indiscretion he rose to a veritable fury of indignation against the Awakening, publishing a broadside of seven letters or sermons, and his magnum opus *Seasonable Thoughts*, within the short span of three years.

To obtain first-hand information on the Awakening, Chauncy set out on an arduous 300-mile circuit throughout New England. The results of his investigations appeared in the early fall of 1743, in a huge octavo volume of 424 pages entitled *Seasonable Thoughts on the State of Religion in New England*. Chauncy began by listing "bad things attending this work," and put the itinerant preaching of Whitefield, Tennent, and Davenport at the top of his list.

> And what is the [meaning] of this going into other men's parishes? Is it not obviously this? The settled pastors are men, not qualified for their office, or not faithful in the execution of it; they are either unfit to take the care of souls, or grossly negligent in their duty to them. . . . Moreover, what is the tendency of this practice, but confusion and disorder? If one pastor may neglect his own people to take care of others, who are already taken care of; and, it may be much better than he can take care of them: I say, if one pastor may do this, why not another, and another still, and so on, 'till there is no such thing as church order in the land?[13]

Whitefield returned to Boston late in 1744 and read Chauncy's many slurring references to him. The two antagonists happened to meet on the street. Chauncy, taking the offensive, stated that he was sorry to see Whitefield return. The latter replied, "So is the devil!"

But the atmosphere of intensity and zeal could not last forever,

---

13. Charles Chauncy, *Seasonable Thoughts on the State of Religion in New-England, a Treatise in Five Parts* (Boston: Rogers and Fowle, 1743), pp. 50-51.

just as Solomon Stoddard had predicted in his revival theology of forty years before, in which he delineated the comings and departures of the Spirit. Another "Testimony" from well over one hundred clergymen in four colonies, which extolled the benefits and blessings of the "late happy Revival," came from the presses. Nevertheless "the extraordinary season" was over, having burned brightly for three years and more. Edwards had foreseen its decline in 1743 when he published his last polemical work, *Some Thoughts Concerning the Present Revival of Religion in New England.*

Edwards then turned his vast intellect to ponder the workings of the Spirit with men in other areas. To him, there was much work to be done and many volumes to be written. He turned to work on the intricate and fascinating books dealing with recondite matters of theology, such as his philosophical treatise *A Careful and Strict Enquiry into the Modern Prevailing Notions of Freedom of Will.*

By the time the Awakening was over, Edwards also was meeting problems in his own parish. He was unhappy with the lax standards of church membership allowed by the Half-Way Covenant and with his grandfather's principles on admission to the communion, which were still in effect. He continued to insist that the membership be composed only of those who had had a genuine experience of conversion. Many opposed him. In 1748, when he proposed to deliver a series of sermons on the qualifications for admission to the Lord's Supper, it was seen that this would challenge Stoddard's ideas; therefore he was not only forbidden to preach the series, but was asked to resign. On July 1, 1750 he preached his farewell message, and its muted strength still conveys Edwards's eminence over against the pettiness of those who could not begin to appreciate him.

Among other offers from churches wishing to secure this distinguished pastor, Edwards accepted a call from the church at Stockbridge, Massachusetts. It was a small frontier congregation, demanding less of a pastor than the very large Northampton congregation, and very likely Edwards chose that church because there he could devote more time to his writing. At Stockbridge he composed his masterly work on *Freedom of the Will* in four and one-half months, and saw it published in 1754. By general agreement it is one of the finest treatments ever written on this profoundly difficult theme. His treatise on *Original Sin* was completed in 1757 and also ranks as an exceptionally able exposition of the biblical doctrine of sin.

In 1757 the New School Presbyterian college in Princeton, New Jersey suddenly needed a president, and the college's corporation extended an invitation to Edwards to serve. After deliberation he accepted and arrived in January 1758 to take up the challenging duties of guiding a thriving college, filled with pro-revivalist students. His first sermon at Princeton was on the subject of the unchangeableness of Christ, and it produced so deep an impression upon the audience that, although two hours long, the congregation was distressed that it concluded so soon.

An epidemic of smallpox was then raging in the area, and it was thought that Edwards should be innoculated as a safeguard. At first his innoculation seemed successful, but a severe fever followed and he died on March 22, 1758.

Thomas Chalmers, the Scottish preacher, expressed the highest admiration for Jonathan Edwards's genius and spirituality, and acknowledged his own indebtedness to Edwards: "He affords perhaps the most wonderful example, in modern times, of one who stood richly gifted both in natural and in spiritual discernment; and we know not what most to admire in him, whether the deep philosophy that issued from his pen, or the humble and childlike piety that issued from his pulpit."

Jonathan Edwards, the classic Puritan preacher in wig and gown behind his sacred desk, facing a stricken congregation and speaking of the anger of a righteous God, was an awesome ambassador of the heavenly powers.

4

The International Catalyst of Awakenings— George Whitefield

In the first half of the eighteenth century every area of British life had large problems. Morality was at a low ebb, and no class of society was untouched by incredible grossness and bestiality. It was the "gin age," when 506 of the 2,000 houses in the London area of Holborn were gin shops. Gin was sold also from wheelbarrows in the streets and secretly from attics and cellars. The results of national drunkenness, Bishop Benson said, had made the English people "what they never were before, cruel and inhuman."[1]

The case of Judith Dufour, recorded in the Old Bailey *Session Papers* for February 1735, is similar to many that could be recited to show the stranglehold the liquor traffic had on multitudes. This woman took her small child to the workhouse, where it was given clothing. She then left the workhouse, strangled the child, threw the body in a ditch, sold the clothes for one shilling and fourpence, and immediately spent the money on gin, which she shared with another woman who had helped in the murder.

Vast fortunes were amassed from the manufacture of cheap alcohol, and alcohol's effects were everywhere. "Gentlemen" squires and judges boasted of being "five-bottle men." Parliament, on numerous occasions, had to adjourn early because "the honourable Members were too drunk to continue the business of State." A protest of 1751 cried out,

---

1. W. E. H. Lecky, *History of England in the Eighteenth Century* (London: Longmans, Green, 1879-1904), 1:479. For an excellent and authoritative life of Whitefield see the recent work by Arnold Dallimore, *George Whitefield: The Life and Times of the Great Evangelist of the Eighteenth-Century Revival.* 2 vols. (Westchester, Ill.: Cornerstone, 1980).

> Gin, cursed Fiend, with Fury frought,
> Makes human Race a Prey,
> It enters by a deadly Draught,
> And steals our Life away.

In any age the treatment of children is an accurate index of morality or savagery. In the late seventeenth and early eighteenth century in England, the death rate of children and the indescribable treatment toward them tells its own pathetic tale. During that time the London Bills of Mortality reveal that 74.5 percent of children of all classes died before their fifth birthday, and the poor classes had their children snatched from them even more than the rich. A petition to Parliament in 1739 to create a foundlings hospital tells of the constant "murder of poor miserable infants," of the custom of exposing new-born babies "to perish in the streets," of the placing of foundlings with "wicked and barbarous nurses" who for a small sum allow them to "starve for want of due sustenance or care," and of the few who survived being turned "into the streets to beg or steal," some being "blinded, or maimed and distorted in their limbs, in order to move pity," thus being "fitter instruments of gain" to "vile, merciless wretches."[2]

The inventory of England's ills at this time is overwhelming: gross poverty, moral depravity, grossness, deistic tendencies, rationalism, abject worldliness, indolence, infidelity, and much more. Such appalling conditions called for revitalization, and in the area of morals the organized churches seemed prepared to give no leadership. Bishop J. C. Ryle, the great evangelical Anglican leader, said of the eighteenth century in England,

> There were some learned and conscientious bishops at this era, beyond question. . . . But even the best of them sadly misunderstood the requirements of the day they lived in. They could not see that, without the direct preaching of the essential doctrines of Christ's gospel, their labors were all in vain. And, as to the majority of the bishops, they were potent for negative evil, but impotent for positive good; mighty to repress overzealous attempts at evangelization, but weak to put in action any remedy for the evils of the age.[3]

Many of the lesser clergy were not even converted to the faith they represented, much less being moral men. Lord Bolingbroke,

---

2. See J. Wesley Bready, *England: Before and After Wesley* (London: Hodder and Stoughton, 1939), p. 144.
3. J. C. Ryle, *A Sketch of the Life and Labors of George Whitefield* (Edinburgh: Johnstone and Hunter, 1850), p. 7.

no friend to Christianity, was moved to wrath at their corruption and ignorance. He addressed a group of Anglican clergymen on one occasion: "Let me seriously tell you, that the greatest miracle in the world is the subsistence of Christianity and its continued preservation as a religion, when the preaching of it is committed to the care of such un-Christian men as you."[4] These were not isolated comments; they could be multiplied over and over again. Even the palace of the Archbishop of Canterbury was so notorious a scene of drunken brawls and feastings that King George II sent this amazing letter to the Archbishop:

> My good Lord Prelate,
>   I would not delay giving you a notification of the great concern with which my breast was affected at receiving authentic information that routs had made their way into your Palace. At the same time I must signify to you my sentiments on the subject, which hold these levities and vain dissipations as utterly inexpedient, if not unlawful, to pass in a residence for many centuries devoted to divine studies, religious retirement, and the extensive use of charity and benevolence; I add, in a place where so many of your predecessors have led their lives in such sanctity as has thrown lustre on the pure religion they professed to adorn.
>   From the dissatisfaction with which you must perceive I behold these improprieties—not to speak in harder terms—and on still more pious principles, I trust you will suppress them immediately, so that I may not have occasion to show any further marks of my displeasure, or to interfere in a different manner.[5]

Unknown to England, the stage was set for God to act again. Even if neither the English church nor the English people knew where to turn for relief from the bad times, God had a genuine remedy.

It was the Evangelical Awakening, far more than any other factor or combination of factors, which lifted the English-speaking world from this moral jungle, began the missionary advance of the nineteenth century, abolished slavery, and furthered every area of social reform. Beginning about 1736 the Evangelical Awakening, led by George Whitefield and John Wesley, was a dynamic tide of gospel proclamation followed by countless conversions and the restoration of decency and morality. The Halévy Thesis, described in the Intro-

---

4. Albert D. Belden, *George Whitefield, the Awakener* (Nashville: Cokesbury, 1930), p. 56.
5. Bready, p. 48.

duction, has convincingly demonstrated that it was the social concern of the Christians, putting into practice compassion for the poor and needy, that in large measure raised English society from the low and depraved state of earlier years. The same concern prevented the horrors of the French Revolution from being duplicated in England.

> Not in the polished irony of Addison, not in the eloquence of Burke, or even in the statesmanship of Walpole or the Pitts, nor, indeed, in the satirical gibes of Samuel Johnson or Dean Swift was deliverance to be found. No, not in these was there any hope, but instead were chosen— a pot-boy out of Gloucester! a son out of the manse! What poetic justice! What romance of reform. The liquor interest and the faithless clergy raided by Providence to provide the twin flames of a heroic selflessness that could purge and cleanse and heal the nation with a divine efficacy.[6]

George Whitefield was born on December 16, 1714, the youngest of seven children of the owner of the Bell Tavern, Gloucester, England. George's father died when the boy was two, and his mother struggled to keep the tavern going, in order to give her youngest son what advantages she could provide.

Inns of that time were rough places for a boy to grow up. Thomas Brown, who lived then, described the average tavern.

> A Tavern is a little Sodom, where as many Vices are daily practiced, as ever were known in the great one: Thither Libertines repair to drink away their brains, . . . Gamsters, to shake their Elbows, and pick the pockets of such Cullies who have no more wit than to play with them; Rakes with their Whores, that by the help of Wine they may be more Impudent and more Wicked, and do these things in their Cups, that would be a Scandal to Sobriety; . . . Thither Young Quality retire to spend their Tradesmens Money, and to delight themselves with the Impudence of Lewd Harlots, . . . Thither Cowards repair to make themselves valiant by the strength of their Wine; . . . Maids to be made otherwise; Married Women to Cuckold their Husbands; and Spendthrifts to be made Miserable by a ridiculous Consumption of their own Fortunes.[7]

It is not surprising, growing up in that environment, that Whitefield in his famous *Journals* confided, "It would be endless to recount the sins and offenses of my younger days. . . . Lying, filthy

6. Belden, *Whitefield, the Awakener,* pp. 56-57.
7. Thomas Brown, *The Works of Mr. Thomas Brown* (London: S. Briscoe, 1715), 3:277-78.

talking, and foolish jesting I was much addicted to, even when very young."[8] Yet God was already at work in his heart, and he felt conviction of sin at an early age. In addition, there were times when he wanted to become a minister, and he imitated in private the clergy saying prayers and preaching. When he was twelve he attended St. Mary de Crypt school in Gloucester and remained there until he was fifteen, but the inn was failing and his mother asked George to come and aid her. So he left school and "washed mops, cleaned rooms, and, in one word, became professed and common drawer for nigh a year and a half."

In 1732, when George was seventeen, he had an opportunity to attend Pembroke College, Oxford. His mother asked him, "Will you go to Oxford, George?" "With all my heart!" was the response, although before he could enter he had to polish up much learning that had almost been forgotten. He did well in preparing himself, but recorded, "All this while I continued in sin, and at length, got acquainted with such a set of debauched, abandoned, atheistical youths, that if God, by His free, unmerited, and especial grace, had not delivered me out of their hands, I should have long since sat in the scorner's chair."[9] So the hand of God was on his shoulder, and he entered Oxford with great anticipation. Again, temptation awaited: "I was quickly solicited to join in their excess of riot with several who lay in the same room. . . . But I soon found the benefit of not yielding; for when they perceived they could not prevail, they let me alone as a singular odd fellow."[10]

At Oxford he joined with some fellow students in what was derisively termed "the Holy Club," or "Methodists." These young men had gravitated together in their common search to find a better life-style than what was commonly being practiced. Their search had hardly begun when Whitefield joined them. John Wesley, then teaching in Lincoln College, was the obvious leader of the group, but he had progressed no further than comprehending the purity imparted by the Christian faith; how this might be attained neither he nor his brother Charles knew. Members of the club devoted themselves to a legalistic set of rules that quickly made them objects of ridicule for all other students and gave them the name "Methodists."

Whitefield, as hampered by superstition in his understanding of

8. George Whitefield, *Journals* (London: Banner of Truth, 1960), pp. 37-38.
9. Ibid., pp. 42-43.
10. Ibid., p. 45.

Christianity as the rest of the group, was given Scougal's *Life of God in the Soul of Man,* by Charles Wesley.

> Though I had fasted, watched, and prayed, and received the sacrament so long, yet, I never knew what true religion was, till God sent me that excellent treatise, by the hands of my never-to-be-forgotten friend. At my first reading it, I wondered what the author meant by saying, "That some falsely placed religion in going to church, doing hurt to no one, being constant in the duties of the closet, and now and then reaching out their hands to give alms to their poor neighbours." Alas! thought I, if this be not religion, what is? God soon showed me; for in reading a few lines further, "that true religion was a union of the soul with God, and Christ formed within us," a ray of divine light was instantaneously darted in upon my soul, and from that moment, but not till then, did I know that I must be a new creature.[11]

"A ray of divine light," though not all of God's truth, fell upon Whitefield. But the practices of the Holy Club were still influential, and he began ascetic rituals to achieve this union of the soul with God.

> God only knows how many nights I have lain upon my bed groaning under the weight I felt, and bidding Satan depart from me in the name of Jesus. Whole days and weeks have I spent lying prostrate upon the ground and begging freedom from those proud hellish thoughts that used to crowd in upon and distract my soul. . . . Having no one to show me a better way, I thought to get peace and purity by outward austerities. Accordingly, by degrees, I began to leave off eating fruits and such like, and gave the money I usually spent in that way to the poor. Afterwards I always chose the worst sort of food, though my place furnished me with variety. I fasted twice a week. My apparel was mean. I thought it unbecoming for a penitent to have his hair powdered. I wore woolen gloves, a patched gown and dirty shoes, and therefore looked upon myself as very humble.[12]

During this time his tutors did not know whether to tolerate his actions, or to send him home as a madman. His bodily punishment brought him to a sickbed, and for seven weeks he despaired. But when he stopped his self-mortification God had a chance to speak to him. "Though weak, I often spent two hours in my evening retirements, and prayed over my Greek Testament, and Bishop Hall's most excellent 'Contemplations.' " Then he discovered the

---

11. Ibid., pp. 46-47.
12. Ibid., pp. 52-53.

true grounds of a sinner's justification. "I found and felt in myself, that I was delivered from the burden that had so heavily oppressed me. The spirit of mourning was taken from me, and I knew what it was to rejoice in God my Saviour."

Thus the joy of Christ came to George Whitefield, and he was the first of the Holy Club to arrive at a full understanding of Christianity's main doctrines. He had found Luther's truth and had rediscovered the power that converted Augustine. But the Wesleys, supposedly the leaders, groped in the darkness for three more years before they had their conversion experiences in 1738.

In 1736, shortly before his graduation from Oxford, George was ordained in the Anglican church by Bishop Benson, one of the few men who condemned the low tone of the age. The twenty-one-year-old Whitefield submitted to ordination only on the Bishop's insistence, who saw the talent in George and waived his own rule that twenty-three was the minimum age for ordination. Soon after, Whitefield preached his first sermon and a complaint was made that he drove fifteen people mad by his oratory. To that complaint Bishop Benson replied that he "wished such madness might not be forgotten till next Sunday."

Whitefield's appearance and abilities even at the youthful age of twenty-one were unusual. He was about average height, his manner graceful, his features regular, his complexion fair. His eyes were small, lively, dark blue, and one had a squint, brought on by the carelessness of a nurse during a childhood bout with measles. To make up for this feature, his voice was a special gift of God. It was incredibly strong, yet Whitefield could modulate it in a great variety of ways, through the whole range of feelings.[13]

Great popularity descended on him even in his early twenties, not only because of his speaking ability, but also because there were few other men in England preaching in such a vital way. Many thousands came from curiosity, to criticize, but remained first impressed, then inspired, then convinced, and finally converted; when they finally left it was with rejoicing.

Between the summer of 1736 and Christmas 1737, Whitefield's preaching became enormously popular in London, Bristol, Gloucester, and Bath. His own vivid accounts give a better idea of what happened than any other description. Whitefield's reaction to his first appearance in London he recorded as follows:

13. Luke Tyerman, *Life of George Whitefield* (London: Hodder and Stoughton, 1890), 1:51.

On Sunday, August 8th [1736] in the afternoon, I preached at Bishopsgate Church, the largeness of which, and the congregation together, at first a little dazed me; but, by adverting to God, and considering in Whose Name I was enabled to speak with power. The effect was immediate and visible to all; for as I went up the stairs almost all seemed to sneer at me on account of my youth; but they soon grew serious and exceedingly attentive, and, after I came down, showed me great tokens of respect, blessed me as I passed along, and made great enquiry who I was.[14]

Similar responses attended his preaching everywhere he went. "On Sunday mornings, long before day, you might see streets filled with people going to church, with their lanthorns in their hands. . . . The tide of popularity now began to run very high. In short time, I could no longer walk on foot as usual, but was constrained to go in a coach, from place to place, to avoid the hosannas of the multitude."[15]

On October 14, 1735, the Wesley brothers had gone to Georgia, Britain's newest colony, to work among the colonists. They were in the same primitive spiritual state that Whitefield had known and outgrown at Oxford. Ritualism was their byword. They asked him to come to Georgia and share their labors, which he did, sailing from England on December 28, 1737. His sensible touch impelled him to take collections in England for the colonists' benefit, and with the money he bought clothing and came to America with it. By then the Wesleys' austerity caused the people to reject them, and they returned to England as bitter men, half aware that their inadequate religion was the cause of their problems. Whitefield met with no such rebuff. The people took to him instantly, and he began to minister to their needs, as well as founding an orphanage for homeless children. The care of the Savannah orphanage was to become the consuming interest of his life, and ever afterward he took collections from congregations in England and America for its upkeep. Whitefield remained a few months and then set sail for home on September 9, 1738, with mixed feelings—reluctance to depart from these new friends, but eagerness to take up once again his preaching ministry.

By 1738 the Wesleys had come into full assurance of their faith, and Whitefield rejoiced in it. The similar experience they had

14. Whitefield, *Journals,* p. 77.
15. Ibid., pp. 88-89.

meant that the association of the three might be even closer. But George was a Calvinist in theology, in conformity to the tone of the Anglican articles, and the Wesleys were influenced by several factors to become Arminians. This resulted in the Methodists' teaching that the Christian could attain sinless perfection in this life, without waiting to achieve it in heaven. Such a teaching Whitefield could not accept, and it remained a bone of contention which was overcome only by their Christian love and regard for each other.

Increasingly, Whitefield met opposition, which was to harass him for years. The Wesleys had become marked men for their propagation of "societies" in cooperation with the Moravian sect, and Whitefield's connection with them put a like odium upon him. These were the formative months of Whitefield's whole ministry, for in them he developed all of the methods he was henceforth to use. After his ordination, he determined to preach to the church at large, which decision was interpreted by some as an irregular thing, wrong simply because it was done by Quakers and other sects. Attempting to preach from church to church, he found the clergy cool and the buildings closed to him. "The clergy had begun to perceive that either his doctrine or theirs, concerning the new birth and the way of a sinner's justification before God, must fall."[16] Soon, pamphlets were published attacking his doctrines of regeneration, and sermons were leveled against him from within his own church. But, predictably, all this had the opposite effect to the intention. "The opposition of the clergy increased the people's inclination to hear; and their crowding to hear increased the opposition of the clergy."[17] At this point, the idea occurred to him of preaching in the open, and on February 17, 1739, at Kingswood, near Bristol, he first attempted it to the ignorant and tough colliers (coal miners), who were the terror of the city.

> "I thought," he said, "it might be doing the service of my Creator, who had a mountain for his pulpit and the heavens for his sounding-board, and who, when his Gospel was refused by the Jews, sent his servants into the highways and hedges." The news spread rapidly among the colliers, and his audience soon increased to twenty thousand. The Gospel was indeed "good *news*" to them, for they had never heard preaching before. . . . The first discovery of their being affected

---

16. Joseph Tracy, *The Great Awakening: A History of the Revival of Religion in the Time of Edwards and Whitefield* (Boston: Tappan and Dennet, 1842), p. 48.
17. Ibid., p. 48.

was, to see the white gutters made by their tears, which plentifully fell down their black cheeks, as they came out of their coal-pits. Hundreds and hundreds of them were soon brought under deep convictions, which as the event proved happily ended in sound and thorough conversion.[18]

After this initial attempt at field preaching, which met with such resounding success and little opposition, Whitefield (and in turn John Wesley) was convinced of its value and used it for the rest of his life. Instances such as the above-mentioned were multiplied, and Whitefield's fame increased throughout England and in America. His amazingly powerful voice was frequently heard, unaided, by crowds of ten thousand to thirty thousand at one time. Not only was Whitefield able to draw that many throughout his entire ministry—incredible congregations!—but he was able to address them without difficulty. This great mass of people, standing tightly together, could not be compacted into a smaller space than six or eight acres. Obviously no building could hold them, and Whitefield turned to open-air preaching not only for the extra space, but also because many churches refused to lend him their pulpits. Ryle says of his speaking abilities, "Unhesitatingly, I believe no living preacher ever possessed such a combination of excellences as Whitefield. Some, no doubt, have surpassed him in some of his gifts. . . . But, for a combination of pure doctrine, simple and lucid style, boldness and directness, earnestness and fervor, descriptiveness and picture-drawing, pathos and feeling—united with a perfect voice, perfect delivery, and perfect command of words, Whitefield, I repeat, stands alone. No man, dead or alive, I believe, ever came alongside of him."[19]

This galvanizing preacher, who was the talk of all England, rapidly broadened his contacts and found sympathy among the Dissenters. He met and exchanged views with Isaac Watts and Philip Doddridge, and greatly impressed them. But his mind was preoccupied with the orphanage, and he sailed for the colonies again on August 14, 1739.[20]

Whitefield was no stranger to the Middle Colonists when he landed the second time in the New World. Two years previously, in 1737, newspapers in Philadelphia had carried notices of his activities with Governor Oglethorpe in Georgia toward the founding of

18. Ibid., pp. 48-49.
19. Ryle, *Life and Labors of Whitefield*, p. 33.
20. Ibid., pp. 49-51; Tyerman, *Life of Whitefield*, pp. 307-11.

the orphanage. Earlier in 1739 they had reported on his revivals in England, his audiences in the thousands, the awful silence that fell upon his hearers, and how people filled the trees nearby to hear him. In mid-October, they reported that Whitefield was returning to Georgia via Pennsylvania, and his arrival was imminent.[21]

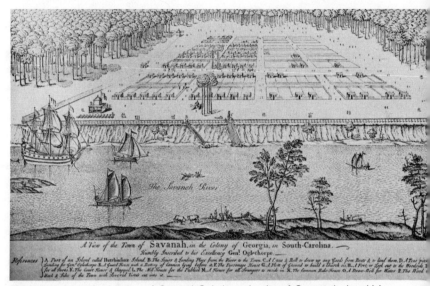

Figure 4.1 An early drawing of General Oglethorpe's city of Savannah, in which George Whitefield's orphanage was located (from an old engraving, c. 1737)

George Whitefield was immediately invited to preach in the churches of Philadelphia when he arrived there from Delaware on November 2, 1739. His only purpose in coming there had been to get some supplies before continuing on to Georgia. Certainly Whitefield had not thought of a preaching tour through the colonies, and probably had not heard of the awakenings in Massachusetts and New Jersey.

Whitefield's success in Philadelphia was overwhelming. The Great Awakening had already spread to the town, largely as a result of the stirring preaching of William Tennent, Sr., and his sons, who were pastors of Presbyterian churches in Pennsylvania and New Jersey. Among many other acquaintances, Whitefield became a lifelong friend of Benjamin Franklin, who described his influence on the town:

21. Tyerman, p. 323.

> In 1739 arrived among us from Ireland the Reverend Mr. White-
> field, who had made himself remarkable there as an itinerant preacher.
> He was at first permitted to preach in some of our churches; but the
> clergy, taking a dislike to him, soon refus'd him their pulpits, and he
> was oblig'd to preach in the fields. The multitudes of all sects and
> denominations that attended his sermons were enormous, and it was a
> matter of speculation to me, who was one of the number, to observe
> the extraordinary influence of his oratory on his hearers, and how
> much they admir'd and respected him, notwithstanding his common
> abuse of them, by assuring them they were naturally half beasts and
> half devils. It was wonderful to see the change soon made in the
> manners of our inhabitants. From being thoughtless and indifferent
> about religion, it seem'd as if all the world were growing religious, so
> that one could not walk thro' the town in an evening without hearing
> psalms sung in different families of every street.[22]

Franklin wrote this account in his *Autobiography* years later, including some other well-known Whitefield stories, and in two instances in the quotation cited above his memory had dimmed a bit. For one, Whitefield was of course not from Ireland, although he did minister there several times. Also, as a deist Franklin was no authority on the churches in Philadelphia. Possibly he was not aware that Whitefield preached from the Anglican pulpit throughout his visit, became friends with the Baptist and Presbyterian ministers, went to the Quaker meeting, and spoke outdoors from the court house steps to great crowds on Market Street when it became difficult to get the large congregations into churches.

Whitefield left Philadelphia on November 12 and then preached at Burlington, New Jersey and at Gilbert Tennent's church in New Brunswick, before reaching New York two days later. At the latter place he was denied the Anglican pulpit by the commissary, but Ebenezer Pemberton, the Presbyterian pastor of the New England party, invited him to preach there, and he did so. "Mr. Pemberton was a native of Boston, and too much of a Puritan to be frightened at Whitefield's doctrine of the new birth. As the house of worship could not hold all that desired to hear, Whitefield preached several times in the fields."[23] In addition, Gilbert Tennent, who had traveled with Whitefield to New York, preached in Whitefield's presence on their arrival in that city, and the Englishman was sincerely

---

22. Benjamin Franklin, "Autobiography," in *A Benjamin Franklin Reader,* ed. Nathan G. Goodman (New York: Crowell, 1945), p. 140.
23. Tracy, *Great Awakening,* p. 52.

impressed. "I . . . never before heard such a searching sermon. He convinced me more and more that we can preach the Gospel of Christ no further than we have experienced the power of it in our own hearts. . . . He has learned experimentally to dissect the heart of a natural man. Hypocrites must either soon be converted or enraged at his preaching."[24]

Leaving New York, Gilbert Tennent took Whitefield on a tour of the Great Awakening in New Jersey and Pennsylvania, where probably the only clergyman Whitefield met who was not Presbyterian was the Dutch Reformed Theodore Frelinghuysen. Whitefield was much impressed with all he saw:

> Tuesday, Nov. 20. Reached here about six last night; and preached to-day, at noon, for near two hours, in worthy Mr. Tennent's meeting-house, to a large assembly gathered together from all parts; and amongst them, Mr. Tennent told me, was a great number of solid Christians. About three in the afternoon, I preached again; and, at seven, I baptised two children, and preached a third time. Among others who came to hear the Word, were several ministers, whom the Lord has been pleased to honour, in making them instruments of bringing many sons to glory. One was a Dutch Calvinistic minister, named Freeling Housen, pastor of congregation about four miles from New Brunswick. He is a worthy old soldier of Jesus Christ, and was the beginner of the great work which I trust the Lord is carrying on in these parts. He has been strongly opposed by his carnal brethren, but God has appeared for him, in a surprising manner, and made him more than conqueror, through His love. He has long since learnt to fear him only, who can destroy both body and soul in hell.
>
> Another was Mr. Cross, minister of a congregation of Barking Bridge, about twenty miles from Brunswick. He himself told me of many wonderful and sudden conversions that had been wrought by the Lord under his ministry. For some time, eight or nine used to come to him together, in deep distress of soul; and, I think, he said, three hundred of his congregation, which is not a very large one, were brought home to Christ. They are now looked upon as enthusiasts and madmen, and treated as such by those who know not God, and are ignorant of the hidden life of Jesus Christ in their hearts.[25]

These pages of Whitefield's *Journal* are full of his amazement and appreciation of the long-standing efforts of many such clergymen to bring revival. Suddenly he became conscious, it is apparent in these

---

24. Whitefield, *Journals,* pp. 347-48.
25. Ibid., pp. 351-52.

paragraphs, that what Solomon Stoddard and Jonathan Edwards had striven for and achieved in Northampton was not unique, but that here in the Middle Colonies was a veritable company of fellow evangelists, diligently working to bring about the Great Awakening. In addition they welcomed him and begged for his help; not to cast his lot with them, however temporarily, would be a mistake. But Whitefield's mentor and guide, Gilbert Tennent, had more to show him. The revivalists recognized the need for an educated ministry, even in a wilderness, and were struggling to fulfill it. Whitefield continued,

> Thursday, Nov. 22. Set out for Neshaminy (twenty miles distant from Trent Town), where old Mr. Tennent lives, and keeps his academy, and where I was to preach today, according to appointment. It happens very providentially, that Mr. Tennent and his brethren are appointed to be a Presbytery by the Synod, so that they intend breeding up gracious youths, and sending them out into our Lord's vineyard. The place wherein the young men study now is, in contempt, called *the College.* It is a log-house, about twenty feet long, and nearly as many broad; and, to me, it seemed to resemble the school of the old prophets. That their habitations were mean, and that they sought not great things for themselves, is plain from that passage of Scripture, wherein we are told, that at the feast of the sons of the prophets, one of them put on the pot, whilst the others went forth to fetch some herbs out of the field. From this despised place, seven or eight worthy ministers of Jesus have lately been sent forth; more are almost ready to be sent; and a foundation is now being laid for the instruction of many others.[26]

So the mutual appreciation of the revivalists and Whitefield increased through such incidents, from the fall of 1739 to the following summer.

In all, Whitefield crossed the Atlantic Ocean thirteen times to visit the colonies and his orphanage at Savannah. He traveled the length of the colonies, becoming the good friend of the great men of America—Benjamin Franklin, Jonathan Edwards, Gilbert Tennent, and others. His effect upon the colonies is fascinating to study. Franklin, then thirty-three but already a leading citizen of Philadelphia, and Whitefield, only twenty-five, were attracted to each other immediately. Whitefield told Franklin of his plans for the orphanage, and Franklin suggested he move it to Philadelphia, then the largest city in America. Whitefield rejected this idea, however, and

---

26. Ibid., p. 354.

so Franklin decided not to give him a penny toward it. But he had not counted on the power of Whitefield's oratory. Franklin told openly,

> I happened soon afterwards to attend one of his sermons, in the course of which I perceived he intended to finish with a collection, and I silently resolved he should get nothing from me. I had in my pocket a handful of copper money, three or four silver dollars, and five in gold. As he proceeded I began to soften and concluded to give the copper. Another stroke of his oratory made me ashamed of that and determined me to give the silver, and he finished so admirably that I emptied my pocket into the collection dish, gold and all.[27]

In 1740 Franklin and other friends erected for Whitefield a hall in Philadelphia, and after he had used it for his own purposes, it was used for an academy, with Whitefield the inspirer and original trustee of the Charity School. Eventually the Charity School developed into the present University of Pennsylvania. A similar demonstration of Whitefield's social concern and interest in education was his encouragement of William Tennent's Log College at Neshaminy, a few miles north of Philadelphia. This school was later moved to New Jersey and became Princeton University.

In 1740, when the Great Awakening was at its height in the Middle Colonies, Whitefield went north and continued his dynamic preaching in New England. At Boston, Ipswich, Newbury, Hampton, Portsmouth, and other towns he addressed huge throngs, such as had not been seen before. Jonathan Edwards welcomed him, for they were kindred spirits.

Only a few of the incidents that crowded Whitefield's life can be recounted. For thirty-four years, until his early death in 1770, his life was one of uniform employment, incessantly preaching, and comforting men. There was hardly a town of any size in England, Scotland, and Wales that he did not visit. As a minister of the Church of England, when churches were opened to him, he preached in them; when churches were closed, he was ready and willing to preach in a field. During that time he always proclaimed the same great gospel, and always he had an immense effect. In one Whitsuntide week he preached in Moorfields and then received one thousand letters from people inquiring about Christianity. He also admitted to the Lord's table three hundred fifty more. It has

---

27. Franklin, "Autobiography," p. 141.

been estimated that in his lifetime he preached eighteen thousand times to more than one hundred million persons. Never, as Ryle remarks, was there a man of whom it could be so truly said that he spent and was spent for God.

Many sermons of Whitefield's were famous, and it is difficult to select one as most representative. But perhaps the following is a good example of his evangelistic style, as well as the humor that could flash through his sermons. It is from a contemporary newspaper account, which sets the scene in Boston, Massachusetts.

After he had finished his prayer, he knelt a long time in profound silence; and so powerfully had it affected the most heartless of his audience, that a stillness like that of the tomb pervaded the whole house. Before he commenced his sermon, long, darkening columns crowded the bright sunny sky of the morning, and swept their dull shadows over the building, in fearful augury of the storm that was approaching.

"See that emblem of human life," said he, as he pointed to a flitting shadow. "It paused for a moment, and concealed the brightness of heaven from our view; but it is gone. And, where will you be, my hearers, when your lives have passed away like that dark cloud! Oh, dear friends, I see thousands sitting attentive with their eyes fixed on the poor unworthy preacher. In a few days we shall all meet at the judgment seat of Christ. We shall form part of that vast assembly which will gather before His throne. Every eye will behold the Judge. With a voice whose call you must abide, and answer He will inquire, whether on earth you strove to enter in at the strait gate; whether you were supremely devoted to God; whether your hearts were absorbed in Him. . . .

"O false and hollow Christians, of what avail will it be that you have done many things? That you have read much in the sacred Word? That you have made long prayers? That you have attended religious duties, and appeared holy in the eyes of men? What will all this be, if, instead of loving God supremely, you have been supposing you should exalt yourself in heaven by acts really polluted and unholy?

"O sinner! by all your hopes of happiness, I beseech you to repent. Let not the wrath of God be awakened! Let not the fires of eternity be kindled against you! See there!" said the impassioned preacher, pointing to a flash of lightning, "it is a glance from the angry eye of Jehovah! Hark!" continued he, raising a finger in listening attitude, as the thunder broke in a tremendous crash, "it was the voice of the Almighty as He passed by in His anger!"

As the sound died away Whitefield covered his face with his hands, and fell on his knees apparently lost in prayer. The storm passed rapidly by, and the sun, bursting forth, threw across the heavens the magnificent arch of peace. Rising and pointing to it the young preacher cried, "Look upon the rainbow, and praise Him who made it. Very beautiful it is in the brightness thereof. It compasseth the heaven about with glory and the hands of the Most High have bended it."[28]

Whitefield was asked to publish this sermon, and he replied that he would consent to it if the printer could manage to include, in addition to the words, the lightning, thunder, and rainbow that went with them!

Many of England's nobility were fascinated by Whitefield, and heard him frequently. Among his most loyal supporters was Lady Huntingdon, but the famous Lord Chesterfield was another great admirer, declaring, "Mr. Whitefield's eloquence is unrivalled, his zeal inexhaustible." Once the worldly Chesterfield attended a service where Whitefield compared the sinner to a blind beggar. Deserted by his dog, the blind man came up to a precipice. But Whitefield so warmed with his subject, and unfolded it with such graphic power, that the whole audience was kept in breathless silence over the movements of the poor old man. Just as the beggar was about to fall to his destruction, the cynical Lord could take no more. He leaped to his feet crying, "He is gone! He is gone!"

Lord Bolingbroke was another greatly influenced by Whitefield, referring to him as "the most extraordinary man in our times. He has the most commanding eloquence I ever heard in any person; his abilities are very considerable; his zeal unquenchable; and his piety and excellence genuine—unquestionable. The bishops and inferior orders of the clergy are very angry with him, and endeavor to represent him as a hypocrite, an enthusiast; but this is not astonishing—there is so little real goodness or honesty among them."[29]

His life was devoted and expended in that highest pursuit, pointing souls to God. In that, Whitefield by human standards was fabulously successful; with his lifelong friend John Wesley, he brought the English-speaking world back from scepticism and immorality to its Christian inheritance. All Christendom benefited immeasurably by his labors.

> Whitefield was the first to essay open-air and field preaching, and the first to get into touch with and realize the potentialities of the Religious Societies of the period which undoubtedly contributed to the

---

28. Belden, *Whitefield, the Awakener,* pp. 110-11.
29. Ibid., p. 5.

Methodist model. He was the first to see the necessity for and to appoint lay preachers and the first to perceive the possibilities of religious journalism. Finally, and perhaps most important of all, he saw very vividly the spiritual need of the wider world of his time, and pioneered the Methodist gospel in Scotland, Ireland, and the American colonies before Wesley had fairly got under way.[30]

This man provided the spark that set England on fire, and he provided the inspiration for the Wesleys who systematized his methods and reaped the benefits of the awakening that Whitefield began.

---

30. Ibid., pp. 233-34.

5

The Methodist Revival—The Wesleys and Francis Asbury

John Wesley (1703-1791), the founder of Methodism, left behind him at his death titanic achievements for God that have seldom been equalled. As one of the principal authors of the Evangelical Awakening, Wesley created a perpetual memorial to his devoted labors. The historian J. R. Green said the Evangelical Awakening "changed, after a time, the whole tone of English society. The church was restored to new life and activity. Religion carried to the hearts of the people a fresh spirit of moral zeal, while it purified our literature and our manners. A new philanthropy reformed our prisons, infused clemency and wisdom into our penal laws, abolished the slave trade, and gave the first impulse to popular education."[1]

During his long lifetime of eighty-eight years, Wesley traveled 250,000 miles on horseback, preached 45,000 sermons, wrote 233 books or pamphlets, and helped with the writing of more than 100 others. His output in all areas was stupendous, and what he accomplished put Christians of all churches in his debt.

John Wesley was born June 17, 1703, at the Anglican rectory in Epworth, Lincolnshire, England. He was the fifteenth child of Samuel and Susannah Wesley. His mother was a remarkable woman of strong Christian faith and character, and under her instruction the children made remarkable progress. Epworth, however, was very rural, and the parishioners became hostile to their minister. During Samuel Wesley's long ministry there, the parishioners crippled his

1. J. R. Green, *A Short History of the English People* (New York: Harper and Brothers, 1878), p. 736.

cattle, burned his crops, and finally on February 9, 1709, someone put a torch to the rectory. As the parents fled the blazing home, they thought all their children had escaped, but suddenly John and his brother Charles were seen at an upper window and rescued just in time.

In 1720 John went to Oxford University, and was ordained a minister in the Church of England on September 22, 1728. He had many friends and loved tennis, riding, and swimming. But increasingly he realized that he lacked a vital, living faith. He came from the high-church party, and rules and works-righteousness were his bywords. Searching for something more dynamic, he and Charles founded the "Holy Club" to include concerned students.

In 1735 Governor James Oglethorpe of the new colony of Georgia persuaded John and Charles to come as missionaries to the New World. There the Wesleys found only disappointment. John's own stiffness and high-handed practices made him very disliked by the colonists. Then he had an unfortunate love affair with a young lady that ended up in a law court. Altogether, most of the Georgia episodes were failures.

All but one. During the voyage over, the Wesleys became acquainted on shipboard with a group of Moravians, followers of Count Nikolaus von Zinzendorf (1700-1760). The Moravians were attempting to rekindle a warm faith and love to Christ in the cold German Lutheranism of the day and were among the first to engage in the modern missionary movement. A group of these sturdy believers showed no fear on the trans-Atlantic journey to America when several great storms threatened to sink the ship, and John Wesley was enormously impressed with their confidence and calm faith in God. On the return voyage he remembered that and could only lament his own lack of faith: "I went to America to convert the Indians; but oh! who shall convert me?"[2]

Back in London on Wednesday, May 24, 1738, Wesley went to a meeting held on Aldersgate Street, and as the preacher spoke, "about a quarter before nine, while he was describing the changes which God works in the heart through faith in Christ, I felt my heart strangely warmed. I felt I did trust in Christ, Christ alone, for salvation; and an assurance was given me that he had taken away *my* sins, even *mine*, and saved *me* from the law of sin and death."[3]

---

2. John Wesley, *The Journal*, ed. Nehemiah Curnock (London: Epworth, 1960), 1:418.
3. Ibid., 1:475-76.

With this conviction overwhelming him, Wesley was from that point to his death a changed man. His old stress on rules and works to please God vanished; from then on he was a proclaimer of faith in the risen Savior alone.

George Whitefield, the first of the "Holy Club" at Oxford to come to a dynamic faith, was already a popular speaker drawing large audiences. In February 1739, Whitefield went to the city of Bristol, where his popularity was enormous; his preaching brought about many conversions, and revival broke out. When some of the churches were closed to him, Whitefield spoke with tremendous success in the open air to the coal miners at Kingswood. John Wesley was invited by Whitefield to observe the vast crowds and the revival at Bristol, but Wesley wrote in his *Journal*, "I could scarce reconcile myself to this strange way of preaching in the fields . . . having been all my life (till very lately) so tenacious of every point relating to decency and order, that I should have thought the saving of souls almost a sin, if it had not been done in a church."[4] The next day Wesley threw aside his caution and tried the new way himself. His fears disappeared as he realized that this was the perfect method for reaching large numbers.

Figure 5.1 Preaching out of doors, John Wesley often faced murderous mobs such as this one at Wednesbury (from an old engraving)

4. Ibid., 2:167.

Soon Wesley developed the society as a way for encouraging converts. By means of prayer and Bible study among a small group, the society leader could discern if each member was growing in grace. Smaller "bands" of five to ten persons were formed for those who wanted even closer fellowship. The only requirement to enter a society was that persons have "a desire to flee from the wrath to come, to be saved from their sins." The Methodist movement grew with great rapidity as a revival movement within the Church of England. Another method that Wesley developed was the use of lay preachers, and eventually riders were recruited who covered a circuit and ministered to the growing societies along it. In combination, all these methods allowed Methodism to make maximum use of its preachers in the establishment and nurture of many societies, and it is easy to understand its rapid growth in the succeeding years.

John Wesley was not an original theologian, but he did emphasize certain doctrines that gave a distinctive tone to Methodism. Many of those emphases may have been in reaction to the immorality and low tone of his day, in his stressing the holiness of the Christian life. Like Edwards, Whitefield, Tennent, and the other awakeners he believed the Scriptures to be infallible and inerrant throughout. He agreed with the Calvinists in the doctrines of the sovereignty of God and the total depravity and lostness of man. But he parted company with them over the questions of limited atonement and an unconditional election of some to salvation and others to reprobation. This is called evangelical Arminianism and must be distinguished from rationalistic Arminianism, which takes an optimistic view of man's abilities and tends to deny original sin. Wesley would never accept this, because he always made it plain that he completely agreed with the Calvinists on the question of original sin and man's hopeless condition without repentance and faith in Christ.

But John Wesley believed that Calvinism painted too gloomy a picture of God's electing only some to salvation. He wanted all to feel that there was hope in conditional predestination—that man was free to choose for or against Christ, and that he therefore had a certain share in working out his own salvation. This became a great area of contention between Calvinists—such as Whitefield—and the Methodists for decades to come.

To Wesley, the Christian life after justification is a continual escape from sin and the unceasing attainment of holiness or sanctification. Here is the distinctive emphasis of Wesleyan Methodism. The constant presence of the Holy Spirit is needed if the Christian life is to be victorious. Once a person is converted he should be very mindful of the Spirit's work within him, and that awareness should express itself in love, joy, devotion, and zeal. Outward evidences of conversion are best shown, Wesley believed, in renouncing the worldly pleasures of the unsaved such as gambling, card playing, dancing, going to the theater, and particularly the use of liquor. The impact these ideas of "Christian perfection" (the avoidance of known sin) would have upon all evangelical Protestant conceptions of morality and the Christian life throughout the nineteenth century in America and England would be immeasurable.

With a leader of such organizational genius and zeal as John Wesley, Methodism forged ahead. John was assisted by his brother Charles (1707-1788) in several vital aspects, particularly in the composing of hymns that sang their way into the hearts of the English-speaking world. Canon Overton called Charles Wesley "the great hymn-writer of all ages," and today most churches still sing "Jesus, Lover of My Soul"; "Hark, the Herald Angels Sing"; "Christ, Whose Glory Fills the Skies"; "O for a Thousand Tongues to Sing"; "Love Divine, All Loves Excelling"; and many more of the approximately 6,500 hymns that Charles wrote. In previous times hymns were not only sung but also memorized by Christians, and it has been said that when people learn theology by the singing of hymns, they retain and understand it far better than by merely hearing it from a pulpit.

As Methodism flourished in England, young men of dedication to God offered themselves as preachers. Francis Asbury was one of those, and he rose in the ranks of Methodism to be one of its most dynamic leaders. Asbury may have taken John Wesley as his model, for he duplicated in his own wilderness diocese of America what Wesley had accomplished in England. He gave his own account of his earliest years:

> I was born in Old England, near the foot of Hampstead Bridge, in the parish of Handsworth, about four miles from Birmingham, in Staffordshire, and according to the best of my after-knowledge on the twentieth or twenty-first day of August, in the year of our Lord 1745.
> My father's name was Joseph, and my mother's Elizabeth Asbury. They were people in common life; were remarkable for honesty and industry, and had all things needful to enjoy; had my father been as

saving as laborious, he might have been wealthy. As it was, it was his province to be employed as a farmer and gardener by the two richest families in the parish. My parents had but two children—a daughter called Sarah, and myself. My lovely sister died in infancy; she was a favorite, and my dear mother, being very affectionate, sunk into deep distress at the loss of a darling child, from which she was not relieved for many years. It was under this dispensation that God was pleased to open the eyes of her mind, she living in a very dark, dark, dark day and place. . . .

God sent a pious man, not a Methodist, into our neighborhood, and my mother invited him to our house; by his conversation and prayers I was awakened before I was fourteen years of age. It was now easy and pleasing to leave my company, and I began to pray morning and evening, being drawn by the cords of love, as with the bands of a man. I soon left our blind priest, and went to West Bromwich Church; here I heard Ryland, Stillingfleet, Talbot, Bagnall, Mansfield, Hawes, and Venn, great names, and esteemed gospel ministers.[5]

The conditions that Asbury described of the spiritual climate in England at that time ("a very dark, dark, dark day and place") are not exaggerated. His mother's conversion to Methodism is a representative commentary of the abject state of religion and the disgust felt by laypeople in the first half of the eighteenth century. Many English ministers were tinged with deism but would not go so far as to reject the orthodox creeds. The clergy became coldly intellectual, unconcerned with the low morals of the majority of Englishmen. In the clergys' books the learning was vast, but in the pulpit it was deadly. "Dull, duller, and dullest" was an estimation of their appeal. Rationalism made the ministers afraid to utter anything that might be construed as an emotional statement or appeal. Deistic tendencies, rationalism, abject worldliness within the churches, indolence, infidelity—all of these characteristics and more described the eighteenth-century English church scene. Any one of them would have been sufficient to call for a revitalization of the church.

English society was even worse, and one may wonder if the church's weaknesses contributed to the grossness and immorality, or if the church simply reflected it. England from the Restoration to the Colonial War was coarse, lawless, ignorant, and vain. Such was the society to which the Wesleys came—and Asbury—as messengers of God's grace. This background is indispensable in understanding their lives and their magnetic appeal.

5. Francis Asbury, *The Journal and Letters of Francis Asbury* (Nashville: Abingdon, 1958), 1:720-21.

Asbury's first contacts with vibrant Methodism came in hearing preachers of note such as John Ryland (1736-1822) and Henry Venn (1725-1797), but he was most influenced later by Benjamin Ingham (1712-1772), and especially by the Swiss John William Fletcher (1729-1785), the vicar of Madeley, ministers of the Church of England, who helped greatly in Wesley's work. Fletcher was a fiery preacher, and to fourteen-year-old Asbury he was powerful and irresistibly attractive. After further contacts with the Methodists near his home, Asbury continued:

> I became very serious, reading a great deal—Whitefield and Cennick's Sermons, and every good book I could meet with. It was not long before I began to inquire of my mother, who, where, what were the Methodists; she gave me a favorable account, and directed me to a person that could take me to Wednesbury to hear them. I soon found this was not the Church, but it was better. The people were so devout, men and women kneeling down, saying "Amen." Now, behold! they were singing hymns, sweet sound! Why, strange to tell! the preacher had no prayer book, and yet he prayed wonderfully! What was yet more extraordinary, the man took his text, and had no sermon book: thought I, this is wonderful indeed! It is certainly a strange way, but the best way. He talked about confidence, assurance, etc., of which all my flights and hopes fell short. I had no deep conviction, nor had I committed any deep known sins. At one sermon, some time after, my companion was powerfully wrought on. I was exceedingly grieved that I could not weep like him; yet I knew myself to be in a state of unbelief. On a certain time when we were praying in my father's barn I believed the Lord pardoned my sins and justified my soul; but my companions reasoned me out of this belief, saying "Mr. Mather said a believer was as happy as if he was in heaven." I thought I was not as happy as I would be there, and gave up my confidence, and that for months; yet I was happy, free from guilt and fear, and had power over sin, and felt great inward joy. After this we met for reading and prayer, and had large and good meetings, and were much persecuted, until the persons at whose houses we held them were afraid, and they were discontinued. I then held meetings frequently at my father's house, exhorting the people there, as also at Sutton Colefield, and several souls professed to find peace through my labors. I met class a while at Bromwhich Heath, and met in band at Wednesbury. I had preached some months before I publicly appeared in the Methodist meeting-houses; when my labors became more public and extensive, some were amazed, not knowing how I had exercised elsewhere. Behold me now a local preacher!—the humble and willing servant of any and of every preacher that called on me by night or by day; being ready, with hasty

steps, to go far and wide to do good, visiting Derbyshire, Staffordshire, Warwickshire, Worcestershire, and, indeed, almost every place within my reach, for the sake of precious souls; preaching generally, three, four, and five times a week, and at the same time pursuing my calling. I think, when I was between twenty-one and twenty-two years of age, I gave myself up to God and his work, after acting as a local preacher near the space of five years.[6]

Asbury was apprenticed to a blacksmith from 1759-1765, at a forge near his home. He had received only a few years of formal schooling, normal for a boy of his class. Lack of more education did not prevent his being accepted as a preacher at local Methodist meetings, to which he preached from three to five times a week. In 1766, when he was twenty-one, he gave up his secular work in the foundry and determined from then on to be a Methodist preacher exclusively, at which time he began to assist on the Staffordshire and Gloucestershire circuits. In August 1767 he gave satisfactory proof of his call to preach[7] and was admitted on trial to a position in Bedfordshire.

Methodism in America was in its early stages when Asbury was appointed missionary to the colonies in 1771. About 1760 a party of German refugees from the Palatinate had landed in New York. For many years they had sojourned in County Limerick, Ireland, where some of their party had been won to Methodism. Among them were Barbara Heck and Philip Embury, the former a woman of devout love for God, the latter a Methodist class leader and local preacher. For some years no attempt was made to conduct services. Finally in 1766 Barbara Heck became alarmed because of the dangers of apostasy, and Embury was impelled to begin preaching. A more inopportune time for the inauguration of Methodism could hardly have been conceived, humanly speaking. The Stamp Act had been passed the preceding year, and the colonies were in the throes of the agitation that was to culminate in the American Revolution. However, the labors of Whitefield had to some extent paved the way for the pioneers of Methodism.

The first services where held in Embury's home, but within a short time a larger room became necessary. Then, a startling thing occurred. Early in 1767 as the society was gathered for worship, a British officer in full uniform with sword came into the room. The

---

6. Ibid., 1:721-22.
7. Herbert Asbury, *A Methodist Saint* (New York: Knopf, 1927), p. 16.

members wondered with apprehension if he had come to put a stop to their worship and to arrest someone. Then they saw this man in his scarlet regimentals join in worship with them. After the service fear turned to delight when he introduced himself as Captain Thomas Webb, barracks master at Albany. He was one of John Wesley's own converts and had been licensed by Wesley as a preacher. Jesse Lee, the first historian of Methodism, described the next events: "The novelty of a man preaching in a scarlet coat soon brought great numbers to hear, more than the room could contain. Some more of the inhabitants joined the society. They then united and hired a rigging loft to meet in that would contain a large congregation."[8]

Captain Webb was an excellent preacher, "a man of fire," Wesley called him. He was just the one to aid the small group of Methodists in New York City, for not only was he a fine preacher, but he was an aggressive leader, well-to-do, and generous. In 1768 Wesley Chapel was built on John Street, with Captain Webb heading the list of 250 contributors with a thirty pound donation. Meanwhile, Webb carried Methodism to Pennsylvania, Long Island, New Jersey, and Delaware. A thriving society sprang up in Philadelphia and bought a half-finished church begun by a German Reformed congregation. This building, St. George's, is the oldest Methodist church still in use in America. In 1768 and 1769 four new missionaries came from England—Richard Boardman, Joseph Pilmoor, Robert Williams, and John King. The eyes of Old World Methodism were beginning to turn to the New World, realizing that there was a huge and fertile territory for expansion.

In 1771, at the Conference in Bristol, England, Francis Asbury volunteered for missionary work in America. He and Richard Wright were selected, and they sailed September 4, landing in Philadelphia October 27. They placed themselves under the direction of Richard Boardman, whose headquarters were in New York; he was general assistant to John Wesley and was in sole charge of the work in America. In dedicating his life to the evangelization of America, Asbury had entertained only the highest aspirations for his own ministry and for the spread of Christianity in general. But he was initially disappointed because Methodism seemed destined to remain in its infancy in America, without growth, vision, or initiative

8. Jesse Lee, *Short History of the Methodists* (Baltimore: Magill and Clime, 1810), p. 24.

(except for the work in Philadelphia and New York). Boardman had no initiative and was lacking in leadership. He possessed the missionary spirit and was a zealous worker for God, but he did not have the vision of an evangelized America that so obsessed Asbury and Wesley. Asbury preached his first sermon in New York from 1 Corinthians 2:2, and alternated with Boardman in the John Street Chapel, each preaching several times a week. But he found little to please him. Discipline was lax, some of the Methodists were addicted to fashionable clothing, and there was a general air of lightheartedness that Asbury found extremely distressing. He was also greatly annoyed because Boardman insisted that both should remain in the city, as well as Captain Webb, and serve the New York congregation. In Asbury's eyes such a scheme was completely wrong, for he was eager to begin his evangelistic campaign and win the lost to Christ.

Asbury's own *Journal*, at that time recently begun and the most valuable record of the growth of Wesleyanism for the next forty-five years, best presents the indignant thoughts of the restless young man.

> Tuesday, November 19 [1771]. I remain in New York, though unsatisfied with our being both in town together. I have not yet the thing which I seek—a circulation of preachers, to avoid partiality and popularity. However, I am fixed to the Methodist plan, and do what I do faithfully as to God. I expect trouble is at hand, This I expected when I left England, and I am willing to suffer, yea, to die, sooner than betray so good a cause by any means. It will be a hard matter to stand against all opposition, as an iron pillar strong, and steadfast as a wall of brass: but through Christ strengthening me I can do all things.
>
> Thursday, 21. At present I am dissatisfied. I judge we are to be shut up in the cities this winter. My brethren seem unwilling to leave the cities, but I think I shall show them the way. I am in trouble, and more trouble is at hand.[9]

It should be remarked here that, although he may have been indolent, Boardman was no troublemaker, and he did not dislike Asbury or punish him in any way for his insubordination. In spite of Asbury's defiance, we are compelled to admit that he had rare insight, for his idea of itinerancy was used as the chief means of Methodism's growth in its first century. The circuit system had been devised by Wesley for English usage, where it was quite successful.

9. F. Asbury, *Journal and Letters,* 1:10.

But in America, where congregations were small and separated by large distances, and settled pastorates were completely impractical, the circuit plan proved singularly adapted to the rural and frontier areas of the United States. After 1784, when he was made head of Methodism in America, Asbury had district superintendents under him and circuit riders under the district superintendents. As the name indicates, circuit riders were assigned areas to cover, some with routes as long as five hundred miles. They had to be traversed by whatever conveyance was possible—on horseback, by canoe, or on foot. This describes the system after Asbury had put it into operation a few years later, but he saw clearly its practicality and followed it himself, from the beginning.

Asbury not only disagreed with how Boardman directed the preachers, but also with the conduct of Methodists in New York and Philadelphia. He believed they were too worldly and of insufficient dedication, and he quarreled with several of the lay leaders in both cities. This situation caused Asbury to ignore the two cities for many years. But just when he seemed to be getting nowhere, a letter arrived from Wesley on October 10, 1772, that appointed him general assistant in charge of America and demoted Boardman to his helper. Asbury stayed in the supreme position until June 1773, and during that period strengthened his hand, especially in Maryland where the Methodists were beginning to flourish far more than in the North. Asbury foresaw that increasing his popularity there might be of use later.

Thomas Rankin was sent from England as general assistant in 1773. Rankin, never before in America, was a strict disciplinarian. In this poor choice Wesley did not see the colonies' need of more than discipline—vision, great energy, tact, and sympathy with the colonists' cause, none of which Rankin possessed. He arrived on June 1, 1773, to find a force of ten preachers and 1,160 Methodists—180 each in New York and Philadelphia, 200 in New Jersey, 500 in Maryland, and 100 in Virginia.[10]

Rankin was bound for failure from the start. His misconceptions of the needs of American Methodism were enormous. His greatest mistake was to think of the societies as forever tied to the Church of England, instead of seeing that in the colonies they were rapidly becoming independent. With the Revolutionary War impending and the dislike for the English clergy growing constantly, such a

10. Ibid., p. 84.

person was exactly the wrong type to lead the movement.

Meanwhile, in 1775 Asbury was stationed in Norfolk, Virginia when John Wesley published his *Calm Address* to the Americans, the climax of his misplaced political campaign upholding England's policies toward the colonies. That writing helped only in putting all Methodists under suspicion as Tories, and merely added more fuel to a fire already out of control. Later, Wesley wrote to Asbury ordering him to return to England, which Asbury would not do. Rankin soon departed with all the other preachers except Asbury, never to return.

The departure of Wesley's English missionaries was a most fortunate thing for American Methodism, not only because it permitted the movement to develop indigenously, but also because it brought to the fore native leaders who were forced to shoulder the burden and develop into good captains on their own.[11] It was a particularly good sign for Asbury, as was to be seen in a short time. He was a man of infinitely greater vision than Rankin. From the beginning he appears to have foreseen the success of the war and the independence of the American colonies, and there is plenty of evidence that he had always intended to side with the colonies. He also foresaw that Rankin's conduct and that of the other British preachers was such that eventually they would either be imprisoned by the colonial authorities or made to leave the country. He knew such a development would again give him control of the Methodists in America.[12]

During the war years, because of the prejudices against Wesley's pamphlets, the Methodists suffered severely. Asbury had to hide out in Delaware for two years. Growth of the movement was suspended if not actually set back, for being a follower of Wesley was dangerous business. Yet even during the war several revivals added members in areas remote from the war zone.

After the war was over, American Methodists took the opportunity of independence to form themselves into a distinct denomination, separate from the greatly weakened Church of England. Wesley himself realized that, with so many of the Anglican clergymen gone, something must be done if the Methodists were to have the sacraments available to them. In 1784 he decided that as a presbyter he had the power to ordain—a precedent he found in the prac-

11. William W. Sweet, *The Methodists,* Religion on the American Frontier, vol. 4 (Chicago: U. of Chicago, 1946), p. 6.
12. H. Asbury, *Methodist Saint,* pp. 93-94.

tices of the early church where presbyters had even ordained bishops. Wesley ordained Richard Whatcoat and Thomas Vasey, who then sailed for America in the company of Thomas Coke, an Anglican clergyman who had greatly assisted Wesley in Methodism. Coke was appointed by Wesley to be "joint superintendent" with Asbury "over our brethren in North America." After the three arrived from England, the famous "Christmas Conference" of 1784 met in Baltimore, and the new Methodist Episcopal Church was founded. While Coke busied himself with several projects, Asbury, now ordained and with Wesley's full support, continued his direction of the American Methodists. In 1787 Coke and Asbury agreed that in the American situation the title *bishop* was more proper than *superintendent*. From then on that term was used by all for the two recognized leaders, although it was contrary to the views of Wesley, who was furious when he heard they were using it without his approval.

The opening frontier, even previous to the Revolution, was the most conspicuous factor influencing the spirit of the colonies. The frontier, that simmering melting pot culture that made up the American West, was enthusiastic, disorderly, rugged, competitive, hard, and sometimes pitiless, without respect for priority or authority. Religion and morals were easily left behind in more civilized areas. Could the churches follow the pioneers to the West?

Throughout the colonies, in the decades before and after the Revolution, there was widespread antipathy toward religion. Such antipathy promised to develop into open atheism, especially in the newer, unchurched areas. There was, of course, much complaint against taxation for the support of the Church of England. Devereux Jarratt, when he became rector of Bath parish, Virginia in 1763, wrote that "ignorance and profaneness prevailed among all ranks and degrees, so that I doubt if even the form of godliness is to be found in one family of this large and populous parish." In Virginia in 1774 James Madison wrote that "poverty and luxury prevail among all sects; pride, ignorance, and knavery among the priesthood and vice and wickedness among the laity." And after a tour of the Middle Colonies Richard Boardman reported that most of the people were "wicked and ignorant to a lamentable degree, destitute of the fear and regardless of the worship of God."[13]

When the war's turbulence had abated and peaceful attention to growth was again possible, Asbury, as undisputed leader of Ameri-

---

13. Ibid., pp. 49-50.

can Methodism, began to consolidate his forces for the great campaign he had anticipated for years. He began to deploy the circuit riders as a military leader moves his troops. Choosing one definite objective, such as a newly-settled area in which there were a few families with Methodist leanings, Asbury would then assemble his itinerants for the assault. He built up a small army of men, often with little education, but well-fitted for the job. Education would have been of little use on the frontier; a powerful speaking voice, a hardy constitution, and massive dedication to the Lord's work were the most important qualities in the itinerants. Their courage and disregard of danger became proverbial. After the territory had been awakened by their exhortations, Asbury often would move them to another area and move in preachers who possessed administrative abilities to organize churches and circuits.

The result of this spectacularly successful system was that revivals were soon in progress throughout the country. The first of the series began in Brunswick County, Virginia in 1787, an area known as a center of Methodist piety. The meetings at times exhibited some emotional excesses—weeping, swooning, and shouting—but the preachers denounced more than hearty shouts and discouraged any wilder behavior.[14]

In 1800 the million or more people who lived along America's advancing frontier were very susceptible to evangelistic preaching. There was an almost complete dearth of intellectual life, and that dearth was accompanied by widespread immorality, gambling, and intemperance. Asbury's shock troops were the very ministry that many an area needed.

The circuit system brought tens of thousands into the Methodist fold. In 1780 there were 42 preachers and 8,504 members; in 1790, 227 preachers, 45,949 white and 11,862 black members; in 1803, 383 preachers, 104,070 white and 22,453 black members; in 1810, 596 preachers and 174,560 members; in 1820, by which time Asbury had passed on, there were 904 preachers and 256,881 members.

Bishop Asbury had still another strategy that would dynamically and efficiently spread the gospel: the camp-meeting. In the camp-meeting, as many as 30,000 people could be reached at once. The people were eager and anxious to attend, and the meetings needed only the most meager preparations. Camp-meetings were intro-

14. William W. Sweet, *Methodism in American History* (Nashville: Abingdon, 1954), pp. 158-59.

duced into the Western field about the middle of 1799 when John and William McGee, brother preachers who were Methodist and Presbyterian respectively, arrived in Logan County, Kentucky and set up a sacramental meeting. Such meetings usually began on a Thursday or Friday and continued until the next Tuesday or Wednesday, with preaching morning, afternoon, evening, and on into the night by the light of torches. Pious and impious came from as far as one hundred miles away, bringing their bedding, provisions, and tents or covered wagons.

Asbury regarded camp-meetings with great favor, for he knew that they brought on some of the greatest revivals. He wrote, "I pray to God that there may be a score of camp-meetings a week. . . . I rejoice to hear that there will be perhaps four or five hundred camp-meetings this year."[15]

During this great expansion, Asbury and the district superintendents were everywhere in the field, directing, planning, and exhorting. It was Asbury's custom until 1816, the year of his death, to make a complete circuit from Georgia to Maine and throughout the frontier territories, inspecting the work, preaching, conferring with his itinerants, and in general furthering the work in each area.

In all this Asbury was compelled to undergo the greatest of hardships and privations. The fact that he was the bishop of American Methodism brought him little glory, and he certainly did not desire any glory. His driving vision of an evangelized America and his disregard of self, made him quite willing to endure privations, constant physical exertion, and exposure to danger. Frequently on the road he went without food; at other times he ate wild vegetables that he picked along the trail and boiled over an open fire. He was forced to stop at inns where the other travelers were rugged and primitive, and their swearing, gambling, and dislike for religion distressed him more than all the dangers of the road. In his later years bronchitis and consumption ravaged his chest, rheumatism racked his legs and arms, his throat and stomach were burned by ulcers, and he itched terribly from skin diseases picked up as he forced himself to journey in all kinds of weather.

From the moment he set foot on American soil, he had no place he could call home. He hardly considered marriage, for he believed that would have hindered his freedom in the Lord's work. Here again his unquestioning loyalty to Wesley's example and indoctrina-

---

15. F. Asbury, *Journal and Letters,* 2:576.

tion was evident. With neither family nor home, he carried his pathetically small and humble belongings in his saddlebags and slept wherever night found him. His saddlebags were also stuffed with the Bibles and books that he urged his followers to read. Asbury was always a great advocate of reading good literature; this largely self-taught man made it a rule to read one hundred pages a day, even when they had to be read on horseback.

After the year 1800 there were several attempts to take some of his autocratic power from him. He was sometimes called a dictator, but upon further questioning his critics willingly admitted that Asbury was a very benevolent dictator. When he saw that there was a move to appoint more than one bishop, if only to care adequately for the huge territory, he finally acquiesced and permitted the election of associate bishops, and in his declining years he left to them more and more of the administration. But his determination to visit as many circuits as possible never abated until the end.

In the last years of his life, wherever he went great crowds gathered to hear him preach, if he was able to do so. Governors and mayors constantly entertained this famous man, and Methodists and others throughout America, contemplating the results of his labors, regarded him with awe and veneration. For almost half a century his gaunt figure, encased in black homespun and wearing a low-crowned beaver hat, was a familiar sight along country roads from border to border.

The years took a heavy toll. When he could not ride his horse, friends lifted him into a cart and hauled him the length of his journey. It was not unusual for a congregation to burst into tears as he tottered or was carried into a church. In return for the steadfast service of this aged and devoted man, whose face was deeply lined with the seams graven by decades of illness and hardship, Asbury was loved as few other men in the United States.

When he died in 1816, Bishop Asbury had traveled 275,000 miles on horseback, preached 16,500 sermons, spoken informally to many times that number of people, ordained more than 4,000 preachers, and had done more to establish Methodism in America than any other figure, by far. And Methodism, in turn, was to be a chief engine of evangelical Protestantism in the nineteenth century, imparting its energy and enthusiasm to all other denominations.[16]

16. Sydney E. Ahlstrom, *A Religious History of the American People* (New Haven, Conn.: Yale U., 1972), p. 372.

6

The Second Great Awakening
in the East—Timothy Dwight

As a direct result of conversions made during the Great Awakening, and in spite of far more demanding requirements for membership, the churches of New England added between twenty and fifty thousand new members to their rolls.[1] Many more also became convinced Christians in the Middle Colonies and in the South. To those churches that supported the Awakening came a new degree of strength that prevailed for some years. In New England particularly, Christian principles were again enthroned in common practice and the general order.

Eventually, the trough period that Solomon Stoddard described came to pass. Facilitating the change was the French and Indian War, which lasted from 1754 to 1763 and had major effects on all Americans, especially in the areas of morals and religion. During this war, for the first time foreigners mingled extensively with the colonists. The colonial soldiers, who often lacked a deep understanding of Christian truth, easily imbibed new ideas and practices in an army composed of those whom they were taught to regard as their superiors.

The British officers and soldiers were often deists or atheists, and often held the colonists in some disdain as unpolished bumpkins. The Americans, on the other hand, respected the British as coming from the "mother country," a place renowned for arts, science, and

---

1. Sydney E. Ahlstrom, *A Religious History of the American People* (New Haven, Conn.: Yale U., 1972), p. 287. These are estimates. Because of lost records or poor record keeping in that period, it is impossible for an exact figure to be arrived at.

wisdom. The British had engaging manners and practiced all those genteel vices, ones that generally fascinate young people and are frequently considered as conferring distinction on those who adopt them. When they returned home, the colonial soldiers had been influenced too deeply by the free-thinking and vices of the British to give them up easily.[2]

As all the uncertainty of impending conflict (Revolutionary War) grew in the early 1770s, faith and morals deteriorated still further until war began. Americans in the Revolution were not exposed to as many foreigners as in the French and Indian War, but those they did meet were of far more dissolute character.[3] Those were Frenchmen, disciples of Voltaire, Rousseau, Diderot, and others of the French Enlightenment, and they were almost invariably atheists. There was a distinction between French and British infidelity. The British infidel at this time usually showed some degree of reverence for God and admitted that there may be an afterlife, whereas the French infidel despised the idea of God and vehemently denied any life beyond. In mannerisms the French were like the British: urbane, very self-assured, but more experienced than the British in silencing with a sneer arguments for morality. In addition, they were the Americans' dear allies in the revolutionary struggle against England, to whom all Americans owed much for their magnanimous help in a time of tremendous need. "They perfectly knew," Timothy Dwight observed, "how to insinuate the grossest sentiments in a delicate and inoffensive manner, to put arguments to flight with a sneer, to stifle conscience with a smile, and to overbear investigation by confronting it with the voice and authority of the great world."[4] Most of the American soldiers had never heard the divine origin of the Scriptures questioned, and they had no answers to even the simplest objections.

In 1782 peace with Great Britain was concluded, and more settled conditions began to prevail. The hopes of Christians that the foreign influences of atheism, deism, and infidelity would lessen were, however, doomed to disappointment. Soon the French Revolution arose, an event that was devastating in its cause and conse-

---

2. Richard J. Purcell, *Connecticut in Transition: 1775-1818* (Middletown, Conn.: Wesleyan U., 1963), pp. 8-9.
3. Timothy Dwight, *Travels in New England and New York* (Cambridge, Mass.: Harvard U., 1969), 4:259. This work by Dwight is a fine description of events in New England from the Revolutionary period to his death in 1817, and would be read with profit by any student of the period.
4. Dwight, *Travels,* 4:261.

quences. Because the Americans had just gone through a revolution of their own, naturally they sympathized with those whom they supposed were aiming at the same desirable goals. Many assumed it would be a release from despotism and superstition for all Frenchmen. The French Revolution, instead, began to produce such horrors and evil consequences, vicious leaders, and successive massacres of innocent people, that Americans were startled.

Because the French were their own reporters of those things, the truth of the accounts was beyond question. The ferocity of the women of Paris, who appeared to be fiends incarnate, was incredible to the women of the United States. The guillotine curdled the blood of even the callous, and the murder of King Louis XVI awakened general disgust. Americans saw the paganism of France and its violation of all moral principles no less amazing than the accounts of its cruelties. There was a grossness of immorality; a brutal atheism in the proceedings of the national legislature; a disregard of evidence, truth, and justice in the courts; a ferocity in the behavior of its judges and juries; and a savagery in the conduct of its new officials, which again would have been unbelievable if it had not been reported by the French themselves.

Under the leadership of Voltaire, Rousseau, and the Encyclopedists, France had been going through the Enlightenment for years before the Revolution. The rallying cry was "Reason," which meant that the unaided human mind was considered the only authority and should bow to no other. Many leaders deliberately intended this as a rejection of Christian revelation, which they considered absurd. They looked upon the Bible as a collection of fairy tales at best, and at worst as an evil book. In the name of reason, the Roman Catholic church was overthrown, its property confiscated and plundered, its priests murdered by the hundreds, and King Louis XVI killed along with his family. Supposedly under the sway of liberated reason, every house in France was prey to inspections by mobs who came to rob, to seek out, and to destroy. In the cause of "liberty" the Bible and the vessels of the Mass were placed on a donkey and marched through the cities to deride and ridicule them before throwing them on a bonfire. In the Jacobin Club of Paris, a formal comparison was made between the Lord Jesus Christ and the Frenchman Jean-Paul Marat—and that twin to Judas Iscariot was adjudged a greater benefactor to mankind than the Savior. For the cause of "liberty" the Lord's Day was abolished and a week of ten days was substituted.

The United States, as a new nation eager to take a place in the councils of the world, was particularly open to foreign influences and ideas at that moment, and France and other European nations were happy to oblige. The *Encyclopedia,* a vast number of volumes composed by Voltaire and other French infidels; the *Systeme de la Nature;* and Thomas Paine's *The Age of Reason* were printed abroad in great quantities to be shipped to America, where they found many eager readers. An enormous edition of *The Age of Reason* was published in France and sent to America to be sold for a few cents per copy. Where it could not be sold it was to be given away. Paine's deism and the ideas of the French Encyclopedists were, for the most part, not closely reasoned arguments for scholars. They were not designed to instruct or convince, but rather to amuse, baffle, and intrigue. They were addressed not to educated people but to the ignorant, the unthinking, and those who already were inclined to loose morals and a hatred of Christianity. The writings were directed not to the intellect but to man's weaknesses, passions, and prejudices.

The deist and atheist writers who produced those works were industrious and bold. Their writings were sometimes clever, but when they came to the question of the authority of Scripture, they were incapable of understanding the nature of evidence. Today their reasonings are for the most part so palpably silly as to deserve no notice from anyone informed. Paine in *The Age of Reason* had attempted to call ridicule to his aid in denouncing the Bible.

> It is upon this plain narrative of facts, together with another case I am going to mention, that the Christian mythologists, calling themselves the Christian church, have erected their fable which, for absurdity and extravagance, is not exceeded by anything that is to be found in the mythology of the ancients. . . . Putting aside everything that might excite laughter by its absurdity, or detestation by its profaneness, and confining ourselves merely to an examination of the parts, it is impossible to conceive a story more derogatory to the Almighty, more inconsistent with his wisdom, more contradictory to his power than this story is.[5]

Responding in kind, the distinguished Presbyterian Ashbel Green characterized Paine's *Age of Reason* as "a book in which the most contemptible ignorance, the grossest falsehood, the most vulgar buffoonery, the most unblushing impudence, and the most daring

---

5. Peter Gay, *Deism: An Anthology* (Princeton, N.J.: D. Van Nostrand, 1968), pp. 171-72.

profaneness are united."[6] Certainly Green was close to the mark. Whereas Paine called Jesus a "virtuous reformer and revolutionist" and regarded Him as a deluded but good man whose teachings were perverted by the apostle Paul and others, Voltaire aimed his many attempts to disprove Scripture directly at Jesus as the chief and deliberate deceiver. "Among the Jews," he declared, "there have always been men from the rabble who played at being prophets in order to distinguish themselves from the mob: here then is the one who made the most noise, and who was turned into a god."[7]

The anger of American churchmen at such books coming from Europe turned to fury when pernicious volumes were first published right at home. In 1784 Ethan Allen, the Revolutionary War hero who had captured Fort Ticonderoga from the British, issued *Reason the Only Oracle of Man* from a printer in Bennington, Vermont. Allen admitted in its preface that his 477-page book was poorly written, but went on to assert that "the doctrine of the Trinity is destitute of foundation, and tends manifestly to superstition and idolatry."[8] As to the atonement Allen declared, ". . . there could be no justice or goodness in one being's suffering for another, nor is it at all compatible with reason to suppose, that God was the contriver of such a propitiation."[9]

An ardent admirer of Paine was Elihu Palmer, who called Paine "one of the first and best of writers, and probably the most useful man that ever existed upon the face of the earth."[10] In 1802 Palmer, a defrocked Baptist clergyman who had been driven from his pulpit for preaching against the deity of Christ, published the third popular book in the library of infidelity, *Principles of Nature*. In it he demanded, "The simple truth is, that their pretended Saviour is nothing more than an illegitimate Jew, and their hopes of salvation through him rest on no better foundation than that of fornication or adultery,"[11] and the Bible is "a book, whose indecency and immorality shock all common sense and common honesty."[12]

---

6. Ashbel Green, *A Sermon Delivered . . . on the 19th of February, 1795* (Philadelphia: Parker and Sharpe, 1795), p. 19.
7. Gay, p. 153.
8. Ethan Allen, *Reason the Only Oracle of Man, or a Compenduous System of Natural Religion* (Bennington, Vt.: Haswell and Russell, 1784), p. 352.
9. Ibid., p. 356.
10. Elihu Palmer, *Principles of Nature; or, A Development of the Moral Causes of Happiness and Misery among the Human Species* (London: Sidwell and Kneas, 1823), p. 112.
11. Ibid., p. 25.
12. Ibid., p. 23.

Those diatribes of Paine, Allen, Palmer, and others were widely discussed. Many of those who agreed with infidelity were gathered into the Democratic-Republican political party being formed under the leadership of Thomas Jefferson, an avowed deist who had openly declared his doubts of Christian truth as early as 1781. Jefferson had been strongly influenced by the French *philosophes* during his years in France from 1783 to 1789. He then became even more an opponent of the Christian ministry and an adherent of deism than before. Soon after his inauguration in 1801, President Jefferson wrote a very cordial letter to Thomas Paine, who was in France, inviting him to return to America on board the naval sloop *Maryland* as the honored guest of the nation. All who had any doubts regarding Jefferson's sentiments were convinced by that action, and when Paine arrived in Baltimore the newspapers of the land teemed with fury. The *New-York Evening Post* and many other papers, angry not only at Paine's anti-Christian militancy but also at his previous attacks on George Washington, resorted to wrathful versification:

TO TOM PAINE

Detested reptile! wherefore hast thou come
To add new evils to our groaning land?
To some wild desert let thy carcase roam,
Where nought can wither by thy blasting hand.

In the dark hour that brought thee to our shore,
The shade of Washington did awful scowl—
Hence, gloomy monster! curse mankind no more
Thy person filthy as thy soul is foul.[13]

The outpouring of public opinion against Paine's coming was so strong that Jefferson was alarmed and soon regretted his connection with Paine's return. Still, many were swept into sympathy with the new ideas, especially during the visit of Citizen Edmond Genêt, representative of the revolutionary French Republic. In 1793 "Jacobin" clubs, named after similar radical clubs in France, appeared everywhere. That was before the numbing insanities of the French Reign of Terror in 1793 and 1794 became well known in America. Of those who were swept into the vortex of infidelity, Timothy Dwight was to reflect,

---

13. *New York Evening Post,* 8 December 1802.

Youths particularly, who had been liberally educated, and who with strong passions and feeble principles were votaries of sensuality and ambition, delighted with the prospect of unrestrained gratification and panting to be enrolled with men of fashion and splendor, became enamored of these new doctrines. . . . Striplings, scarcely fledged, suddenly found that the world had been involved in a general darkness through the long succession of preceding ages, and that the light of wisdom had but just begun to dawn upon the human race. . . . Men reluctantly conscious of their own inferiority of understanding rejoiced to see themselves without an effort become in a moment wiser than those who had spent life in laborious investigation.[14]

As might be expected, new ideas from Europe were welcomed particularly in the colleges by students. The colleges were indeed a trial to godly people. Transylvania College in Kentucky, which had been founded by Presbyterians, was perhaps the most extreme example of a departure from its founding principles, as it was taken over by a faculty and student body that banished Christian teaching from the campus and instituted deism in its place. At Bowdoin College in Maine there was but one professed Christian in the student body in the 1790s. Bishop Meade of Virginia said, "Infidelity was rife in the state, and the College of William and Mary was regarded as the hot-bed of French politics and religion. I can truly say that then and for some years after in every educated young man in Virginia whom I met I expected to find a skeptic, if not an avowed unbeliever."[15]

Dr. Ashbel Green, who enrolled at Princeton in 1782, described a similar state of affairs in that college. "While I was a member of college, there were but two professors of religion among the students, and not more than five or six who scrupled the use of profane language in common conversation, and sometimes it was of a very shocking kind. To the influence of the American war succeeded that of the French revolution, still more pernicious, and I think more general."[16]

Lyman Beecher, in describing the condition of Yale College prior to the presidency of Timothy Dwight, said, "Before he came college was in a most ungodly state. The college church was almost extinct.

---

14. Dwight, *Travels*, 4:266-67.
15. Daniel Dorchester, *Christianity in the United States* (New York: Hunt and Eaton, 1895), p. 316.
16. William B. Sprague, *Lectures on Revivals of Religion* (Edinburgh: Banner of Truth, 1958), p. 131.

Most of the students were skeptical, and rowdies were plenty. Wine and liquors were kept in many rooms; intemperance, profanity, gambling, and licentiousness were common. . . . That was the day of the infidelity of the Tom Paine school. Boys that dressed flax in the barn, as I used to, read Tom Paine and believed him. . . . most of the class before me were infidels, and called each other Voltaire, Rousseau, D'Alembert, etc., etc."[17]

In addition to Thomas Jefferson, multitudes of others prominent in public affairs and the councils of state embraced the new views. Washington, John Adams, Patrick Henry, and many others had no sympathy with deism and atheism, but they seemed to be in the minority at times. Jefferson's secretary of war, Henry Dearborn, was an avowed atheist and said of the country's churches, "So long as these temples stand we cannot hope for good government." General Charles Lee was so violent in his opposition to Christianity that in his will he stipulated he not be buried "in any church or church-yard, or within a mile of any Presbyterian or Anabaptist meeting-house."

Not all the leaders of the nation were sympathetic with the enemies of Christianity. So serious had the situation become for public morals and decency that President John Adams set aside a national fast day for April 25, 1799, declaring in his proclamation, "The most precious interests of the people of the United States are still held in jeopardy by the hostile designs and insidious acts of a foreign nation, as well as by the dissemination among them of those principles, subversive of the foundation of all religious, moral, and social obligations, that have produced incalculable mischief and misery in other countries."[18] Here was official recognition and alarm from the highest level of government that many things were wrong in the country, and that European anarchy and immorality had already gone far in subverting Americans.

The situation in the churches was indeed very low and depressed. There were many churches along the Eastern seaboard that were taking in almost no new members and were at the same time losing multitudes to the allurements of the opening frontier. By 1800, nearly one million people had deserted the East for a new life and, it was hoped, riches in the Ohio and Allegheny River valley areas.

---

17. Lyman Beecher, *Autobiography* (Cambridge, Mass.: Harvard U., 1961), 1:27.
18. James D. Richardson, ed., *A Compilation of the Messages and Papers of the Presidents, 1789-1904* (New York: Bureau of Natl. Literature and Art, 1904), 1:285.

That number increased greatly in the next few decades as new states were formed from the large increase in United States territory after 1803, the year of the Louisiana Purchase.

As he saw the people of Virginia leaving for an unchurched and unevangelized wilderness in 1794, the Episcopal rector of Bath, Devereux Jarratt (1733-1801), wrote sadly, "The present time is marked by peculiar traits of impiety and such an almost universal inattention to the concerns of religion that very few will attend except on Sunday, to hear the word of the Lord. . . . The state of religion is gloomy and distressing; the church of Christ seems to be sunk very low."[19] Such a state was a new situation for Jarratt, for he had become used to great congregations (because of his dynamic preaching).

Jarratt was influenced early by his fellow Anglican George Whitefield, and when Jarratt went to England for ordination he met both Whitefield and John Wesley. When he returned to Virginia he began an unusual ministry of vibrant evangelism and zealous preaching, with the result that his three churches became so crowded that he was compelled to hold services outside, following the Methodist pattern. He also followed the Methodists in meeting with the most earnest Christians in small groups. When the Methodists came to Virginia, Jarratt was of inestimable help to them for years. But by 1794 all that had changed; the churches were once again depressed.

The ministers of the Presbyterian church agreed. For years the annual General Assembly had issued pastoral letters to all its churches lamenting the decline of zeal and morals, but the pastoral letter of 1798 showed greater alarm than any of its predecessors:

> Dear Friends and Brethren: The aspect of divine providence, and the extraordinary situation of the world, at the present moment, indicate, that a solemn admonition by the ministers of religion and other church officers in General Assembly convened, has become our indispensible duty. . . . A solemn crisis has arrived, in which we are called to the most serious contemplation of the moral causes which have produced it, and the measures which it becomes us to pursue. . . . Formality and deadness, not to say hypocrisy; a contempt for vital godliness, and the spirit of fervent piety; a desertion of the ordinances, or a cold and unprofitable attendance upon them, visibly pervade every part of the Church, and certain men have crept in amongst us, who have denied, or attempt to explain away the pure doctrines of the gospel; to

---

19. Dorchester, *Christianity,* p. 348.

introduce pernicious errors which were either not named, or named with abhorrence, but which have, within a few years since, been embraced by deluded multitudes. The Lord's day is horribly profaned, and family religion and instruction lamentably neglected. . . . God hath a controversy with us—Let us prostrate ourselves before him! Let the deepest humiliation and the sincerest repentance mark our sense of national sins; and let us not forget, at the same time, the personal sins of each individual, that have contributed to increase the mighty mass of corruption.[20]

Only one year later the Presbyterian General Assembly's annual pastoral letter called to the attention of its churches that although there was still much vice and immorality, "amidst this generally unfavourable aspect, there are several particular circumstances peculiarly comforting and encouraging. . . . We have heard from different parts the glad tidings of the outpourings of the Spirit, and of times of refreshing from the presence of the Lord. We have heard from several parts of our church, and elsewhere, of the late hopeful conversion of many. From the east, from the west, and from the south, have these joyful tidings reached our ears."[21] Still greater joy was expressed by the General Assemblies of 1800 and 1801.

What was happening?

It was not a revulsion from the horrors of the French Revolution or disgust at the scurrilities of the deist and atheist writers that was calling the nation back from the brink of infidelity. The Lord God was moving again, in convicting power.

Particularly in the West—areas of Kentucky, Tennessee, Ohio, and western Pennsylvania—the Spirit of God was working to bring renewal. The Presbyterians reported in 1800, "The success of the missionary labours is greatly on the increase. God is shaking the valley of dry bones on the frontiers, a spiritual resurrection is taking place there."[22] But in the East also, similar movings of God were occurring. "Thus," as E. H. Gillett has described, "the century which was just closing, and which had threatened to close with dark and dismal prospects, was destined to leave behind it a brighter record. A new era had dawned upon the Church—an era of revivals."[23]

---

20. William M. Engles, ed., *Minutes of the General Assembly of the Presbyterian Church, 1789-1820* (Philadelphia: Presbyterian Board of Pubiication, 1847), pp. 152-53.
21. Ibid., p. 177.
22. Ibid., p. 209.
23. E. H. Gillett, *History of the Presbyterian Church in the United States of America* (Philadelphia: Presbyterian Board of Publication, 1864), 1:299.

While a new era was indeed dawning, in which awakenings would eclipse anything known in the eighteenth century, in actuality occasional revivals had never ceased. In addition to the remarkable revival among the Methodists in 1787, there had been general awakenings in New England in 1763 and 1764, although for numerical results they could not compare with the Great Awakening of the 1740s. Then in 1787 Hampden-Sydney, a small Presbyterian college in Virginia founded during the Revolution, became the center "of the great inter-denominational Awakening which marked the final triumph of evangelical Christianity in Virginia, and . . . left Hampden-Sydney throbbing with a new zeal for its mission."[24] Again in New England local revivals broke out in several towns of Connecticut for several years: Norfolk in 1767, Killingly in 1776, Lebanon in 1781, New Britain in 1784, East Haddam and Lyme in 1792, Farmington and New Hartford in 1795, and Milford in 1796. Suddenly, revivals seemed to be everywhere in New England. The Reverend Edward Dorr Griffith, a perceptive observer of those events, wrote that the period of awakening dated from 1792 and that he "saw a continued succession of heavenly sprinklings at New Salem, Farmington, Middlebury, and New Hartford . . . until, in 1799, I could stand at my door in New Hartford, Litchfield County, and number fifty or sixty contiguous congregations laid down in one field of divine wonders, and as many more in different parts of New England."[25]

One of the most important of those revivals occurred in the small town of Lee, Massachusetts in 1792. As its pastor, Alvan Hyde (1768-1833), reported, "This people had been for nine years without a pastor, and were unhappily divided in their religious opinions. Some were Calvinists, and favored the church, but the largest proportion were Arminians. . . . Contrary to my expectations, I found, on my first visits, many persons of different ages, under serious and very deep impressions. . . . Before I was aware, and without any previous appointment, I found myself, on these occasions, in the midst of a solemn and anxious assembly. . . . All our religious meetings were very much thronged, and yet were never noisy or irregular, nor continued to a late hour. They were characterized with a stillness and solemnity, which, I believe, have rarely been witnessed."[26] The awakening lasted for eighteen months, and fur-

---

24. W. M. Gewehr, *The Great Awakening in Virginia, 1740-1790* (Gloucester, Mass.: Peter Smith, 1965), p. 230.
25. Sprague, *Lectures on Revivals,* appendix, pp. 151-52.
26. Ibid., pp. 269-73.

ther revivals occurred in the town in 1800 and 1806.

Those seeking awakening in New England soon found their leader and theologian in Timothy Dwight. A grandson of Jonathan Edwards through his mother, Dwight was born at Northampton, Massachusetts in 1752. A precocious lad as might be expected, he graduated from Yale in 1769 and immediately thereafter began teaching grammar school, at the age of seventeen. After two years of teaching, he received an appointment as tutor at Yale in 1771 and found that at the age of nineteen he was younger than most of his students. But he faced the situation undismayed and overcame the handicap of youthfulness by energy, tact, and firmness—qualities that served him well throughout life.

Always a prodigious worker, Dwight threw himself into his teaching with enthusiasm, and his students loved him for it. He allowed himself four hours' sleep each night and no time for exercise, that he might be as good a teacher as possible. Under the heavy regimen of a meager diet, long and exacting hours, and little exercise, his eyesight and general health failed him at the same time, and he became almost blind. He was forced to abandon his position at Yale for a time, during which his health recovered, but his eyes were weak for the remainder of his life. As he returned to his teaching duties, the stirring days of the Revolution's beginnings were upon the college, and the students felt the continual upset of threatened coastal raids and general distraction.

Timothy Dwight had by that time decided to follow the Edwardsean footsteps into the ministry, and on June 9, 1777, he was ordained. Shortly before, on March 3, 1777, he had married Mary Woolsey, and his uncle Jonathan Edwards, Jr. had officiated. Patriotism and confusion then combined to close Yale (many of the students were joining the army), and Dwight became a chaplain on October 6, 1777. In service with the First Connecticut Brigade Dwight saw much of the misery of war's desolation. He exhibited his patriotism as well as his poetic abilities in composing songs and hymns for the use of the army, many of which attained wide popularity.

At the war's end Dwight opened his own academy at Northampton, which prospered. In 1777 Ezra Stiles was made president of Yale, although some favored the election of Dwight because of the excellent work he had performed as tutor before the war. Despite his success as an educator, Dwight still cherished his ministerial inten-

Figure 6.1 Timothy Dwight the Elder. Dean Keller, after John Trumbull (Yale University Art Gallery)

tions, and in May 1783 he was called by a unanimous vote of the congregation to Greenfield Hill, a parish in Fairfield, Connecticut. He had a very successful ministry there until June 1795, when the corporation of Yale College elected Dwight president after the death of Stiles. Ministerial and public opinion throughout Connecticut immediately acknowledged Dwight as the obvious man for the post. Yale at that time was not a large and thriving institution. With only one hundred and ten students it was struggling, and in many ways Ezra Stiles had not provided answers to its problems. Dwight expressed his sentiments on this in a letter written just before his election: "I do not court the appointment; let those who do, take it. I am already happily settled, and in a station little exposed to envy or obloquy. To build up a ruined college is a difficult task."[27] Nevertheless, when Dwight was chosen he accepted, and immediately threw his characteristic energies into the task.

There was an enormous amount to be done. Discipline was notoriously slack and, as Lyman Beecher noted, infidelity was the students' creed. Stiles, as an older man of declining vigor, had clung tenaciously to the methods of the mid-eighteenth century.

Timothy Dwight came to the presidency in the prime of life (forty-three); he possessed a great deal of experience, boundless energy, and an openness to new ideas. Although he was certainly unhappy with the licentiousness of the students, he had no intention of alienating them and making his work harder. By example he would show the rebellious student body the integrity and dignity of the Christian position.

The students felt the change immediately. One reported home, "We now see the advantage of having an able director at the head of affairs, one whose commands are energetic, respected, and obeyed. . . . It is surprising to see what a difference there is in the behavior of the students since last year; at present there is no card playing, at least but little of it, no nightly revellings, breaking tutors' windows, breaking glass bottles, etc. but all is order and quietness, more so I believe than was ever known for any length of time in this college."[28] Other students testified—their own amazement showing through—to the studiousness of all, and that most were "much more steady at prayers than formerly." Although his instruction and

---

27. Cited in E. E. Beardsley, *History of the Episcopal Church in Connecticut* (Boston: Houghton Mifflin, 1883), 2:212.
28. Cited in Charles E. Cuningham, *Timothy Dwight, 1752-1817* (New York: Macmillan, 1942), pp. 178-79.

administration impressed the students greatly, above all they soon came to admire Timothy Dwight's character, his "sound understanding," "open, candid and free behavior," his "handsome and graceful person," and "engaging manner."[29]

Although Dwight continued to introduce new methods, new textbooks, and new courses, and the college by 1800 had achieved much greater prestige than ever before, his purpose was not merely to make the academic machinery hum briskly. Concern with the honor of the Christian faith and the students' spiritual condition led Dwight to place the highest priority on building faith and character. The students began to sense that and began to appreciate his concern for their souls' welfare. Among his many admirers was Lyman Beecher (1775-1863), patriarch of a distinguished family and leader of the forces of revivalist preaching after Dwight's death. In later years Beecher would exemplify the intimate association of evangelism with moral reform and social benevolence. Looking back on his days at Yale, he said of Dwight,

> They [the students] thought the Faculty were afraid of free discussion. But when they handed Dr. Dwight a list of subjects for class disputation, to their surprise he selected this: "Is the Bible the word of God?" and told them to do their best.
>
> He heard all they had to say, answered them, and there was an end. He preached incessantly for six months on the subject, and all infidelity skulked and hid its head.
>
> He elaborated his theological system in a series of forenoon sermons in the chapel. . . . To a mind appreciative like mine, his preaching was a continual course of education and a continual feast. He was copious and polished in style, though disciplined and logical.
>
> There was a pith and power of doctrine there that has not been since surpassed, if equaled. I took notes of all his discourses, condensing and forming skeletons. He was of noble form, with a noble head and body, and had one of the sweetest smiles that ever you saw. He always met me with a smile. Oh, how I loved him! I loved him as my own soul, and he loved me as a son. And once at Litchfield I told him that all I had I owed to him. "Then," said he, "I have done a great and soul-satisfying work. I consider myself amply rewarded."
>
> He was universally revered and loved. I never knew but one student undertake to frustrate his wishes.[30]

After Dwight's inauguration as president of Yale the battle lines

---

29. Ibid., p. 181.
30. Beecher, *Autobiography,* 1:27.

were soon drawn. There were two alternatives, Christianity or infidelity, and there was no middle ground. Not only were the students generally without faith, but even some of the faculty could not claim to be Christian (tutor Benjamin Silliman was regarded as a deist). Thereupon, President Dwight took it as his most important duty to begin a sledge-hammer attack on infidelity, and he entered with customary zeal into a battle that gave no quarter for seven years. In his sermons, so that no one could misunderstand, he carefully explained the dangers to church, state, and morals of all departures from revealed truth. In debate he encouraged free and open discussion of religious doubts and difficulties, thereby having opportunity to refute points raised by his opponents, as Beecher has described. He then entered upon the preparation of a great series of sermons given in the college chapel, which series lasted for the four years that a student would be at Yale. The sermons, which constituted a large system of divinity in which the whole philosophy of skepticism was answered and overthrown, would be repeated for the next group of students.

At Dwight's coming, most of the students denounced divine revelation and organized religion as loudly as Voltaire had shouted down superstition. Christianity was dead at what had once been its proudest Connecticut fortress; infidelity reigned. The recovery of Yale was of the highest priority not only for the new president but for all of Connecticut's clergy. After the students had learned to admire and appreciate Dwight's abilities, a perceptible change took place in the atmosphere. Early in 1796 a group of undergraduates organized to improve moral conditions, and in 1797 the Moral Society of Yale College was founded. Many students turned to the president as their favorite counselor after realizing that he was a sympathetic and concerned listener, and a number left his study with a new determination and direction, often to enter the ministry.

Early in the spring of 1802 two seniors were overwhelmed with conviction of their sins. In a short period they came to faith in Christ and assurance of forgiveness. After making a public profession of their faith they joined the college church. This made an impact on others, and they in turn sought peace and consolation. In the ten days preceding vacation fifty young men declared themselves "serious inquirers." On the day of junior exhibitions a student reported the "greater part of the scholars" felt more like attending "a prayer meeting than anything of a sportive kind."

Conviction multiplied; wherever the students gathered, in their rooms, at meals, and around New Haven, the great subject of conversation was eternal salvation. "The convictions of many were pungent and overwhelming; and 'the peace in believing' which succeeded, was not less strongly marked," Professor C. A. Goodrich reported after an intensive study.[31] During the awakening that followed, no regular college activities were suspended, nor was preaching more frequent than usual. Dwight disapproved of "enthusiasm," or displays of emotion such as had been seen during the Great Awakening; orderliness and lack of fanaticism typified all that was done.[32]

Many feared that when the students dispersed for the spring vacation the revival might cease. The reverse occurred. The young men carried home with them news of Yale's turnabout and the impulse spread. When they reassembled in New Haven, more offered their lives to God. Half of the seniors were by then rejoicing in salvation, and one-third of the class eventually entered the ministry. With great happiness Dwight witnessed the formal conversion of eighty men out of the total enrollment of one hundred and sixty students. Among the converts was tutor Benjamin Silliman, who wrote to his mother, "Yale College is a little temple, prayer and praise seem to be the delight of the greater part of the students, while those who are still unfeeling are awed into respectful silence."[33]

The Brothers and Linonian debating clubs were transformed into centers of spiritual exhortation and prayer. As they were about to separate on graduation day the seniors signed an agreement to pray for one another on a certain hour of each day. Because the student body changed constantly, the revival effects gradually faded. However, under Dwight's concerned ministry for his students, a new awakening came in April 1808. That one was almost as powerful as the one of 1802, and succeeding revivals came to the students in 1813 and 1815.

Those revivals in Yale and New Haven marked only the beginning of a movement that swept Connecticut. Thereafter, there was

---

31. Chauncey A. Goodrich, "Narrative of Revivals of Religion in Yale College," *American Quarterly Register* 10 (1838):295-96.
32. Cuningham, *Timothy Dwight,* pp. 329.
33. Charles R. Keller, *The Second Great Awakening in Connecticut* (New Haven, Conn.: Yale U., 1942), p. 42.

little danger of a pagan Yale. As Dwight's biographer Cuningham has commented,

> God having thus again blessed Yale, an ardent student carried the news from that favored institution to Dartmouth, where soon afterwards a revival was in full swing. That same year, Princeton, too, enjoyed a shower of grace. In giving thanks for these events the editors of the *Connecticut Evangelical Magazine and Religious Intelligencer* lamented that Harvard, founded with many prayers, and nurtured by the strong faith of pious progenitors, had been, for many years, passed by. At Yale, President Dwight, skilled gardener that he was, labored in a fruitful vineyard. No weeds of infidelity throve long there.[34]

A proper understanding of Dwight's influence, however, makes it clear that he was not only the central figure in the collegiate revivals that radiated from Yale to other New England schools, but that he was also the crucial innovator in making revivals a permanent feature of American Protestantism from 1800 until the beginning of the Civil War. Through his writings, his devoted students took up and carried on his work as well as his leadership of Connecticut Congregationalism. Timothy Dwight thus represents a watershed in the history of awakenings in America.

To understand this, it is necessary to review what had happened in theological development after the death of Jonathan Edwards. For decades Edwards's theological descendants had taken his many works and from them developed the Edwardsean or New Divinity School. Another and larger group were the "Old Calvinists," who counted themselves completely orthodox but did not hold Edwards as their mentor. Still a third group were the rationalists, early represented by Charles Chauncy, who would eventually turn unitarian and repudiate Calvinism.[35]

Interestingly, Timothy Dwight agreed more with the Old Calvinists than with the Edwardseans in his and their stressing the "means of grace": prayer, the preaching of the gospel, the searching of the Scriptures, fellowship with Christians, and attendance at divine services. Through these and other available ways the efficacious grace of the Holy Spirit could descend upon the soul and rouse it from spiritual stupor to be aware of guilt and open to salvation. In his multivolumed *Theology* Dwight firmly rejected the utter sinful-

---

34. Cuningham, *Timothy Dwight,* p. 334.
35. A good discussion of these three parties is found in Ahlstrom, *A Religious History,* beginning on p. 403.

ness of all "unregenerate doings" and held, "it is the soul, which is thus taught, alarmed, and allured, upon which descends" the Holy Spirit; therefore "the Means of Grace ought to be used by sinners, and by Christians, for the purpose of promoting the salvation of sinners." And pastors "ought to advise, and exhort, sinners to use the Means of Grace."[36] In that regard Dwight ran directly counter to the tenets of most Edwardseans, especially those of the more rigid Hopkinsian school.

It was not that Dwight believed the prayers of a convicted sinner had any moral goodness; that could not come until the Holy Spirit imputed the righteousness of Christ to the soul in regeneration. But, said Dwight, the sinner's agonized prayers for deliverance and the experience of being under conviction of sin had a definite purpose. Unless a sinner knew his guilt and danger and recognized his total dependence upon God's grace in Christ, he could not appreciate the love and goodness of God in rescuing him. Indeed, it was to every person's eternal interest to use the means of grace, for they were plainly seen as the usual methods by which God regenerated the lost soul. God would not have provided them if they were forbidden.

Thus Dwight prepared the way for free will by trying to break the logjam of human inability behind which Calvinism had been stultified. In effect, he enhanced the possible role of man's choice in salvation. This dramatically changed the old Puritan idea of a prolonged period of convictions to one in which conversion could come within a relatively brief period. The text most dear to the heart of the evangelist was "Whosoever will may come," and his revision of Puritan evangelism presented a new program behind which he hoped Calvinists could unite. It was, of course, an "Arminianized Calvinism" that would surely erode crucial doctrines of the Reformed view and fall in largely with John Wesley's ideas. But it was to be the wave of the future for most American Protestantism, and it would come to fruition in the teachings of Charles Grandison Finney and Nathaniel W. Taylor.

The second great change brought about largely by Timothy Dwight went to the very heart of how awakenings were understood to operate. Sidney Mead has expressed the change well:

---

36. Timothy Dwight, *Theology: Explained and Defended* (Middletown, Conn.: Clark and Lyman, 1818-1819), 4:43, 58, 60.

As for the revivals, Edwards' connection with the First Awakening was much different from Dwight's connection with the Second. Edwards preached sincerely and vividly of what he had experienced and apparently was genuinely surprised when the revival began. Dwight deliberately set out to start a revival in the college and among the eminent men of the state, and Beecher and Taylor perfected methods of fostering them. To Edwards the revival was a by-product of his shared experience; to the latter men revivals were the calculated means to an end.[37]

All these men would have been utterly convinced that awakenings were the work of the Holy Spirit, but there was the increasing feeling that God *invited* men, by their praying and preaching for revival, to cooperate with Him. It is a fascinating study in American church history to note what five generations of an eminent family line—Stoddard, Edwards, and Dwight—contributed to the theology of awakenings.

As any good strategist would do, Dwight organized his forces while he was still at the peak of his powers to assure that the work would be effectively continued after his demise. He was fortunate in having several very capable lieutenants, not only Lyman Beecher but also Asahel Nettleton (1783-1844) and Nathaniel William Taylor (1786-1858). Nettleton was probably the more influential of these latter two in the realm of evangelism. During his postgraduate theological studies at Yale he was asked to take a temporary preaching assignment in eastern Connecticut. Therefore he took some time off from his academic preparation to engage in this evangelistic opportunity. Nettleton began by adopting methods reminiscent of the strongly intellectual approach practiced by Edwards, and he immediately achieved phenomenal success. Conservative in practice, retiring, and determined to bring about revival by involving the local pastor in every aspect, he found himself in great demand as an itinerant evangelist throughout New England and New York. For some years Nettleton shared the leadership of the revivalist forces with Beecher, until his health failed in 1820. Taylor was a prominent pastor in New Haven and later became the first professor of theology at Yale Divinity School.

---

37. Sidney Earl Mead, *Nathaniel William Taylor, 1786-1858: A Connecticut Liberal* (Chicago: U. of Chicago, 1942), p. 101.

7

The Second Great Awakening in the West—James McGready, Barton Stone, and Peter Cartwright

The awakening that fell upon Virginia from 1787 through 1789 soon wore off in the turbulent era of the 1790s. In that decade great growth was seen on the frontier as thousands of easterners poured westward in search of cheap land and a new existence. Kentucky was opened up, after the French and Indian War, when the first permanent settlement was established at Harrodsburg in 1774, and the next year Daniel Boone, as agent for the Transylvania Company, blazed the trail for the Wilderness Road and founded Boonesboro. Meanwhile, the steady penetration of fur traders and "long hunters" from Virginia and the Carolinas into Tennessee led to the first settlement there, in the Watauga River valley, in 1769. Jonesboro, the oldest town in Tennessee, was founded in 1779. At the same time, settlers were coming into Ohio on flatboats and barges and overland by wagon. The town of Marietta, founded in 1788, was the first permanent American settlement in the Old Northwest. By 1800 the census counted 220,955 people in Kentucky; 105,602 in Tennessee; 51,006 in the Northwest and Indian Territory; and tens of thousands more in western Virginia, North Carolina, and other parts of the expanding frontier territory. Then the crowning achievement of President Jefferson's first administration was the Louisiana Purchase in 1803, which doubled the area of the United States and gave an enormous new impulse to western migration.

What appeared to be auspicious for national expansion, however, seemed dark for the future of the Christian faith. How, church people wondered, could the resources of religion possibly keep abreast of the vast movement to the new lands? Here were farmers, land speculators, hunters, lawyers, miners, "merchants, millers, blacksmiths, artisans, rogues and saints—all rubbing elbows on the trails that led to the mecca beyond the mountains."[1] The churches of the eastern states were greatly weakened as many members followed the siren song. The circular letter of the Charleston Baptist Association in 1799 pointed to one of the causes of the decline in the churches being "that prevailing spirit of moving from place to place, just as fancy, whim, or supposed interest may dictate, without a due regard to the call of providence, or the interests of religion; by which churches are often greatly weakened, or, as it were, wantonly, and sacrilegiously, broken up."[2]

Not only was this profound social disruption causing unrest in the East, but the lawless and violent nature of the new territories became of even greater concern to Christians. Original hopes that the faith would take quick hold in the new settlements, as the southern revivals of the 1780s promised, were soon dashed. The tours of Bishop Francis Asbury in behalf of Methodist expansion convinced him of the great danger of the unchurched wilderness to the souls of those unevangelized people. "When I reflect," he wrote in his *Journal*, "that not one in a hundred came here to get religion, but rather to get plenty of good land, I think it will be well if some or many do not eventually lose their souls."[3] In every southern state, leaders of the denominations voiced their concerns.

In addition to deistic propaganda, postwar materialism, and westward migration, all of which impeded the growth of the Christian faith in the South and West, the denominations themselves did not always help the situation. Intradenominational squabbling and rivalries were also frequent, although eventually the various groups cooperated to some extent in the common task. Little wonder that one commentator in 1794 described Kentucky "with concern . . . that religion appears to be at a very low ebb with every denomination in this state."[4] The same was true in Tennessee, where one respected citizen said that, "especially among the upper classes, deism and irreligion ruled beyond all bounds."[5]

---

1. Ray A. Billington, *Westward Expansion* (New York: Macmillan, 1949), p. 246.
2. Wood Furman, ed., *A History of the Charleston Association of Baptist Churches* (Charleston, S.C.: 1811), p. 145.
3. Francis Asbury, *The Journal and Letters of Francis Asbury* (Nashville: Abingdon, 1958), 2:125.
4. John Rippon, *The Baptist Annual Register* (London, n.d.), 2:201.
5. Steiner and Schweinitz, "Report of the Journey of the Brethren" (N.p., n.d.), p. 513.

Christians in the East were confronted with an appalling problem. The evils that prevailed throughout the country to some extent were appearing in an aggravated form along the frontier. Lawlessness seemed to be the order of the day. The Christian faith was mocked and disregarded, deism and infidelity were rife, and morals were low. The early settlers of Kentucky named some of their towns after eminent French infidels, as Altamont, Bourbon, La Rue, Rousseau, and other names testify. In 1793 the Kentucky legislature voted to dispense with the services of a chaplain as being no longer necessary. In many towns of considerable size, no place of worship could be found, and religious services had never been held. Therefore, several hundred thousand people were beyond the reaches of the gospel and were "hair-hung and breeze-shaken over the pit of hell," as the saying was.

And why? What was the purpose of the Almighty in all of this? In 1795 Silas Mercer surveyed the lamentable situation in Georgia, comparable to the rest of the South and West, and in one of the more profound interpretations of the time endeavored to trace the finger of God.

> But why are these things so? To which we answer. The great Governor of the Universe does not always work by miracles, neither offers violence to the human will. It cannot be thought, but that he could have made his people perfect in soul, body, and spirit, at the same time when he converted their souls. But it appears to us, that Jehovah, in his wise providence, saw proper to continue them in connection with an old corrupt nature, in order to properly discipline them, that by the various combats between flesh and spirit, they may be weaned from sensual delight, and learn to trust their all in him. But again: in a lively time of religion, hypocrites and formalists are apt to creep into the Church, therefore, a time of trial is necessary to purge these, as dross from the pure gold or real Christians. And further: the Lord intends, it may be, by this way to prove that salvation is by grace alone; for in a time of declension no man or set of men, no, not all the people in the world, can make a stir of religion. So this proves that religion is of the Lord.[6]

Well and good; God undoubtedly has His seasons. The East had seen both lean years and fat in spiritual harvests. But that was not the situation for the new lands of the West: these vast areas had never known the Christian faith, and the pressing question was,

---

6. Jesse Mercer, *A History of the Georgia Baptist Association* (Washington, Ga., 1838), pp. 145-46.

Would the West ever be evangelized? As wild and dangerous as it was, could it be *impervious* to the gospel? Certainly no Christian of real faith could believe that.

Increasingly, another dimension of thinking and belief began to enter the picture as the enormity of the West became more and more apparent—the divine mission of America, as a light to the other nations of the world. In one sense, there was nothing new about this conviction, for the Puritans of New England were confident that in setting up a theocracy in the New World God had fulfilled His long-concealed purpose. Edward Johnson had declared to his fellow Puritans in 1650, "When England began to decline in religion," Christ had raised "an army out of our English nation, for freeing his people out of their long servitude under usurping prelacy," and created "a New England to muster up the first of his forces in." The New World, Johnson continued, "is the place where the Lord will create a new heaven, and a new earth in, new churches, and a new commonwealth together."[7] The role of God's people in America, John Winthrop had instructed them, was to be "a city set on a hill" to exemplify before "the eyes of the world" God's new purpose and the power of His gospel.

But in another sense, there was a new meaning and urgency in the conviction of an increasing number that America was meant to be God's light to the world. In Puritan days the concept of missions was still embryonic, and the sending of missionaries was an occasional thing. By 1800, however, a new dynamic had arrived, and ambassadors of the cross were going to distant lands. That was undoubtedly an extension of God's original purpose in colonizing the New World. It was hoped that in time, as America matured, it might send missionaries back to Europe and throughout the world to spread the good news of Christ. Therefore, as Charles Hodge proclaimed, the character of America was of "unutterable importance to the world." If God's purpose was to use America as a major base for the evangelization of all men, Hodge asked "whether a generation ever lived on whose fidelity so much depended?"[8] The corollary of this was the imperative that the American West be won for Christ. If it were not evangelized, Professor Hodge argued, in time it threatened to paganize the rest of the country.

---

7. Cited in P. Miller and T. Johnson, eds., *The Puritans* (New York: Harper & Row, 1963), 1:143-45.
8. Cited in Peter G. Mode, *Source Book and Bibliographical Guide for American Church History* (Menasha, Wis.: George Banta, 1921), pp. 430-32.

Such earnestness, such zeal, such powerful persuasion, enforced by the joys of heaven and miseries of hell, I had never witnessed before. My mind was chained by him, and followed him closely in his rounds of heaven, earth, and hell with feeling indescribable. His concluding remarks were addressed to the sinner to flee the wrath to come without delay. Never before had I comparatively felt the force of truth. Such was my excitement that, had I been standing, I should have probably sunk to the floor under the impression.[9]

Thus, young Barton W. Stone (1772-1844) recalled his first exposure to a central figure of the Awakening in the West, James McGready. Of Scottish-Irish parentage, McGready (1762?-1817) was a fiery Presbyterian preacher whose evangelical theology had been nourished at John McMillan's academy in western Pennsylvania. He had spent some time observing the interdenominational revival of 1788 in Virginia and was greatly influenced by the dignified evangelistic preaching of John Blair Smith, president of Hampden-Sydney College. The awakening at that Virginia college showed McGready that revivals could be conducted without emotionalism and with lasting results. As a result of the Hampden-Sydney revival more than thirty men had gone into the ministry.

The frontier people, however, lived, worked, and died hard, and they were not patient with the fine theological points that eastern congregations could cope with. McGready was well aware of this, and he discarded Smith's model of dignified evangelism. Although he began his sermons in a calm and orderly way, as he went on he warmed to the topic and, with his thunderous voice, achieved an intensity that thrilled his backwoods congregations and brought the desired results. In 1796 McGready became pastor of three small churches at Muddy River, Red River, and Gasper River in Logan County, Kentucky. This was in the southwestern part of the state and, as Peter Cartwright described it, "was called Rogues' Harbor. Here many refugees from almost all parts of the Union fled to escape justice or punishment. . . . Murderers, horse-thieves, highway robbers and counterfeiters fled here, until they combined and actually formed a majority."[10]

McGready's preaching in this dangerous area had a telling effect. With utter directness he went immediately to the heart of the spiri-

9. Barton W. Stone, "A Short History of the Life of Barton W. Stone," in James R. Rogers, *The Cane Ridge Meeting-House* (Cincinnati: 1910), p. 121.
10. Peter Cartwright, *Autobiography of Peter Cartwright* (London: Wesleyan-Methodist Book House, 1856), p. 5.

tual problem. He described heaven so magnificently that his calloused hearers would "almost see its glories and long to be there." When he came to speak of hell, he preached no subtleties; he would "so array hell and its horrors before the wicked, that they would tremble and quake, imagining a lake of fire and brimstone yawning to overwhelm them, and the wrath of God thrusting them down the horrible abyss."[11] The response to this powerful preaching was not long delayed, and by the summer of 1798 many were "struck with an awful sense of their lost estate." But it was not until June 1800 that the first manifestation of divine power occurred.

On that occasion four or five hundred members of McGready's three congregations gathered for a Communion service. For many it was the third year they had been praying for a display of God's power. Three Presbyterian ministers (McGready, William Hodge, and John Rankin) were joined by two brothers, the Presbyterian William McGee and the Methodist John McGee. The first three days of the meetings were solemn and reverent as the pastors spoke, but nothing unusual occurred. On the final day John McGee, the Methodist, began to exhort the people that "there was a greater than I preaching" and that they should "submit to him." At this insistence that God was at work the congregation joyously and frantically began to shout and cry.

The preachers stood amazed at what was happening; even though they were New Side (prorevival) Presbyterians, they agreed it was beyond anything they had previously experienced. When one woman "shouted" for mercy, John McGee moved toward her.

> Several spoke to me: "You know these people. Presbyterians are much for order. They will not bear this confusion. Go back and be quiet." I turned to go back and was near falling; the power of God was strong upon me. I turned again, and losing sight of the fear of man, I went through the house shouting, and exhorting with all possible ecstasy and energy, and the floor was soon covered with the slain; their screams for mercy pierced the heavens.[12]

Although McGready was a forceful preacher who was accustomed to some emotional response from his people, he was astounded at the results. Eventually, as John Rankin wrote, "On

---

11. Franceway R. Cossitt, *The Life and Times of Rev. Finis Ewing* (Louisville, 1853), p. 44.
12. John McGee to Thomas L. Douglas, in the *Methodist Magazine* (London, 1821), vol. 4, p. 190.

seeing and feeling [John McGee's] confidence, that it was the work of God, and a mighty effusion of his Spirit, and having heard that he was acquainted with such scenes in another country, we acquiesced and stood in astonishment, admiring the wonderful works of God."[13]

Convinced that the Lord was moving, McGready and the other ministers planned another sacramental service to be held in late July 1800 at Gasper River. Unprecedented crowds began assembling at the appointed time, many from distances as great as one hundred miles. Although the term *camp meeting* was not first used until late 1802,[14] and large outdoor services had had a long history, this was the first true camp meeting in which the continuous outdoor service was combined with the planned practice of camping out. Tents were set up everywhere, wagons with provisions brought in, and the underbrush near the church cleared. The preaching went well, with anticipation and hopes building that God would perform a mighty work.

Figure 7.1 A typical camp meeting of the mid-nineteenth century (From *Harper's Weekly*, September 10, 1859. Drawing of actual meeting held at Sing Sing, Upper New York state, August 1859.)

13. John Rankin, "Autobiographical Sketch, Written in 1845," cited in J. P. McLean, "The Kentucky Revival and Its Influence on the Miami Valley," *Ohio Archaeological and Historical Publications* 12 (April 1903):280.
14. Charles A. Johnson, *The Frontier Camp Meeting: Religion's Harvest Time* (Dallas: Southern Methodist U., 1955), p. 36. This work and John B. Boles, *The Great Revival: 1787-1805* (Lexington, Ky.: U. of Kentucky, 1972) provide the finest studies available on the camp meeting and the Kentucky revival.

The continuous preaching evoked much response, and the clergy was kept active counseling the multitudes of convicted penitents seeking conversion. On a Sunday, after three long, tense days, the pent-up emotions of the huge throng were ready to burst forth. At the evening meeting, with the rude pulpit lighted by flaming torches, William McGee preached a throbbing message on a doubting Peter sinking beneath the waves. McGready recalled:

> The power of God seemed to shake the whole assembly. Towards the close of the sermon, the cries of the distressed arose almost as loud as his voice. After the congregation was dismissed the solemnity increased, till the greater part of the multitude seemed engaged in the most solemn manner. No person seemed to wish to go home—hunger and sleep seemed to affect nobody—eternal things were the vast concern. Here awakening and converting work was to be found in every part of the multitude; and even some things strangely and wonderfully new to me.[15]

Later it would become apparent that the Gasper River camp meeting was the turning point in the Awakening in the West. In the months after that, in meeting after meeting, similar revivals broke out, until the area affected spread into Tennessee also. But the full force of the new work was yet to be felt. Barton W. Stone, a Presbyterian minister in Bourbon County, Kentucky, had met and been influenced by McGready some years before. (His impression of McGready is quoted earlier in this chapter.) Stone was pastor of the Cane Ridge and Concord churches, northeast of Lexington. That area was still sunk in spiritual deadness and lethargy. Having heard of the work in Logan County, Stone traveled across the state in the spring of 1801 to view for himself what God was doing. He reported that in the camp meetings "the scene was new to me and passing strange. It baffled description." Much impressed that this was indeed a good work, Stone returned to his own people and made plans for a similar protracted meeting to be held at Cane Ridge in August 1801.

The Cane Ridge camp meeting was memorable because, being better publicized than its predecessors, the numbers who responded gave it greater fame throughout the country. The multitude was

---

15. James McGready, "A Short Narrative of the Revival of Religion in Logan County, in the State of Kentucky, and the Adjacent Settlements in the State of Tennessee, from May 1797, until September 1800," *New York Missionary Magazine* 4(New York, 1803):193.

estimated between ten and twenty-five thousand, coming from as far as Ohio and Tennessee. Even ten thousand was an astonishing figure at a time when Lexington, the largest town in Kentucky, had fewer than 1,800 inhabitants.

Stone, dumbfounded at the numbers pouring in, reported that "the roads were crowded with wagons, carriages, horses, and footmen moving to the solemn camp." Arrangements had been carefully made so that the crowds could be dispersed into several congregations of somewhat manageable size, although this was strained to the breaking point by the unanticipated throngs that poured in. Invitations had been sent by the Presbyterians to Baptist and Methodist preachers from distant points, and Stone rejoiced that "all appeared cordially united in it. They were of one mind and soul: the salvation of sinners was the one object. We all engaged in singing the same songs, all united in prayer, all preached the same things."[16]

Numerous descriptions of the Cane Ridge meetings remain, and one of the best is from John Finley to his uncle, dated September 20, 1801:

> I attended [Cane Ridge] with eighteen Presbyterian ministers, and Baptists and Methodists, I do not know how many, all either preaching or exhorting the distressed with more harmony than could be expected. The Governor of our state was with us and encouraging the work.
>
> The number of the people computed from 10 to 21,000 and the communicants 828. The whole people serious, all the conversation was of a religious nature, or calling in question the divinity of the work. Great numbers were on the ground from Friday until the Thursday following, night and day without intermission engaged in some religious act of worship. They are commonly collected in small circles of ten or twelve, close adjoining another circle, and all engaged in singing Watts' and Harts' hymns; and then a minister steps upon a stump or log and begins an exhortation or sermon, when as many as can hear, collect around him. On Sabbath night I saw above one hundred candles burning at once—and I saw I suppose one hundred persons at once on the ground crying for mercy of all ages from eight to sixty years. When a person is struck down he is carried by others out of the congregation, when some minister converses with and prays for him; afterwards a few gather around and sing a hymn suitable to his case. . . . The sensible, the weak, learned and unlearned, the rich and the poor are the subjects of it. At Cynthiana, Paris, Flat Creek, Point Pleasant, Walnut Hill and Georgetown, great congregations are

---

16. Rogers, *Cane Ridge Meeting-House*, p. 165.

in all these places, and exercised in the manner as above described.
... I see several things I do disapprove; but can say, if only the tenth person convicted is truly converted, 'tis a great work. In Cumberland the work is also great; they often meet in congregations of twenty-five thousand, and spend sometimes two weeks together.[17]

Cane Ridge also witnessed the beginning of excesses that had been generally condemned, especially by the Congregationalists and Presbyterians, ever since the wild antics and frenzies of James Davenport and others had brought discredit on the Great Awakening of New England in the 1740s. Excesses, or "enthusiasms," were viewed with great distaste and suspicion by most prorevival evangelists, and since Davenport the years had brought awakenings admirable by the absence of excesses, with some minor exceptions in the rural South. Beginning with the Kentucky revivals of 1800-1801, however, two factors combined to break down the resistance of men like McGready to uncontrolled emotionalism: (1) the bleak roughness of pioneer life, its absence of restraint, and the sparsity of social contact; (2) the traditionally slow cycle of conviction of sin, despair, faith, and assurance of salvation was compressed into a few days at the camp meeting, and the pent-up emotion would be agonizingly intensified when finally released. Recognizing these elements, McGready and the others accepted the inevitable.

At later camp meetings shouting, crying, and falling down were the only physical reactions to rousing preaching. With the release of tidal waves of feeling in those early camp meetings, however, convulsive physical "exercises" became somewhat common. Hysterical laughter, occasional trances, the "barking" exercise, and the "jerks" (of which more will be said later) were witnessed in Kentucky. Those reactions did not produce the disastrous results they would have engendered in more settled communities. Professor John Boles states, "These grossly exaggerated revival exercises, which have been cited widely to discredit the revival, were probably restricted to a comparative few. Only among some of the splinter groups that developed in Kentucky did they become ultimately respectable. ... Except at the very start, they were never a significant factor in the camp meetings."[18] Professor Bernard Weisberger agrees: "Many stories of unusual transports of holy joy and anguish were undoubted-

---

17. Cited in William W. Woodward, *Surprising Accounts of the Revival of Religion in the United States of America* (Philadelphia: 1802), pp. 225-26.
18. Boles, *Great Revival,* p. 68.

ly stretched. Some came from supporters. . . . Others were planted by opponents, who were trying to underscore the element of caricature in the meetings."[19]

The awakening spirit, with many conversions, spread over the entire South and West with amazing speed. Portions of the Ohio Territory, western Pennsylvania, Maryland, Tennessee, Georgia, and the Carolinas received showers of divine grace within a short time, although the vast congregations of Cane Ridge and Gasper River were seldom repeated. In time, the moral tone of the frontier was raised. The sins that McGready, Stone, the McGees, and others scourged—drunkenness, profanity, gambling, horse racing, cockfighting, dueling, fornication, and adultery—dramatically declined. In the East, the church people were jubilant, particularly on hearing reports from eminent eyewitnesses like George A. Baxter, president of Washington College, Virginia, who toured Kentucky in 1801 and declared:

> On my way I was informed by settlers on the road that the character of Kentucky travelers was entirely changed, and that they are as remarkable for sobriety as they had formerly been for dissoluteness and immorality. And indeed I found Kentucky. . . the most moral place I have ever seen. A profane expression was hardly ever heard. A religious awe seemed to pervade the country. Upon the whole, I think the revival in Kentucky the most extraordinary that has ever visited the church of Christ; and all things considered, it was peculiarly adapted to the circumstances to the country into which it came. Infidelity was triumphant and religion was on the point of expiring. Something extraordinary seemed necessary to arrest the attention of a giddy people who were ready to conclude that Christianity was a fable and futurity a delusion. This revival has done it. It has confounded infidelity, awed vice into silence, and brought numbers beyond calculation under serious impressions.[20]

One of the most eminent of the frontier evangelists, after the first years of the awakening in the West, was Peter Cartwright. His importance for the historian is that Cartwright was a frontiersman himself, one who had to adapt no methods from more cultured areas to the needs of the advancing frontier. As a native he understood its people as no outsider could and tailored his evangelism accordingly.

19. Bernard A. Weisberger, *They Gathered at the River* (Boston: Little, Brown, 1958), p. 35.
20. *Methodist Magazine* 26 (1803):93.

Peter Cartwright was born September 1, 1785, in Virginia, and in a few years his relatively poor parents joined the migrants moving west. They settled in Kentucky, a few miles from the Tennessee border. This was Logan County, the infamous area called "Rogues' Harbor," in the description given by Cartwright in his *Autobiography* (see p. 133). Here had gathered a multitude of desperadoes, out of the reach of law. To control that element, a vigilante group had been formed, and one of the most exciting episodes of Cartwright's boyhood was on a court day in Russellville, Kentucky when the two groups met head-on. The vigilantes had named themselves the "Regulators," and "a general battle ensued between the rogues and Regulators, and they fought with guns, pistols, dirks, knives, and clubs. Some were actually killed, many wounded, the rogues proved victors, kept the ground, and drove the Regulators out of town."[21] Such was frontier life.

Figure 7.2 Peter Cartwright, pioneer circuit rider (from an old engraving)

21. Cartwright, *Autobiography*, p. 5.

Young Peter grew up to assist his father on the farm, which was surrounded by wilderness, and people were seldom seen except on occasional journeys to towns. The few towns that existed were sparsely settled. In 1800 Nashville, Tennessee could boast of only 350 citizens, and most of the towns were much smaller than that. "When my father settled in Logan County," Cartwright recalled, "there was not a newspaper printed south of Green River, no mill short of forty miles, and no schools worth the name."[22] Because the awakening had not begun as yet, Sunday was used for hunting, fishing, horse racing, dancing, and anything else. Meat for the family table was killed in the woods, and much of the remainder of their food was from nature. The farm raised cotton and flax, and from these Peter's mother and sisters made all the family's clothing.

On the whole, frontiersmen were a hardworking group. They were rough and ready in speech, impatient with hypocrisy and ceremony, and conditioned to severe situations and toughness. Their entire lives were simple and direct. No churches existed as yet. And Cartwright reported that he knew of men forty-five years old who had never seen a wagon.

The men spent at least part of their time trapping and hunting; some did little else. Hunters might be seen with their long rifles over their shoulders, perhaps some small game hung from their belts, and a pack of bear-dogs yelping after them. The days would be spent hunting or at work on a farm, and the evenings given to storytelling interspersed with the consumption of hard liquor.

Thomas Paine's deism made a great impact among those who were literate. But to the far greater number who were not readers of books, infidelity was not a reasoned system. In Kentucky and Tennessee a large number of the migrants had come from Virginia, where the churches had some strength. In Ohio many hailed from Pennsylvania and New England, again areas where the Christian faith was widely followed. For the most part the frontiersmen were not determined against Christianity, but they had been in something of a moral and spiritual vacuum since their moving to the frontier and leaving the churches behind. Many of the pioneers had some knowledge, however inadequate, of Christian teachings. But on the frontier to that time the spiritual life was not cultivated, Bibles and other literature in the rude homes were few, and worship services fewer yet.[23] It was not until 1783 that the first itinerant

---

22. Ibid.
23. Boles, *Great Revival,* pp. 45-46.

preacher entered Kentucky. Later, when they came in greater force, they were still inadequate to the great distances and meager congregations.

Peter Cartwright's mother was one of those who longed for the ministrations of the church of Christ, and any missionary who came by was invited to hold services in their cabin. To her great joy a Methodist congregation was organized about four miles from the Cartwright farm, and young Peter and his mother attended regularly. Yet Cartwright declared that he was "a wild, wicked boy, and delighted in horse-racing, card-playing, and dancing. My father restrained me but little, though my mother often talked to me, wept over me, and prayed for me."[24] His father presented Peter with a racehorse, which was a delight for several years. When he was sixteen Peter became convicted of sin. "It seemed to me, all of a sudden, my blood rushed to my head, my heart palpitated, in a few minutes I turned blind; an awful impression rested on my mind that death had come, and I was unprepared to die."[25] After several days of agonizing over his lost condition, during which his friends came "to try to divert my mind from those gloomy thoughts of my wretchedness," he heard a voice from heaven saying, "Peter, look at Me." He took that as encouragement from the Lord to hope for His mercy.

It was widely taught from Puritan days onward that although conversion could be almost instantaneous (as in the apostle Paul's case), because of its crucial importance the time of preparation should last for a sustained period. That emphasized the seriousness of conversion, even for young people who would have less sin to repent of than adults. When sins were understood and repented of for the guilt and misery they brought, renouncing them meant a real determination to commit them no more. Peter followed that pattern and underwent a further period of three months' searching for the pardon of his sin. After that time notices of a camp meeting to be held in the vicinity were circulated and Peter went, feeling "a guilty, wretched sinner." There, with many other "mourners," he found release. "Divine light flashed all round me, unspeakable joy sprung up in my soul. My mother raised the shout, my Christian friends crowded around me, and joined me in praising God."[26] Peter Cartwright was a redeemed soul.

24. Cartwright, *Autobiography,* p. 6.
25. Ibid., p. 10.
26. Ibid., p. 11.

Thereafter, although he was only sixteen, Cartwright seemed destined for the ministry. Sooner than he expected he was given a license "to exercise his gifts as an exhorter in the Methodist Episcopal Church." The idea in practice was that exhorting could be done by anyone, not necessarily an ordained person. Those exhorters, however, often showed more zeal than knowledge. Cartwright had until that time almost no formal education. He had attended in a catch-as-catch-can fashion two small schools, but had left after a short time. Rather than depreciating education, he realized his lack. Cartwright followed the pattern set by Francis Asbury for traveling preachers and for the rest of his life attempted to supplement his meager schooling by continual reading. In that regard he was typical of all the circuit riders: their library consisted of a pocket Bible, the hymnbook, and the Book of Discipline. The three standard books were carried in the saddlebags, along with the Bibles and books the circuit riders sold or gave away as they traveled.

Cartwright was so successful as an exhorter that in October 1803 he was made a preacher, the next higher rank, and placed on a wide circuit. It was a hard life, full of danger; but for a young man of eighteen it was a great challenge to serve the living God in this way. It meant constant travel through barely cut trails and across unbridged rivers, in the heat of summer as well as the storms, cold, and snow of winter. It meant not knowing, literally, where your next meal might come from, unless you happened to be near friendly Christians. Near the end of his long life Cartwright reported, "We walked on dirt floors for carpets . . . had forked sticks and pocket or butcher knives for knives and forks; slept on bear, deer, or buffalo skins before the fire, or sometimes on the ground in open air . . . and one new suit of clothes of homespun was ample clothing for one year."[27]

The life of a traveling preacher also meant poverty, accepted as cheerfully as possible. Cartwright and his fellows were supposed to receive eighty dollars a year, but he declared, "I think I received about forty dollars this year; but many of our preachers did not receive half that amount. These were hard times in those Western wilds; many, very many, pious and useful preachers were literally starved into a location. I do not mean that they were starved for food; for, although it was rough, yet the preachers generally got enough to eat. . . . Money was very scarce in the country at this

27. Ibid., p. 243.

early day."[28] In spite of that trifling salary, Cartwright thought it his duty to marry, and on August 18, 1808, he was wed to Frances Gaines. Nine children were born to that marriage, and all but one lived to maturity.

As he became a seasoned circuit rider and preacher, Cartwright became one of the most famous evangelists and planters of new churches that the West knew. In a life that was never dull, he found himself constantly in difficult situations. As he conducted worship several times each day on his circuits, the substance of his message was "a text that never wore out nor grew stale: 'Behold the Lamb of God, that taketh away the sin of the world.' " Contemporaries recorded that he had a booming voice that made women weep and strong men tremble. His methodology in evangelism was shared with the other successful preachers of the West: portray in the most vivid terms the terrors of hell, and then proclaim the gospel of God's love, grace and forgiveness, and the beauties of the Lord Jesus Christ in His resurrected power and glory. Eager congregations demanded exactly that format, and if the preacher was weak or derelict, woe unto him. Usually those in the congregation who were converted "got happy and shouted aloud for joy," and prayed for those outside the kingdom.

One reason Cartwright became so well known was his dexterity in handling difficult occasions and disturbances caused by rowdies, which sometimes called for bare fists. At one camp meeting in Tennessee in 1814 a gang threatened.

> The ringleaders of the rowdies went by the names of J. P. and William P., two brothers. . . . I found it would be hard to keep order, and I went to J. P., and told him I wanted him to help me keep order. Said I, "These rowdies are all afraid of you; and if you will help me, you shall be captain, and choose your own men." He said he did not want to engage in that way; but if I would not bind him up too close, but left him have a little fun, away off, he would then promise me that we should have good order in the encampment through the meeting. I said, "Very well . . . ."
>
> Then came into the congregation a young, awkward fellow, that would trespass on our rules by seating himself all the time among the ladies. It was very fashionable at that time for the gentlemen to roach their hair; and this young man had a mighty bushy roached head of hair. I took him out several times from among the women, but he would soon be back again.
>
> I told J. P. I wished he would attend to this young man. "Very well,"

---

28. Ibid., p. 41.

said he, and immediately sent off and got a pair of scissors, and planted his company about a half-mile off; then sent for this young fellow under the pretence of giving him something to drink. When they got him out there, two of them, one on each side, stepped up to him with drawn dirks, and told him they did not mean to hurt him if he would be quiet; but if resisted or hallooed, he was a dead man. They said they only wanted to roach his hair, and put him in the newest Nashville fashion. The fellow was scared almost to death, but made no resistance whatever. Then one with the scissors commenced cutting his hair, and it was haggled all over at a masterly rate. When they were done shearing him, they let him go; and he came straight to the camp ground. Just as he entered it, I met him; he was pale as a cloth. He took off his hat, and said, "See here, Mr. Cartwright, what those rowdies have done!" I had very hard work to keep down my risibilities [laughter]; but I told him he had better say nothing about it, for if he did, they might serve him worse. He soon disappeared, and interrupted us no more during the meeting.[29]

For decades, Peter Cartwright was a leader in organizing camp meetings throughout the area of his circuits: Ohio, Kentucky, Tennessee, Indiana, and Illinois. He fervently believed they were the most expedient way to bring sinners to Christ and into the membership of the church, and to back up his claim he could quote statistics to prove that tens of thousands had been converted through them.

In addition, Cartwright became something of an authority on the excesses that occurred in the awakening in the West. He declared that "the old starched Presbyterian preachers" and "the Methodist preachers generally preached against this extravagant wildness." But there was no denying that some illiterate preachers and ranters, with their ignorant blusterings, brought discredit on the awakening by allowing or encouraging excesses.

The "jerks" were the most notorious and memorable of those physical manifestations, and Cartwright witnessed them occasionally in early Kentucky camp meetings.

No matter whether they were saints or sinners, they would be taken under a warm song or sermon, and seized with a convulsive jerking all over, which they could not by any possibility avoid, and the more they resisted the more they jerked. If they would not strive against it and pray in good earnest, the jerking would usually abate. . . . To see these proud young gentlemen and young ladies, dressed in their silks, jewellery, and prunella, from top to toe, take the jerks, would often excite

29. Ibid., pp. 64-65.

my laughter. The first jerk or so, you would see their fine bonnets, caps, and combs fly; and so sudden would be the jerking of the head that their long loose hair would crack almost as loud as a waggoner's whip. . . .

I will relate a very serious circumstance . . . at a camp meeting. . . . The jerks were very prevalent. There was a company of drunken rowdies who came to interrupt the meeting. These rowdies were headed by a very large drinking man. They came with their bottles of whisky in their pockets. This large man cursed the jerks, and all religion. Shortly afterward he took the jerks, and he started to run, but he jerked so powerfully he could not get away. He halted among some saplings, and although he was violently agitated, he took out his bottle of whisky, and swore he would drink the . . . jerks to death; but he jerked at such a rate he could not get the bottle to his mouth, though he tried hard. At length he fetched a sudden jerk, and the bottle struck a sapling and was broken to pieces, and spilled the whisky on the ground. There was a great crowd gathered around him, and when he lost his whisky he became very much enraged, and cursed and swore very profanely, his jerks still increasing. At length he fetched a very violent jerk, snapped his neck, fell, and soon expired, with his mouth full of cursing and bitterness.[30]

Peter Cartwright completed one of the longest and most useful ministries in the West, living to see area after area he first knew as wilderness grow to become settled and civilized. When in 1824 his circuits in Kentucky and Tennessee vexed him because of his distaste for slavery, he requested transfer to Illinois, where he served as presiding elder for forty-five years. Twice he was elected representative to the Illinois legislature, and in 1846 he lost an election campaign against Abraham Lincoln for an Illinois seat in Congress.

During his life he calculated that he had preached at least 14,600 sermons, had received into the church at least 10,000 members, and had baptized almost as many children. Until the close of the Civil War he served his people well and contributed greatly to saving the American West of his day for Christianity. Hundreds of churches had been built under his direction, and his friends were everywhere. His great stamina carried him to the age of eighty-seven, and he laid down his labors for the Master, confident that they would be revealed favorably at the Last Day.

---

30. Ibid., pp. 17-18.

8

The Worldwide Evangelical
Awakening—Samuel J. Mills

"Run for that haystack! Hurry, men, or we will get soaked through!"

The five fellows dashed for the makeshift shelter and, laughing at how they must appear, each tore aside enough loose hay to pry a hole for himself.

Thunder caroomed across the hills. The rain, unleashed like a torrent, slatted at the earth and the wind-tossed trees. It was a typical summer thunderstorm on this hot, sultry August day of 1806 in western Massachusetts. The haystack did not give total protection, but it was the only convenient haven for some distance, and like a thatched roof house, it could divert most of the downpour and keep the young men dry.

These five had gone to the grove for a prayer meeting. On Wednesday afternoons some of the students at Williams College gathered to pray near one of the halls under some willow trees, while on Saturdays they met in this thick grove of maples known as Sloan's Meadow. On this day only five were present—Samuel J. Mills, Harvey Loomis, Byram Green, James Richards, and Francis L. Robbins. Robbins and Green were sophomores, the others freshmen at Williams.

While the lightning flashed and the thunder echoed across the hills, they tried to divert their minds to serious conversation. India had recently been studied in the geography course they were taking, and its peoples, religions, and needs were discussed. Reports sent back by the East India Company spoke of a land of great poverty, famine, and superstition. The horrors of the caste system, with its teeming millions of untouchables and pariah castes so abhorred that physical contact with them was considered polluting, had also been reported. They were interested in the work of the East India Company, which was opening up that closed continent. The moral degradation and darkness of India so disturbed these young men that the humor and fun of their haystack shelter was forgotten. Samuel J. Mills, leader of the group, saw that the discussion presented an opportunity: "Why should *we* not be the ones to take the gospel to these who are so oppressed and benighted under the weight of sin?" Mills grew more earnest. "*We can do it if we will!*"

The others, except for Harvey Loomis, greeted this with a chorus of agreement and support. Loomis, although he agreed that India was in a tragic condition, said that the time was not ripe. Missionaries would be in great danger, he believed, and would probably be murdered.

"But Harvey," Francis L. Robbins objected, "God is always willing to have his kingdom advanced, and if Christian people would only do their part, God can be relied on to protect his workers in any dangerous place, and to accomplish his work."

Mills did not want to see the meeting devolve into an argument. "Fellows," he said, "we came here to talk with God. I have great faith in prayer. Come, let us make India and foreign missions the subject of prayer under this haystack, while the dark clouds are leaving and a clear sky is coming."

Robbins, Byram Green, and James Richards lifted up their hearts to God that their vision of an evangelized India might become a reality, through their own labors, if possible. All prayed except Loomis. Mills prayed last, referring to Loomis's objection that missionaries would be killed in India: "O God, strike down the arm, with the red artillery of heaven, that shall be raised against a herald of the Cross." When they concluded their devotions, they closed by singing a stanza of an Isaac Watts hymn.

> Let all the heathen writers join
> To form one perfect book;
> Great God, if once compared with thine,
> How mean their writings look!*

---

*The preceding narrative, beginning at the start of the chapter, is reconstructed from an August 22, 1854, letter by Byram Green to Professor Albert Hopkins of Williams College. The letter was published in *Proceedings of the Missionary Jubilee Held at Williams College* (Boston: T. R. Marvin, 1856), pp.7-9.

As the skies cleared, anyone who chanced to walk across that meadow and hear loud singing coming from a haystack would have been astonished, until he realized that he was near a college and those must be students at one idiocy or another. The actions could be dismissed with a tolerant smile, as all college antics could be. But if our walker were then told that he had just overheard one of the most important prayer meetings in all history, the smile might be replaced by complete bewilderment. Unnumbered thousands of prayers have pled to God on behalf of missions and the unsaved, but a world shaking movement begun and vast numbers saved in foreign places because of prayers in a haystack during a thunderstorm? Most unlikely.

It was so. The God of the impossible honors such as this. Not from dignified, starched clergymen following rigid agendas in important meetings did the impetus and thrust of foreign missions begin in the United States, but—parallel to Paul and the other apostles outraging "the wisdom of the world" with "the foolishness of God" (1 Cor. 1:18—2:13)—from the daring of consecrated young manhood challenged by God's work, and the craziness of prayer under a haystack, issued one of the most glorious movements of all human history. It is amazing what God can do with a slingshot, a rod, or a jawbone; they are such trifling things, as the world counts them.

The one who organized the haystack prayer meeting, and the founder of foreign missions in America, Samuel John Mills, Jr., was born April 21, 1783, in the Congregational parsonage in Torringford, Connecticut. His father graduated from Yale in 1764, was ordained the first pastor of the Torringford church in 1769, and remained there until his death in 1833 at the age of ninety. Samuel Mills, Sr. was a tall man of commanding appearance, much loved in the Torringford area, and universally known as "Father Mills." His wit in the pulpit was unusual for that day; during one of his sermons the boys in the balcony turned their attention elsewhere, and Father Mills stopped his sermon and said, "Boys, you must make less noise in the gallery; if you don't you will wake up the fathers below." Samuel, Jr., grew up in a happy household with older brother, Jeremiah, and sister, Florilla.[1]

This was a time of moderate renewal of interest in missions.

1. Thomas C. Richards, *Samuel J. Mills: Missionary Pathfinder, Pioneer and Promoter* (Boston: Pilgrim Press, 1906), pp. 4-10.

Certainly the concept of missions was nothing new; it emanated from the book of Acts and the apostle Paul's epochal labors to plant churches around the Mediterranean. That fulfillment of Christ's Great Commission in Matthew 28:19-20 was pursued with some vigor in the first few centuries of the church's existence. After the Reformation, sporadic efforts were made to win the heathen. The Society for the Propagation of the Gospel (S. P. G.) was organized within the Church of England in 1701 with the full support of the Archbishop of Canterbury, and over three hundred of its missionaries labored in the American colonies until 1783.[2] The Moravians, under the leadership of Nikolaus von Zinzendorf, launched a far-flung campaign after 1730 to evangelize those in foreign lands; one of their projects was the establishment of a settlement in Georgia for work among the blacks and Indians.[3] Roman Catholic priests such as Isaac Jogues (1607-1646) accompanied French trappers and traders on their far-ranging travels into the interior of America, and attempted, with only moderate success, to work with the Indians. Missions to the Indians were attempted with greater success by the Congregationalists, notably in the work of John Eliot (1604-1690), Eleazer Wheelock (1711-1779), and David Brainerd (1718-1747). The Baptists, Presbyterians, Quakers, and Moravians also had Indian missions.

Most Christians in the United States before 1800, however, were only slightly concerned about distant peoples. But the mood was beginning to change, stimulated in part by America's own westward migration. In 1800 one distressed Easterner lamented, "All America seems to be breaking up and moving Westward." In 1775 there were approximately 5,000 white people west of the Alleghenies. By 1800 there were almost one-half million, and by 1830, three million settlers. Within one generation the western territories were settled by more people than had come from Europe in the previous one hundred years. All of this awakened the missionary interest of Christians.

Another factor in stimulating concern was the example of Europe in establishing missionary societies. During the decade 1790-1800, in Great Britain and on the Continent, missionary agencies had

2. C. F. Pascoe, *Two Hundred Years of the S. P. G.: An Historical Account of the Society for the Propagation of the Gospel* (London: S. P. G., 1901), pp. 86-87.
3. See J. R. Weinlick, *Count Zinzendorf* (Nashville: Abingdon, 1956), and Edward Langton, *History of the Moravian Church* (London: Allen and Unwin, 1956).

been formed by the Baptists, Presbyterians, Congregationalists, and others. In England when William Carey (1761-1834), "the Father of Modern Missions," published his 1792 pamphlet *An Enquiry into the Obligations of Christians to Use Means for the Conversion of the Heathens* and preached his famed sermon "Expect Great Things from God; Attempt Great Things for God" before a group of ministers, a Baptist pastor from Philadelphia became vitally interested. Four months later he witnessed the founding of the Baptist missionary society that sent Carey and John Thomas to India. When the Philadelphia pastor returned home he became an ardent supporter of foreign missions in America. In addition, when European missionaries began to go to the Orient in greater numbers after 1800 they frequently sailed first to American East Coast ports en route, and thus they came into contact with American Christians.

A third factor that stimulated missionary concern was the development in Europe of a new literature—travel books. Those books portrayed exotic lands and dusky people, often with flagrant inaccuracies, but they did alert Americans and Europeans alike to the existence of those without the gospel. Books and journals of geographical and anthropological research enjoyed an increasing vogue, and magazines often carried articles describing real or supposed customs of strange tribes and nations. Sixty-three new magazines appeared within one decade (1801-1810) in the United States. They gave various amounts of space to such travel articles, testifying to the new tastes of the reading public. Among the most popular articles were narratives sent home by missionaries, but some of those were dry reports not intended for publication. Therefore some were only slightly edited for popular consumption.

The new awareness of an immense world where the name of Christ was totally unknown reached even to Torringford, Connecticut. As he grew, Samuel Mills, Jr. was told by both parents of the great missionary heroes of the past, such as Eliot and Brainerd. He was especially close to his mother, and one day as she spoke of great men of God he heard her say of himself, "I have consecrated this child to the service of God as a missionary." In 1798 an awakening came to his father's parish, and Samuel came under great conviction. No confidence of salvation came to Mills, and for the next two years or more he labored for assurance that his sins had been forgiven. At length, in the fall of 1801, he enrolled in Morris Academy. Before leaving home, he had a serious talk with his mother and told her "I have seen to the very bottom of hell."

With a heavy heart, Mills started for the new school. On the road, he had a vision of God's love and acceptance, and a new confidence that he was born anew. When he next saw his father, Samuel told him, "I could not conceive of any course in which to pass the rest of my days that would prove so pleasant as to communicate the gospel of salvation to the poor heathen."[4] To be a Christian meant to him from the first to be a missionary.

The time arrived to choose a college, and, because his father had attended Yale, it would seemingly have been first choice. Instead, Williams College was chosen. Located in Williamstown, a town of two thousand inhabitants in northwestern Massachusetts, Williams had been founded in 1791 in what was wilderness. It would remain very remote for years to come. Convinced that everything about Williams was impossible—its location, its funds, its enrollment—President Moore in 1821 abandoned it and led a group of students to a new college known as Amherst. In the spring of 1806, when Samuel Mills entered, the Williams campus boasted two large, plain brick buildings.

Actually, there were strong reasons, to the Mills family, why Williams College had the edge over Yale. For one, it was known for the high moral character of the college and the community. Second, Williamstown was a secluded place, and therefore it was thought by many to be safer against habits of dissipation and extravagance. Perhaps of highest priority, the expenses at Williams were less than at Yale or Harvard. Undoubtedly, that influenced the choice, for the largest salary the elder Mills ever received was less than $350 a year, payable half in money and half in wheat, rye, corn, and firewood. The low cost at Williams at that time was illustrated by the fact that Charles Sedgwick, class of 1813, got through the entire four years on expenditures of $600. But the scanty means of the Mills family induced Samuel to scrimp through, in some inexplicable way, paying only $88.19 to the college over the entire four years.

Williams College had undergone an awakening similar to Yale's in 1805, and that was still underway as Mills entered the school. He was twenty-three, older than most of the students, and possessed the magnetism of a great enthusiasm. He was shorter than his father and lacked a good speaking voice, yet he became a leader in the college life. Although he had an excellent mind, he did not excel at his studies, but he continued his preoccupation with foreign mis-

4. Richards, *Samuel J. Mills*, p. 26.

sions. Prayer meetings had already begun during the revival, and those were continued, with missions becoming their chief concern after the decisive haystack meeting. At times the prayer group would number two dozen or more.

Samuel Mills's enthusiasm for evangelizing the heathen was contagious; he used every method that he could devise to stimulate the interest of the aroused students. In wintertime, a dozen men crowded into Byram Green's home in Williamstown to read and discuss missionary reports and letters they had gathered. Revival had made the Christian faith a vital thing at Williams, and that faith found what it needed most—an outlet, an expression in life and work for others. Fifty years after the haystack meeting, Abner Phelps remembered well several talks with Samuel Mills, particularly one in which Mills talked of the deplorable state of Africa and the slaves in America. "His plans were new to me," Phelps recalled, "and uttered with so much self-devotion and piety they made a lasting impression on my memory."[5]

In addition to his plans and new ideas, Samuel Mills also had great organizational ability that was to be essential in the years ahead. He recognized that something must be done to concentrate the energies of those who had already dedicated their lives to foreign missions. At the beginning of his senior year in college, Mills organized a "Society of Brethren," not for the purpose of sending others, but "to effect, in the persons of its members, a mission to the heathen." The first five members were cautious about advertising their existence or soliciting recruits, so they determined to keep the group secret, lest they be charged with rashness or overheated zeal and fanaticism. In addition, Mills felt he could best influence others in a quiet manner. Ezra Fisk, elected vice-president, said later, "Mills desired to be unseen in all his movements on this subject, which I am well persuaded arose from his unaffected humility, never desirous to distinguish himself, but to induce others to go forward."[6]

Yet they felt no need of secrecy in regard to promoting missions. That should move ahead with all deliberate speed. One of the members left Williams, became a student at Middlebury College, and started a similar society there. And so the movement began to spread. A constitution was adopted and written in code, as were the records.

5. Ibid., p. 34.
6. Ibid., p. 38.

After he graduated from Williams College, Samuel Mills entered the newly-founded Andover Seminary in 1810 to study theology prior to becoming a missionary. At Andover he found a number of college classmates and members of the Society of Brethren. Mills was accepted by the faculty and students as a remarkable person, "an extraordinary man," and that acceptance was not after he had become famous, but at the time. Roommate Timothy Woodbridge wrote to his brother about Mills, "He has a great heart and great designs. His great thoughts in advance of his age are not like the dreams of a man who is in a fool's paradise, but they are judicious and wise."[7]

Feeling that at Andover Seminary there was a need for some public means of disseminating information on missions, in addition to the secret Society of Brethren, the Brethren organized the "Society of Inquiry on the Subject of Missions" on January 8, 1811. But there was still no real foreign missionary agency in America. Christians in the United States were at this point sending large sums to the London Missionary Society, and when it was proposed that Adoniram Judson, who had recently graduated from Providence College, should offer himself as a missionary to the British society, Mills wrote:

> What! is England to support her own missionaries and ours likewise? O shame! If brother Judson is prepared, I would fain press him forward with the arm of an Hercules, if I had the strength, but I do not like this dependence on another nation, especially when they have already done so much and we nothing. I stand that each of the brethren will stand at their several posts, determined, God helping them, to show themselves *men*. Perhaps the fathers will soon arise and take the business of missions into their own hands. But should they hesitate, let us be prepared to *go forward*—trusting to that God for assistance who hath said, "Lo, I am with you always, even to the end of the world."[8]

By the "fathers" Mills meant the professors at Andover, Edward D. Griffin, Moses Stuart, and Leonard Woods, and two pastors of the area, Dr. Samuel Spring and Dr. Samuel Worcester, all of whom were then consulted. In that meeting the students were advised to present the entire matter before the General Association of Massachusetts, which was to meet the next day, June 27, 1810, in Bradford. On Dr. Spring's motion before the Association, the students

7. Ibid., p. 60.
8. Ibid., pp. 70-71.

presented their case, concluding with the following questions:

> Whether with their present views and feelings, they ought to renounce the object of Missions as visionary or impracticable; if not, whether they ought to direct their attention to the eastern or the western world; whether they may expect patronage and support from a Missionary Society in this country, or must submit themselves to the direction of a European Society; and what preparatory measures they ought to take previous to actual engagement?

(Signed)   Adoniram Judson, Jr.
Samuel Nott, Jr.
Samuel J. Mills
Samuel Newell[9]

The petition was referred to a committee of three, which next day reported in favor of the institution of an agency to be named "The American Board of Commissioners for Foreign Missions" (ABCFM)—the first such group in the United States. There were to be nine commissioners, five from Massachusetts and four from Connecticut, and this was later extended to include representatives from several Reformed persuasions. The students were advised to give themselves to "earnest prayer and diligent attention to suitable studies." So the dream of Samuel Mills and the Brethren was approaching fruition.

Funds were next sought, and a plea was sent forth to all the

Figure 8.1 Ordination of Rice, Hall, Nott, Newell, and Judson by the American Board of Commissioners for Foreign Missions (from an old engraving)

9. Ibid., pp. 72-73.

churches of New England to join with the ABCFM in obtaining money. On February 8, 1812, in Dr. Worcester's church in Salem, five men—Judson, Nott, Newell, Luther Rice, and Gordon Hall— were ordained missionaries.

Why was Samuel Mills not ordained and sent as a missionary? With characteristic consideration for others, he had given way to Gordon Hall, whom he believed was better fitted to be sent. Two reasons for the decision to defer Mills's ordination were given: first, Mills himself stated that he was not as well equipped as the others (difficulty with foreign languages, not a strong voice); second, the Brethren believed that Mills would be more useful to the cause of world evangelism if he remained for the present in America, be- cause he was a tireless activist, a fine organizer, and was superlative in presenting the cause of missions to the churches at home.

Thus Luther Rice and Gordon Hall, members of the Brethren at Williams College, were joined by Samuel Nott, Jr., a graduate of Union College, Samuel Newell, a graduate of Harvard, and Adoni- ram Judson from Providence College. Judson was a brilliant stu- dent and graduated valedictorian of his class at the age of nineteen, but in college he was not a Christian. He had imbibed some skepti- cal views, and the sudden death of an intimate friend and classmate, also a skeptic, overwhelmed Judson. He began to seek after faith, and at that time several ministers met him and were impressed with his abilities. They invited him to become a student at Andover Seminary, even though he was not a Christian or a candidate for the ministry, and he was admitted only by a waiver of the seminary rules. On the second of December, 1808, he made a solemn dedica- tion of his life to Christ, and soon after began to feel the call of God to the foreign mission fields.

The salary of the married men, Judson, Nott, and Newell, was to be $666.66, and that of Rice and Hall $444.44. It was estimated that the expenses for the five, including passage, salary, and all equipment would be $5,000 for the first year. Although there was at that point only $1,200 in the treasury, the Board went ahead on faith that the balance would come in. Soon the group set sail for India as agents of the ABCFM. Unexpectedly, two of them were converted to Baptist views, Adoniram Judson on board ship and Luther Rice shortly after arriving in Calcutta, and they were im- mersed by the Baptist church there.

Judson's and Rice's change to Baptist views gave a powerful challenge to American Baptists to get behind the work of foreign missions. Judson and his wife remained to begin a work that eventually led to great achievements in Burma.[10] Rice returned to the United States to sever relations with the American Board and to begin moves that culminated in May 1814 with the founding of "The General Missionary Convention of the Baptist Denomination in the United States of America for Foreign Missions."

During the next few years the American Board went ahead with plans for establishing missions in Ceylon and the Hawaiian Islands. Of special interest is the story of Henry Obookiah, a Hawaiian boy who was orphaned and shipped as a common sailor to Connecticut in 1809. There he met Samuel Mills, who described him in a letter to Gordon Hall: "Obookiah was at this time without a home, without a place to eat or sleep. The poor and almost friendless Hawaiian would sit down disconsolate, and the honest tears flowed freely down his sunburnt face." The outcome of a friendship with Mills was almost predictable: Obookiah decided to become a missionary to his own people. A foreign missions school was founded at Cornwall, Connecticut to train persons like him for such work, but unfortunately Obookiah's life was cut short by typhus while Samuel Mills was in Africa. However, as is often the case, when one dedicated person can no longer bear the load, others are inspired by his sacrifice to take up the burden. Three of Obookiah's classmates were successful in winning King Kamehameha II to Christ, thus beginning an awakening in Hawaii. With the founding of the Baptist board of missions and the expanding work of the ABCFM, the repercussions of the haystack meeting were indeed beginning to have a worldwide effect.

After the ordination of his five friends in February 1812, Mills eagerly searched for the Lord's will regarding his own future. His own will aside, it soon became evident that God's work involved home missions, not foreign, for the immediate future. Actually, that was not so strange a departure for the organizer of foreign missionary forces as it might seem, for he had talked with the Brethren of a mission "to our own continent," "to the heathen tribes to the westward." He entertained a great concept of home missions. To

---

10. Judson's immense labors in Burma, which cannot be traced here, included translation of the entire Bible from Greek and Hebrew into Burmese, pioneering language studies, and the compilation of a massive two-way lexicon. For a fine biography of Judson, see Courtney Anderson, *To the Golden Shore* (Grand Rapids: Zondervan, 1972).

him, the American West should be carefully surveyed with an eye to its particular needs and demands, if a full-fledged assault by missionaries was to be successful.

Actually, Mills's plan precisely filled a crying need. In the churches of America there *was* no accurate conception of the people and towns of the remote West and of what it would take to evangelize the immense territories. He saw that a survey of all the Western conditions was needed, one which could be printed and placed in the hands of any interested Christians so that personnel recruitment and funds collection could be done intelligently. To that end, on July 3, 1812, Mills and John F. Schermerhorn began a journey that covered 3,000 miles through Ohio, Kentucky, Tennessee, and down the Mississippi River to New Orleans. They then journeyed overland to Georgia and South Carolina, and finally to Connecticut. After he reached home, Mills began with his customary zeal to describe in reports to the Christian public the areas traversed. He began corresponding with Bible and missionary societies, urging them to send men and Bibles into that "God-forgetting and God-provoking portion of our country."

The trip, the first of its kind, had taken a year and three days. Mills and Schermerhorn had surveyed nearly every state and territory in the Union. They had investigated the numbers, location, and history of each of the Indian tribes west of the Allegheny Mountains. By swimming their horses across the rivers and creeks, sleeping on the deck of a Mississippi flatboat, tramping through nearly impenetrable swamps, they brought back an accurate picture of the West, the Indian tribes, and the small towns and settlements to a concerned reading public.

So concerned were they over Mills's investigations, the Massachusetts Missionary Society, the Philadelphia Bible Society, and the Philadelphia Missionary Society contributed $1,300 in total to finance Samuel Mills on a second western journey. On August 13, 1814, Mills and Daniel Smith left Philadelphia in a wagon loaded with 5,000 French New Testaments, 600 English Bibles, and 15,000 tracts, to be met at points west by other consignments of Bibles and literature. Early in November they reached St. Louis, then a tumble-down French village of 2,000 people, about one-third of whom were Americans.

St. Louis was not hospitable to morals. Another missionary pioneer found that its population was "a low, indecent grade and utterly worthless. Their nightly orgies were scenes of drunkenness and revelry. Among the frantic rites observed were the mock celebration of the Lord's Supper and burning the Bible. . . . The boast was often made that the Sabbath had never crossed and never should cross the Mississippi."[11] Yet Mills also saw the strategic importance of the town. "No place in the Western Country, New Orleans excepted, has greater natural advantages. No place, therefore, has higher importance, considered as a missionary station," he said.

Mills left St. Louis and pressed on to New Orleans, while Daniel Smith stayed at Natchez, Mississippi to organize a Presbyterian church and become its first pastor. Mills reached New Orleans February 10, 1815, a month after the famous battle and the day before the British captured the American fort on Mobile Bay. While finding abundant opportunity to minister to English soldiers held prisoner and to American wounded, he called on the most influential Roman Catholic priest to explain the plan of giving away the French Testaments. The priest expressed great satisfaction and promised to do all in his power to make a wise distribution of the Scriptures among those who could read.

Stimulated by all that he had observed concerning the state of the West, Mills arrived back in New England to begin pouring forth a stream of reports, letters of appeal, and addresses before groups.

> Ever since we came back to this land of Christian privileges we have been endeavoring to arouse the attention of the public, and to direct it toward the West. These exertions have been stimulated by a deep conviction of the deplorable state of the country. Never will the impressions be erased from our hearts that have been made by beholding these scenes of wide-spreading desolation. The whole country, from Lake Erie to the Gulf of Mexico, is as the valley of the shadow of death. Darkness rests upon it. Only here and there a few rays of gospel light pierce through the awful gloom. This vast country contains more than a million of inhabitants. Their number is every year increased by a mighty flood of emigration. . . . Yet there are at present only a little more than one hundred ministers in it. Were these ministers equally distributed throughout the country, there would be only one to every ten thousand people. But now there are districts of country, containing from twenty to fifty thousand inhabitants, entirely destitute. And how shall they hear without a preacher?[12]

11. Richards, *Samuel J. Mills,* p. 133.
12. Ibid., pp. 146-47.

As much as the West needed teachers of the Word to bring the civilizing and redemptive effects of the gospel, it also desperately needed the Bible itself. In so much of his journeys, Mills had encountered not only fearful ignorance of the simplest spiritual truths, but also a complete absence of the Scriptures. There were in 1816 132 Bible societies in the United States, but they were not able to supply even their own local demands.

What was needed was an institution like the British and Foreign Bible Society, which had been organized in 1804 to coordinate the efforts of local groups. "Old England has no brighter jewel in her crown," said Mills. "It is thought that half a million of Bibles are necessary for the supply of the destitute in the United States. It is a foul blot on our national character. Christian America must arise and wipe it away. The existing societies are not able to do it. They want union; they want cooperation; they want resources. If a national institution cannot be formed, application ought to be made to the British and Foreign Bible Society for aid."[13]

Mills brought all the pressure he could to bear upon men such as Elias Boudinot, president of the New Jersey Bible Society, and a meeting was called of all the societies for May 8, 1816, in New York City. The American Bible Society was formed, whose "sole object shall be to encourage a wider circulation of the Holy Scriptures without note or comment." The society itself was a great triumph, for it brought together in its founders and officers members of all the Protestant denominations, and that was the first time they had worked together in such concerted action. As with previous projects, Mills wanted and took no credit, yet Lyman Beecher, secretary of the convention, said that it was Mills's own "profound wisdom, indefatigable industry, and unparalleled executive power in the excitement and combination of minds in benevolent combinations that made him the primary agent in this movement."

Despite the magnificent achievements that this young man of thirty-three had already accomplished for his Lord, Samuel Mills was not yet ordained as a minister of the gospel. In the assumption that his service to home missions was over and that he would take up his first concern, the foreign field, he was ordained June 21, 1815. But he never did marry because he believed that the demands of mission work were too pressing. When asked regarding this, he stated that he would gladly have taken a wife, if he did not feel that

13. Ibid., pp. 160-61.

he must set himself against everything that would possibly stand in the way of his efficiency in the missionary cause.

Now that he had done all he could for the American West and the distribution of the Scriptures, Mills turned to foreign evangelization. From the time of the haystack meeting until the day of his death, the passion of Mills's heart was Africa. On his tours of the Southern states, Mills had been stirred by the miserable plight of the slaves held there, and now his concern was rekindled. He estimated that there were a million and a half blacks in the United States, and he discovered in the South many slaveholders ready to emancipate their slaves if some good solution regarding the slaves' future might be arrived at.

The first proposal from Mills was that a large tract of territory in the thinly settled West be set aside as a black colony, to which all freed slaves could go. He then tried hard to get such a tract in Ohio, Indiana, or Illinois, but the plan failed, not because anyone thought it would not work, but because it was believed that the whites would eventually want all the region.

The next proposal advanced by Mills was to pursue actively a plan with a long history—African colonization. Several years before the Revolutionary War, Dr. Samuel Hopkins, Congregational pastor in Newport, Rhode Island, believed that some compensation ought to be made to Africa for the evil and misery of the devastating slave trade. His purpose was to educate several blacks, and send them back to their native lands as teachers and preachers of the gospel. While the war interrupted that plan, Hopkins was an intimate friend of Samuel Mills's father, and there is no reason to doubt that Mills's early interest in Africa was because of Dr. Hopkins. From then on innumerable suggestions were made for the colonizing of Africa by blacks from America. In 1800 the Virginia legislature asked Governor James Monroe to correspond with President Thomas Jefferson in regard to purchasing land for colonizing free blacks. Various places were discussed, but the project eventually died.

Another attempt to promote the plan was made by the Virginia legislature in 1816. Hearing of it, Dr. Robert Finley called a meeting of influential friends in Washington for December 21, 1816. Henry Clay presided, and Francis Scott Key was chairman of the committee on constitution. Mills attended and was one of the fifty signers of the constitution of "The American Society for Colonizing the

Free People of Color in the United States." A pamphlet, written by Mills, was distributed outlining the plan. He then volunteered for the dangerous duty of visiting Africa and finding a suitable place on its west coast for the proposed colony. His offer was gratefully accepted.

With understandable apprehension, and yet a total confidence in the Lord God who is able to do all things, Mills wrote,

> I never engaged in an object before, which laid me under so vast a responsibility. I have entered upon it with no ordinary degree of trembling, though I have generally been satisfied with respect to what is my duty. The object is, I think, a noble one; and we have reason to hope it will be approved by God. On his approbation it must rely for success.[14]

Mills then chose as his companion on the long voyage Ebenezer Burgess, professor of mathematics and natural philosophy at the University of Vermont. To Burgess he wrote, "It is confidently believed by many of our best and wisest men, that, if it succeeds, it will ultimately be the means of exterminating slavery in our country." Whatever may be the current attitude toward a plan for colonizing blacks who volunteered, the intentions of Samuel Mills and the society were only benevolent in trying to ameliorate their wretched condition as slaves. The gracious spirit of Mills must be admired as he started out to blaze a trail for an enterprise that enlisted the support of many of the ablest statesmen from Jefferson to Abraham Lincoln.

The first intention of Burgess and Mills was to visit England and consult with those who had experience in the administration of Sierra Leone, a colony for blacks in Africa. William Wilberforce, the great evangelical who led Parliament to abolish slavery throughout the British Empire, took them under his care and introduced them to the Duke of Gloucester and other important officials, seeking to give them all possible guidance and help. Bearing their letters of introduction, Mills and Burgess left England for Africa on February 2, 1818, in the ship *Mary*.

"At 4 P.M. we exulted at the sight of Africa," wrote Mills in his journal under the date of March 12, 1818. We can hardly imagine his feelings summed up in those few words. The dream of his life had become real, and he saw Africa for the first time. Perhaps, he prayed, the accomplishment of this mission might result in the eventual winning of Africa to Christ. What greater project could

14. Ibid., p. 200.

Figure 8.2 Samuel Mills surveys the coast of Africa, searching for an appropriate site for his colony (from an old engraving)

possibly be envisioned—Africa, with its tens of millions of primitive peoples, finding a magnificent hope at the throne of God?

They first inspected Sierra Leone, England's experiment for colonizing blacks. In 1787 the first settlement had been made, and after 1807, when the slave trade was abolished, those liberated from slave ships were brought there. Schools and churches had been established, five towns had grown up, trade and agriculture were thriving. Nowhere else but in Sierra Leone could conditions instead of theories of colonization be studied. One-sixth of the entire population of 12,000 attended schools that Mills judged to be excellent. The Americans were convinced and encouraged by what had been accomplished.

Burgess and Mills left Sierra Leone and started down the coast in a fifteen-ton schooner with a native crew and several from the English colony who volunteered to come along to advise and translate. After numerous parleys with native chiefs and much exploring, they determined that the country along the Bagroo River seemed the most attractive for a colony. There was much unoccupied land that could be bought for six dollars an acre. There was good water, rolling countryside, and the climate appeared to be as healthy and temperate as in any area they had visited. Native wars and the slave trade had decimated the population; Mills passed places with scarcely a hut to be found, where large towns had previously existed. The land was suited to rice, sweet potatoes, corn, and cassada. Many tropical fruits grew in abundance. The region seemed ideal.

For five weeks Mills and Burgess explored, gathered much information, and palavered with tricky natives. On May 7, 1818, they arrived back at Sierra Leone and laid the results of their investigation before Governor McCarthy. "I am every day more convinced," wrote Mills, "of the practicality and expediency of establishing American colonies on this coast." Although the American Society for Colonizing subsequently saw fit not to make the territory American, the first colony was landed at Sherbro in April 1822, and in July 1847 Liberia became an independent nation, with a government patterned after that of the United States. Many freed slaves voluntarily came to its shores, making Liberia the jewel of Africa.

Mills's mission was ended. On board the brig *Success* he wrote on May 22, 1818, "The continent of Africa recedes from our view." However, two weeks after they sailed, he began to display symptoms of fever. A racking cough had begun in the damp climate of England, but at sea and in Africa he seemed to be relieved enough to accomplish an immense amount of work. Leaning on the taffrail of the *Success*, despite the increasing symptoms of tuberculosis, he said to Ebenezer Burgess, "I have now transcribed the brief journal of my visit to the coast of Africa and turned my face toward home. If it please God that I may arrive safely, as I may reasonably hope, I think that I shall take Obookiah and go to the Sandwich Islands, and there I shall end my life."

It was not in the will of God for this great servant. On June 15, 1818, in the afternoon, Samuel J. Mills, Jr., his face calm and peaceful, met his Lord. That evening at sunset his body was committed to the ocean, whose waves have borne his influence to the "remotest corner of this ruined world."

He was thirty-five at his death. What Samuel Mills had accomplished in six incredible years staggers the imagination. Leonard Bacon, a professor at Andover Seminary, paid the following tribute to Mills in 1824:

> A ship returning from a distant quarter of the globe paused in her passage across the deep. There stood on her deck a man of God, who wept over the dead body of his friend. He prayed, and the sailors wept with him. And they consigned the body to the ocean. It was the body of a man who, in the ardor of youthful benevolence, had aspired to extend his influence throughout the world. He died in youth, but he had redeemed his pledge, and at this hour his influence is felt in Asia, in Africa, in the islands of the sea, and in every corner of his native country. This man was Samuel John Mills, and all that know his history will say that I have exaggerated neither the grandeur of his aspirations nor the results of his efforts. He traversed our land like a ministering spirit. . . . He explored in person the desolations of the West, and in person he stirred up to enterprise and effort the churches of the East. He lived for India and Hawaii, and died in the service of Africa. He went to heaven in his youth, but his works do follow him, like a long train of glory that still widens and brightens, and will widen and brighten forever. Who can measure the influence of one such minister of the gospel?[15]

---

15. Ibid., pp. 241-42.

9

The Benevolence Empire in America—Charles G. Finney

Before his conversion Charles Grandison Finney had been described by one writer as a "splendid pagan—a young man rejoicing in his strength, proudly conscious of his physical and intellectual superiority to all around him."[1] He was six feet two inches tall and weighed one hundred eighty-five pounds. Striking and handsome, he was regarded by the opposite sex in the area of Jefferson County, New York as a most eligible bachelor. Young Finney was well known for his dancing, cello playing, and athletic prowess. As a man studying for a legal career, and as the leader of the church choir, his leadership influence was especially large among the young people. There was, however, one problem. Finney was not a Christian. He might have been unconcerned with that in the light of his many capabilities, but increasingly it gnawed at him.

In the autumn of 1821, Finney related in his *Memoirs*, he resolved to settle the issue of his soul's salvation. Because no one was in the law office but himself on Monday and Tuesday, he had opportunity to study his Bible and engage in prayer a great deal. He stopped up the key hole so he could not be heard praying. "During Monday and Tuesday my convictions increased; but still it seemed as if my heart grew harder. I could not shed a tear, I could not pray. . . . Tuesday night I had become very nervous; and in the night a strange feeling came over me as if I was about to die. I knew that if I did I should sink down to hell."[2]

---

1. William C. Cochran, *Charles Grandison Finney* (Philadelphia: Lippincott, 1908), p. 13.
2. Charles G. Finney, *Memoirs of Rev. Charles G. Finney* (New York: A. S. Barnes, 1876), p. 13.

On Wednesday morning Charles Finney started for the office with the questions of the previous evening weighing on his mind. Convinced that he could no longer evade the issue, he turned to go to the woods north of town. Resolving to "give my heart to God, or I never will come down from there," Finney found a spot near a tangle of fallen trees where he hoped to escape from prying eyes. As he dropped to his knees the verse from Jeremiah 29:12 came to him which gave him assurance: "Then shall ye call upon me, and ye shall go and pray unto me, and I will hearken unto you" (KJV). Until then he had believed the Bible intellectually, but the truth had not come to him that faith was a voluntary trust and not an intellectual state. Now, by faith he had become a Christian.

After hours of prayer Finney left the woods to go to the office. There he attempted to play his bass viol, as he often did, and to sing some sacred pieces, "but as soon as I began to sing those sacred words, I began to weep. It seemed as if my heart was all liquid."[3] His law partner Benjamin Wright came in and they spent the rest of the day moving furniture. After Wright left for the day, the emotional impact of Finney's decision struck him again. One of the choir members dropped by and was amazed to see Finney weeping loudly. On inquiry, Finney said that he was not in pain, "but so happy that I cannot live."

The next morning Finney returned to the office, as he described,

> And there I was having the renewal of these mighty waves of love and salvation flowing over me, when Squire Wright came into the office. I said a few words to him on the subject of his salvation. He looked at me with astonishment, but made no reply whatever, that I recollect. He dropped his head, and after standing a few minutes left the office. I thought no more of it then, but afterward found that the remark I made pierced him like a sword; and he did not recover from it till he was converted.
>
> Soon after Mr. Wright had left the office, Deacon B——came into the office and said to me, "Mr. Finney, do you recollect that my case is to be tried at ten o'clock this morning? I suppose you are ready?" I had been retained to attend this suit as his attorney. I replied to him, "Deacon B——, I have a retainer from the Lord Jesus Christ to plead his cause, and I cannot plead yours."[4]

Soon after his conversion, therefore, Charles Grandison Finney

---

3. Ibid., p. 19.
4. Ibid., p. 24.

made his first definite step in the direction of the Christian ministry.

Four years had passed, at the time of Finney's conversion, since the death of the leader of New England's awakenings, Timothy Dwight. The Yale president's carefully organized campaign to promote dignified, orderly revivals in the settled East had met with unexpected success after he had begun it in 1800. He chose and carefully groomed promising Yale men to succeed him so that his influence might be perpetuated. The most outstanding of those men were Lyman Beecher, Asahel Nettleton, and Nathaniel W. Taylor. These men and dozens of other Yale graduates had provided excellent leadership under Dwight's paternal encouragement. Things seemed very hopeful after 1801 when the Congregational churches of New England and the Presbyterian churches in the remainder of the states agreed on the Plan of Union "to promote harmony and to establish as far as possible a uniform system of Church government." Thus, the Yale pastors and the Presbyterians of Finney's New York had officially been members of the same ecclesiastical body since 1801. Ministers from the two regions easily intermixed, and there was general agreement among them on matters of church government.

In response to the efforts of such pastors, great numbers had been converted and were energizing the churches of the East. Between 1800 and 1835, while the national population tripled, church membership increased five times over. In 1800 seven percent of the population belonged to Protestant churches, whereas in 1835 the proportion had jumped to twelve and one half percent. Membership in Protestant churches soared from 365,000 in 1800 to 3,500,000 by 1850.[5] Evangelism flamed in the healthiest churches of America, and an expectant spirit of awakening made the clergy and the laity alike vitally concerned for the salvation of the lost. The future of the churches appeared bright indeed.

With that dynamic spirit surging onward, a successor to Timothy Dwight was sought after his death. Lyman Beecher had been Dwight's lieutenant in the leadership of the campaign for awakenings, and he appeared to be the likely commander of aggressive evangelism for the future. Not only did Beecher enlarge the existing structure of institutional revivalism in New England and New York

5. Garth M. Rosell, *Charles Grandison Finney and the Rise of the Benevolence Empire* (Ann Arbor, Mich.: University Microfilms, 1971), p. 23.

by utilizing the Plan of Union network, but in 1826, by which time he was one of the well-known preachers of America, he was called to the Hanover Street Church of Boston. There he was able to carry his campaign for revivals into the heartland of Unitarianism. In Boston he found a distressing situation, with many of the congregations split between trinitarians and unitarians and court battles in progress over church property. Joining forces with the Baptists, Beecher began "inquiry" meetings in various parts of town, and he was rewarded at the next communion with seventy converts in his church alone.

But Dwight's mantle was not to fall upon the shoulders of Beecher or any other of Dwight's protegés. Rather, it was an unknown young lawyer, Charles Finney, who was to become the chief evangelist of America, and the head of the "Benevolence Empire" of reform movements in the nation. "No religious leader in America since [Jonathan] Edwards commanded such attention," the historian Perry Miller has declared, "and no one was to do it again until Dwight Moody."[6]

Finney was born in Warren, Litchfield County, Connecticut on August 29, 1792, in the very path of the migration that was taking thousands of New Englanders into the beckoning lands of New York. "When I was about two years old," Finney recalled, "my father removed to Oneida County, New York, which was at that time, to a great extent, a wilderness. No religious privileges were enjoyed by the people. . . . My parents were neither of them professors of religion. . . . I seldom heard a sermon, unless it was an occasional one from some traveling minister."[7] Finney was the seventh child, and when he was sixteen the family settled in Henderson, on the Lake Ontario shore. After receiving the training available from the backwoods schools of his boyhood, Finney attended the Hamilton Oneida Academy at Clinton, New York for two years (1806-1808). Although regular church attendance was not his lot, he must have been inspired by the academy's headmaster, Samuel Kirkland, the famous missionary to the Oneida Indians.

Increasingly, Finney was convinced he wanted to be a teacher, not a farmer, and that he needed more education to attain his goal. He left the academy and taught school from his sixteenth to his twentieth year. In the fall of 1812 he enrolled in a school at Warren,

6. Perry Miller, *The Life of the Mind in America: From the Revolution to the Civil War* (New York: Harcourt, Brace and World, 1965), pp. 9, 22-24.
7. Finney, *Memoirs,* p. 4.

Figure 9.1 Charles Grandison Finney (Allen Memorial Art Museum, Oberlin College, Oberlin, Ohio. Gift of Lewis Tappan, 16.6)

Connecticut, where he lived with one of his uncles. He contemplated attending Yale College, but a teacher advised him against it, saying he could master the entire curriculum by himself in two years. Finney then set himself to acquiring some knowledge of Latin, Greek, and Hebrew and was offered a position teaching school in New Jersey, which he accepted. Again, as before, he was a successful teacher, but much of his formula for success came from his ability to win the students' unbounded admiration. One former student declared,

> There was nothing which anyone else knew, which Mr. Finney didn't know, and there was nothing which anyone else could do, that Mr. Finney could not do—and do a great deal better. He was the idol of his pupils. . . . He was very dignified, and kept perfect order. Should any boy attempt to create a disturbance, one flash of Mr. Finney's eye would quell the sinner at once. Oh, I tell you, they all loved and worshipped him, and all felt that some day he would be a great man.[8]

This admirer went on to say that in the school yard, Finney kept the students' loyalty by out-wrestling and out-fighting the best of them, even taking on several of the boys at once. But after a time, teaching paled; Finney was in his mid-twenties, and turned his interests toward a career in law. The custom at that time was to study under the tutelage of a local lawyer, and he entered the law office of Benjamin Wright in Adams, New York, not far from his parents' farm. This, then, was to be his life work—or so he thought. But the Christian faith had a strange allure.

> Thus when I went to Adams to study law, I was almost as ignorant of religion as a heathen. I had been brought up mostly in the woods. I had very little regard for the Sabbath, and had no definite knowledge of religious truth.
>
> At Adams, for the first time, I sat statedly, for a length of time, under an educated ministry. Rev. George W. Gale, from Princeton, New Jersey, became, soon after I went there, pastor of the Presbyterian Church in that place. His preaching was of the old school type; that is, it was thoroughly Calvinistic.
>
> In studying elementary law, I found the old authors frequently quoting the Scriptures. . . . This excited my curiosity so much that I went and purchased a Bible, the first I had ever owned. . . . This soon led to my taking a new interest in the Bible, and I read and meditated on it much more than I had ever done before in my life. However, much of it I did not understand.[9]

Finney's musical talents enabled him to take the position of choir director in the Adams Presbyterian Church, even though he was all too aware he was not yet converted. The pastor, George Gale, in time became a good friend of his popular choir director. Gale probably thought Finney needed special efforts at conversion, for his influence was keeping some of the choir out of the Kingdom. In their many discussions over theology, the core of disagreement was Gale's Calvinism, which stressed the sovereignty of God and man's

8. Cochran, *Finney,* pp. 17-18.
9. Finney, *Memoirs,* pp. 7-8.

depravity and utter inability to bring about his own salvation. Whatever Finney's own views, through those discussions he was "brought face to face with the question whether I would accept Christ as presented in the Gospel, or pursue a worldly course of life."

Finney's own intense study of the Bible at this point, as he debated theology with Gale, seemed to be leading him to different conclusions about human ability than those of strict Calvinism. He agreed that he and the remainder of mankind were at enmity with God, as the Scriptures teach throughout. But Finney became convinced from his own study that this broken relationship with God could be healed if mankind would turn in repentance to Christ. His innate self-assurance asserted itself and Finney's understanding of the gospel showed him that it was a matter of man's admitting that he was a sinner, and of his acceptance of what Christ had done on the cross of Calvary, that brought him salvation. What was holding him back was not that he was not one of the elect, but his own obstinacy and lack of determination. "Gospel salvation seemed to me to be an offer of something to be accepted; and that it was full and complete." All that was necessary to receive it "was to get my own consent to give up my sins, and accept Christ."[10]

Those were the thoughts that overwhelmed him on that October Wednesday in 1821 and drove him away from the route to his office and into the nearby woods to seek God and settle the matter forever. When he emerged, his heart and mind at peace with God and confident of salvation, the conversion experience epitomized the influences of his formative years—his confidence in himself and his free will and the theology he had been hammering out in discussions with George Gale. Regeneration was much simpler than the version Gale had presented; it involved only the admission of one's lostness and sin and then the willing acceptance of the Savior's redeeming grace and forgiveness. With that—in all its beautiful simplicity—the believer immediately was regenerated, through God's grace.

Charles Finney now turned about completely from his irreligion; wherever he went he told people of his conversion and urged them to think seriously of Christ and His salvation. When he found the son of a church elder advocating universalism—that all men would go to heaven—he demolished the young man's arguments in short order. Finney seemed from his conversion to be destined for the

10. Ibid., p. 15.

ministry, and one witness remembered him saying that if he ever served God he would be in earnest and "pull men out of the fire."[11]

The news spread quickly that Finney was professing conversion. Although some of his friends counseled him not to leave a most promising career in law, others such as George Gale recognized that if Finney could bring all the intensity he focused on other areas to the Christian faith, he would have much to offer. As it was, his legal training had already given him much valuable experience in dealing with people and in speaking. Indeed, his style in preaching for the rest of his life showed his law training, for most who heard him preach saw that he owed much of his pulpit success to the conversational, direct, argumentative, and persuasive modes of address that he had cultivated as a lawyer. That electrifying style was in marked contrast to the written sermons then in vogue.

At Gale's urging, Finney placed himself under the care of the local presbytery as a candidate for the ministry in the spring of 1822. The presbytery's assembled clergy put the usual queries to him, and then urged him to enroll at Princeton to study theology. Doubtless they were dumbfounded when he informed the august body, "that I would not put myself under such an influence as they had been under; that I was confident they had been wrongly educated, and they were not ministers that met my ideal of what a minister of Christ should be. I told them this reluctantly, but I could not honestly withhold it."[12]

After they regained their composure and dignity following that demolition, the leaders of the presbytery saw that they were not dealing with the average young man. Reluctantly they agreed to allow Finney to pursue studies under Gale's direction. The two friends were delighted with this arrangement and continued the discussions that had begun even before Finney's conversion. But their views remained as far apart as ever.

The Presbytery of St. Lawrence was again called together at Adams in December 1823 for the purpose of licensing Finney to preach and checking his progress. When asked if he received the Westminster Confession of Faith, Finney answered that he did as far as he understood it, but that in actuality he had never seen it. In March 1824 the Female Missionary Society of the Western District of New York retained Finney as a missionary to Jefferson County, a

---

11. *New York Evangelist,* May 23, 1850.
12. Finney, *Memoirs,* pp. 45-46.

very rural northern district bordering on Lake Ontario. On July 1, 1824, he was ordained a Presbyterian minister, and he began pastoral work in the towns of Antwerp and Evans Mills.

Already he was consolidating the techniques he would use as an evangelist for the rest of his life. His criticisms of the presbytery revolved around two complaints: his disagreements with the Calvinism of the Westminster Confession, and the ornate, elevated preaching style practiced by Gale and most of the Congregational and Presbyterian clergymen of the time. *His* preaching style, Finney determined, would reach people where they were.

But the established clergymen also aimed criticisms at Finney. They were not pleased by his preaching performances, which in their view destroyed the dignity of the pulpit by his colloquial and familiar speech, and vivid, energized homiletics. He was hurt that "Mr. Gale, when I preached for him immediately after I was licensed, told me that he should be ashamed to have any one know that I was a pupil of his. . . . They would reprove me for illustrating my ideas by reference to the common affairs of men. . . . I sought to express all my ideas in few words, and in words that were in common use."[13] Whether preachers of the time liked his ways or not, he was the voice of the future, and the days of the older methods were numbered.

Soon, under Finney's direct and challenging preaching, the communities of Antwerp and Evans Mills were ablaze with an awakening. As he preached throughout the area, his experiences in those upper reaches of New York taught him evangelistic techniques that avoided the howls and shrieks of the Cane Ridge tradition; his methods were based on civilized decorum. Directness, real life, and animation, yes, but without sensationalism.

In October 1824 Finney married Lydia Andrews of Whitestown in Oneida County. A year later, having left the revivals in Jefferson County, Finney and his wife planned to return home from a synod meeting in Utica in time to celebrate their first year of marriage. While they were unaware of it, events were shaping that would change their lives and catapult Finney from an unknown evangelist into national prominence.

In the small town of Western, on Lake Oneida, they happened to meet George Gale, who had retired to a farm near the village and was concerned with the low moral condition of the area. Finney,

13. Ibid., pp. 67-68.

already known in the region, was implored by Gale and the church leaders to stay a short time to preach. As a result, he began conducting services almost every evening and three times on Sundays. The result was the setting of a revival fire that brought thousands of converts to God and began the Oneida County revivals of 1825-1827.

Immediately after that, the Reverend Moses Gillet invited Finney to preach at his Congregational church in Rome, New York. In a short while Gillet declared "religion was the principal subject of conversation in our streets, stores, and even taverns." Finney's personal and extemporaneous pulpit style had a rapid-fire impact on the packed congregation, but perhaps it was his uncannily penetrating and hypnotic eyes that most riveted his audience. Set under firm brows in a handsome face, those eyes were "large and blue, at times mild as an April sky, and at others, cold and penetrating as polished steel."[14] In addition to those unforgettable eyes, observers were always impressed with Finney's grace in the pulpit, his fitting illustrations, his appropriate but not exaggerated gestures that dramatized his delivery, and his majestic voice, which was a fitting companion to the eyes. One theology student described Finney giving a sermon on those who believed that hell was not perpetual punishment, but that men might serve some time there for their sins and then be released. Finney, of course, held that Scripture taught *eternal* punishment for unbelievers.

> The tones of the preacher . . . became sweet and musical, as he repeated "Worthy is the Lamb that was slain, to receive power, and riches, and wisdom, and might, and honor, and glory, and blessing." No sooner had he uttered the word "blessing" than he started back, turned his face . . . fixed his glaring eyes upon the gallery at his right hand, and gave all the signs of a man who was frightened by a sudden interruption of the divine worship. With a stentorian voice he cried out: "*What* is this I see? What means that *rabble-rout* of men coming up here? Hark! Hear them shout! . . . 'Thanks to hell-fire! We have served out our time. Thanks! Thanks!' " . . . Then, after a lengthened pause, during which a fearful stillness pervaded the house, he said in gentle tones: "Is this the spirit of the saints? Is this the music of the upper world?"[15]

Finney was able to modulate his rich voice to be immensely

---

14. Cochran, *Finney,* p. 13.
15. George F. Wright, *Charles Grandison Finney* (New York: Houghton Mifflin, 1891), pp. 71-74.

persuasive, as well as to be explosive with his verbal pyrotechnics. Many warned him at first that being dramatic in the pulpit might woo the lower classes, but it would turn away the educated. As Finney suspected, just the opposite proved to be the case. "They would say, 'You will not interest the educated part of your congregation.' But facts soon silenced them on this point. They found that, under my preaching, judges, and lawyers, and educated men were converted by scores; whereas, under their methods, such a thing seldom occurred."[16]

Another factor that worked in Finney's favor in the promotion of awakenings was the socio-economic. He came into an area, beginning with the time of the revivals at Rome and Western, that was being turned upside down by rapid industrial development, led by the completion of the Erie Canal in 1825. That, plus the opening of multitudes of small factories, mills, distilleries, and packing houses, attracted thousands of migrants, some bound for the Midwest, and some destined to settle along the canal. As Bernard Weisberger has stated, "Steadily, upstate New Yorkers watched the crumbling of certain eternal verities—fixed land tenure, a stable populace, small class distinctions, isolation from the outside world."[17]

People searched for certainties they could cling to, and enthusiastic religion among other items filled the bill admirably, although it was not always orthodox Christianity they chose. New York west of the Hudson River Valley was termed the "Burnt-over District" before Finney's time, because of the number of scorchings it had received from various religious excitements. Just as it was in Kentucky and Tennessee, the winter of 1799-1800 was called the time of the "great revival," although the New York awakening was far more decorous and well-behaved (to suit the Yankee taste) than it was in the West. That was the beginning. From then on one enthusiasm after another agitated the area. During the quarter century 1825-1850, New York state in some remarkable way produced Mormonism; various forms of perfectionism, spiritualism, and millennialism; as well as the anti-Masonic, Liberty, and Free Soil political parties.

When Finney left Rome, five hundred converts had been made. The Reverend Samuel C. Aiken, pastor of the First Presbyterian

---

16. Finney, *Memoirs,* p. 84.
17. Bernard A. Weisberger, *They Gathered at the River* (Boston: Little, Brown, 1958), p. 108. An excellent treatment of the situation is given in Whitney R. Cross, *The Burned-over District* (Ithaca, N.Y.: Cornell U., 1950).

Church in Utica, New York, begged for Finney to preach there, and soon that city was ablaze with spiritual concern. Aiken reported that the services were made "solemn and sometimes terribly so by the presence of God which made sinners afraid and Christians humble and still."[18] By May 1826, four hundred new members had been added to Aiken's church, and in the surrounding area over one thousand converts were added to the rolls of other churches. Demands for Finney's increasingly famous preaching came faster; in the summer of 1826 he led meetings in Auburn, and in September in Troy. Again spiritual concern flooded those New York cities, and multitudes of converts were made.

As Charles Finney's fame grew, his practices came under increasing criticism. Asahel Nettleton, particularly, charged that Finney had introduced "new measures"—measures that were changing previous evangelistic practices in which awakenings had been kept firmly in the hands of settled pastors, and only ordinary "means of grace" had been used. The new measures included praying for persons by name, allowing women to pray and testify, encouraging persons to come forward to an "anxious seat" (a front pew for those under conviction), mobilizing the entire community through groups of workers visiting homes, and displacing the routine services of the church by "protracted meetings" (special services held each night for several weeks' duration).

Yet for every critic who might find fault, Finney found supporters who lauded his aggressive evangelism, and especially his insistence on order and dignity. "Beyond some unaffected, yet striking peculiarities of voice and manner," wrote one observer of Finney's preaching, "there is nothing to attract curiosity, or offend even the most fastidious or carping sense of propriety."[19] The new measures were successful and logical extensions of evangelistic techniques, his supporters urged. The real difference, it was claimed, between Finney's efforts and those who disagreed with him was in the "power and passion" that attended his meetings.

In still another way, Finney made a significant change from the ways of older evangelists, and that was to gather around himself a

18. *A Narrative of the Revival of Religion in the County of Oneida, Particularly in the Bounds of the Presbytery of Oneida, in the Year 1826* (Utica, N.Y.: Hastings and Tracy, 1826), pp. 23-24.
19. Thomas Seward, "Address: A Memorial of the Semi-Centennial of the Founding of the Sunday School of the First Presbyterian Church, Utica, New York" (Utica, N.Y., 1867), pp. 126-27.

group of like-minded associates for the promotion of the work. At some point in 1826 Finney; Daniel Nash, a retired pastor; Herman Norton, a recently ordained evangelist; George W. Gale (his views by now in line with Finney's); and Nathaniel Smith, another Presbyterian preacher, joined together to form the Oneida Evangelical Association. That society's purpose was "to send forth . . . evangelists" to "establish and benefit the Redeemer's Kingdom."[20] As Garth Rosell says, "For the first time in the nation's history, professional evangelists banded together for the 'salvation of the world.' "[21]

In addition to the members of the Association, a circle of friends was gathering around Finney to support his work. Nicknamed the "Holy Band," it consisted mainly of pastors in whose churches Finney had ministered, such as Nathaniel Beman of Troy, Dirck Lansing of Auburn, Samuel C. Aiken of Utica, and Moses Gillet of Rome. As the work progressed, others became convinced that God's hand was upon Finney. Among those who later joined the effort were John Frost, pastor at Whitesboro; Charles Stuart, principal of the Utica Academy; Noah Coe, pastor in New Hartford; Edward N. Kirk, pastor at Albany (and destined later to arouse the spiritual concern of the young Dwight L. Moody); Horatio Foote, evangelist in New York; and Theodore Weld, who would become one of the most famous abolitionists in America. Thus many of the most important leaders of the Presbyterians and Congregationalists in New York were rallying around Finney and moving their denominations closer to the new kind of evangelism he used.

The methods and increasing impact of the Oneida Association were bound to stir controversy. Lyman Beecher, who recently had become pastor in Boston, called for a meeting of concerned evangelical leaders on July 18, 1827, at New Lebanon, just west of the Massachusetts line in New York. Rumors of Finney's deviation from accepted evangelistic practices had been filtering into New England, as a result of the concerns of Asahel Nettleton, coleader

---

20. A. B. Johnson to Charles Finney, 5 December 1826, Finney Papers, Oberlin College Library, Oberlin, Ohio.
21. Rosell, *Finney and Rise of Benevolence Empire.* p. 36. It is true that this was preceded by the shaky coalition of pro-revival pastors and evangelists pieced together by Lyman Beecher, which made up the New England contingent at the New Lebanon Conference. But those, with the exception of Asahel Nettleton, were settled clergymen, not itinerant evangelists, and they received salaries from the churches they pastored. But the members of the Oneida Association were paid for the awakenings they conducted here and there.

with Beecher of New England orthodoxy. Beecher sensibly did not want to be stampeded into anything rash, and he wrote to Nathaniel Beman, "Satan, as usual, is plotting to dishonor a work which he cannot withstand. I have confidence in the piety and talents of brother Finney, and have no doubt that he brings the truth of God to bear upon the conscience with uncommon power."[22]

After some discussion of Finney's methods, the first formal resolutions that were passed by unanimous vote stated in part:

> That revivals of true religion are the work of God's Spirit, by which, in a comparatively short period of time, many persons are convinced of sin, and brought to the exercise of repentance towards God, and faith in our Lord Jesus Christ.
>
> That the preservation and extension of true religion in our land has been much promoted by these revivals.
>
> That . . . greater and more glorious revivals are to be expected, than has ever yet existed.[23]

Then followed a discussion upon possible extravagances and enthusiasm. Finney and the other New Yorkers, as Presbyterian evangelists, made clear to the New Englanders that they were as firmly opposed to the ignorant bombast and physical excesses of the Cane Ridge tradition as Beecher was. It was again unanimously agreed that it was wrong to condemn settled pastors, to depreciate education, to justify any measure simply because it might be successful, to hold inquiry meetings until late at night, to exaggerate accounts of revivals, to encourage "audible groaning, violent gestures and boisterous tones" among the congregation, or to name particular individuals in public prayer.

More discussion followed concerning alleged extravagances during Finney's past revivals, but it soon became apparent that those problems had been exaggerated, and none of the New Yorkers retained a disposition to condemn Finney in any way, whatever their sentiments had been when they came to the meeting. The discussion then turned to the question of the propriety of women speaking and praying in public. Here the New Englanders were adamant. The apostle Paul forbade women from speaking in church (1 Corin-

22. Lyman Beecher to N. S. S. Beman, January 1827, cited in Lyman Beecher and Asahel Nettleton, *Letters on "New Measures" in Conducting Revivals of Religion* (New York: Astley and Smith, 1828), p. 81.
23. James E. Johnson, "The Life of Charles Grandison Finney" (Ph.D. diss., Syracuse University, 1959), pp. 143-44.

thians 14:34; 1 Timothy 2), and that ended the matter. Then it was shown that the First Presbyterian Church of Utica had been encouraging women to pray in public before Finney arrived to begin his meetings, and Finney simply went along with the practice. Three days were spent in debate on this, but the two groups could not agree. Howard Morrison has said of that debate, "Still, the female issue was not in any way a question of an excess which could discredit Finney. Indeed, although Beecher and Nettleton had planned to use the convention to put Finney in his place, none of the resolutions passed by the delegates were in any way a censure of Finney . . . but actually supported and reinforced him."[24] After a great deal of prayer the group adjourned, and Charles Finney emerged the victor, his views exonerated.

Lyman Beecher left New York with the recognition that younger men, led by Finney, with newer ways were supplanting those represented by Nettleton and himself. As he said, he had "crossed the mountains expecting to meet a company of boys, but . . . found them to be full-grown men."[25] He then took actions to silence the dissention and to align himself with Finney. At the General Assembly of the Presbyterian Church in May 1828, an agreement was drawn up between the two sides that stated, "The subscribers . . . are of the opinion that the general interests of religion would not be promoted by any further publications on these subjects, or personal discussions."

Charles Finney thus emerged, at age thirty-six, as the leader of the Congregational-Presbyterian campaign for awakening in America. He became the recognized head of the Second Great Awakening and the inheritor of the mantle of Timothy Dwight. Demands for his preaching in the major cities of the Eastern seaboard drew him first to Wilmington, Delaware in the fall of 1827. There, in the Philadelphia-Princeton area, he came into the heart of the Old School views of Calvinism. That view believed that Christ had

---

24. Howard A. Morrison, "The Finney Takeover of the Second Great Awakening During the Oneida Revivals of 1825-1827," *New York History* 59, no. 1 (January 1978):47.
25. Beecher in his *Autobiography,* ed. Barbara Cross (Cambridge, Mass.: Harvard U., Belknap Press, 1961), claimed that he said during the Convention, "I know your plan, and you know I do. You mean to come into Connecticut, and carry a streak of fire to Boston. But if you attempt it, as the Lord liveth, I'll meet you at the State line, and call out all the artillery-men, and fight every inch of the way to Boston, and I'll fight you there" (2:73). But Finney had no recollection of such a thing being said, and it is doubtful it was uttered.

made atonement for the elect only and that it was entirely up to the Holy Spirit to initiate faith in an elect person, who in complete passivity had no means or will to pursue faith. Finney, sharing the "New Divinity" of Yale's Nathaniel W. Taylor, held that sin was a voluntary act and theoretically avoidable. He taught at the very outset of his *Revivals of Religion*, "A revival is not a miracle, nor dependent on a miracle, in any sense. It is a purely philosophical result of the right use of the constituted means—as much so as any other effect produced by the application of means."[26] As Christians could use scriptural means to bring about revivals, so could the unregenerate exercise their wills—actively—to choose or reject Christ and His claims. Old-school adherents were horrified.

During the Wilmington meetings, Finney received an invitation to preach in the pulpit of the Reverend James Patterson in Philadelphia. In the fortress of old-school theology, Finney had some misgivings—for a while.

> But I was preaching to please the Lord, and not man. I thought that it might be the last time I should ever preach there; but purposed, at all events, to tell them the truth, and the whole truth, on that subject, whatever the result might be.
>
> I endeavored to show that if man were as helpless as their views represented him to be, he was not to blame for his sins. If he had lost in Adam all power of obedience, so that obedience had become impossible to him, and that not by his own act or consent, but by the act of Adam, it was mere nonsense to say that he could be blamed for what he could not help. . . . Indeed, the Lord helped me to show up, I think, with irresistible clearness the peculiar dogmas of old-schoolism and their inevitable results.[27]

Surprisingly, Finney soon received invitations to speak in several of the leading Presbyterian pulpits of Philadelphia, including the First Church of Dr. James P. Wilson. As a friend wrote to Finney in February 1828, "Dr. Wilson having taken you into his pulpit it has almost petrified opposition here. He has more weight here than perhaps any Minister in the Presbyterian Church."[28] Opposition did continue, but Finney moved on to preach to great crowds in the largest German Reformed church in the city.

---

26. Charles G. Finney, *Revivals of Religion* (Westwood, N.J.: Revell, n.d.), p. 5.
27. Finney, *Memoirs*, pp. 235-36.
28. William G. McLoughlin, Jr., *Modern Revivalism: Charles Grandison Finney to Billy Graham* (New York: Ronald Press, 1959), p. 43.

Meanwhile, a group of new measure laymen in New York City were appealing for his aid there. Zephaniah Platt wrote in March 1828, "Our New York churches are generally in a cold stupid state but I am happy to tell you there is a very general change of sentiment here in regard to yourself and the Western Revivals."[29] Finney responded in the fall of 1829 and preached for a year in New York under the patronage of Anson G. Phelps. He received an invitation to conduct a city-wide campaign in Rochester, New York in the fall of 1830, and welcomed the opportunity to return to the area where his first successes had occurred. Whitney Cross has said,

> No more impressive revival has occurred in American history. Sectarianism was forgotten and all churches gathered in their multitudes. . . . But the exceptional feature was the phenomenal dignity of this awakening. No agonizing souls fell in the aisles, no raptured ones shouted hallelujahs. . . . The great evangelist, "in an unclerical suit of gray," acted "like a lawyer arguing before a court and jury," talking precisely, logically, but with wit, verve, and informality. Lawyers, real-estate magnates, millers, manufacturers, and commercial tycoons led the parade of the regenerated. . . .
>
> Finney later quoted Lyman Beecher's testimony that a hundred thousand in the nation made religious affiliations within a year, an event "unparalled in the history of the church."[30]

The life of the entire area was profoundly influenced. Former enemies and critics became firm supporters, acknowledging that there was little or nothing to criticize, but much to praise. The awakening in time spread far beyond Rochester as other evangelists and pastors carried its message and fervency back to their own areas.[31]

Finney then accepted invitations to conduct meetings in New England, first in Providence, then in Boston. After becoming convinced that Finney would not give the Unitarians anything to condemn, Lyman Beecher and the Congregational ministers' association of Boston requested that he come "as a general labourer among the Evangelical churches in this city." He stayed in Boston for nine months, from August 1831 to April 1832, but was quite critical of the spiritual climate there. When Lewis Tappan, a

29. Platt to Finney, March 1828, Finney Papers, Oberlin College Library, Oberlin, Ohio.
30. Cross, *Burned-over District*, pp. 155-56.
31. McLoughlin, *Modern Revivalism*, p. 57.

wealthy businessman, rented the Chatham Street Theater for another series of meetings in New York City, Finney gladly accepted the call and named the place the Second Free Presbyterian Church, inasmuch as it had issued from his earlier work there.

Since the late 1820s, Finney had been moving in the direction of including reform in his program for awakening, and his evangelism meant that converts would immediately be put to urgent work in the battle against sin. "Every member must work or quit. No honorary members," was a motto of his. During the first three decades of the nineteenth century, evangelical Christians organized thousands of societies toward what they were convinced would become an empire of benevolence that would begin alleviating every vice and problem. By 1834 the total annual income of the benevolence societies reached the then-incredible amount of nine million dollars.[32] Finney entered zealously into the leadership of the movement, sharing it with reformers like Weld, Tappan, and many others. Almost no phase of life in America was untouched. Temperance, vice, world peace, slavery, education, Sabbath observance, profanity, women's rights, the conditions in penal institutions—all those and more had specific societies devoted to their betterment. In the Rochester awakening of 1830-1831, Finney had introduced his new concern by paying much attention to the temperance crusade, and from then on he lent his influence to the entire spectrum of causes. In his first sermon in the Chatham Street Chapel of New York City, during the May "anniversary meetings" of 1832, Finney assumed the role of spokesman for the benevolence empire by outlining the framework within which American benevolence might function.

Finney first borrowed the concept of "universal benevolence" from Jonathan Edwards. It pictured America as the center of a theocratic world, a nation ruled by the moral government of God. "Laws of benevolence" are deeply graven into human society, he declared, and Christ commanded specifically that men love both God and neighbor. The obligation of each Christian is therefore inescapable, he thundered; every child of God is to "aim at being useful in the highest degree possible," preferring the interest of

---

32. For books dealing with the "benevolent empire," see Perry Miller, *Life of the Mind*, pp. 78-84; Whitney Cross, *Burned-over District;* and especially Clifford S. Griffin, *Their Brothers' Keepers: Moral Stewardship in the United States, 1800-1865* (New Brunswick, N.J.: Rutgers U., 1960).

God's Kingdom above all other interests. In that way God's millennium will be hastened by each faithful Christian.[33] It was a great vision. And to a remarkable degree the reform movements achieved their goals in the middle third of the nineteenth century, making genuine and lasting contributions to national life, eliminating much evil, and bringing transcendent Christian values into the mainstream of society. Charles Grandison Finney, in his alliance of awakenings and the reform impulse, was worthy of receiving a large portion of credit and public notice.

However, it must also be stated that Finney created some problems, the results of which have carried over to today. His statement, "A revival . . . is a purely philosophical result of the right use of the constituted means," with its emphasis on the human production of revivals and conversions, is consistent with his self-confident conviction that the only thing needed for God to save a sinner is the man's own consent. In time this idea led to his stress on perfectionism, the doctrine that since sin is a voluntary act it is theoretically avoidable. With this concept, holiness becomes a human possibility. In the 1800s this was a startling and dangerous idea in those parts of the United States that had long been influenced by Calvinism, and it has since led many to have grave difficulties with Finney's theology.

In addition it also must be stated that, for all of his many contributions Finney was also somewhat of a divisive person. He took advantage of his great popularity when he consistently went his own way, without regard for his peers in the ministry.

Finney began another phase of his career in 1835 when he left New York and became professor of theology (and later president) of Oberlin Collegiate Institute in Ohio. Oberlin did not get all of his time, however, for in March 1836 he became the pastor of the Broadway Tabernacle in New York. He held that position simultaneously with his work at Oberlin, and from 1837 he set aside a period each winter to hold evangelistic meetings in various places. But changes were in the wind. The Second Great Awakening was over by then, and Finney summarized all he had learned in his evangelistic career when he published his *Lectures on Revivals of Religion* in 1835. In effect, this was a professional manual of techniques for the promotion of revivals, and for the next hundred years

33. Charles G. Finney, *Sermons on Various Subjects* (New York: Benedict, 1835), pp. 96-103.

its impact upon evangelism was enormous.

After 1835, with Finney's encouragement and blessing, a large number of professional evangelists came to the fore from the ranks of every major denomination. Jabez Swan conducted five or six large campaigns every year from 1840 until the 1870s, and Jacob Knapp did much the same in the important cities of the East. Edward N. Kirk, James Caughey, Daniel Baker, Lewis Raymond, Orson Parker, Emerson Andrews, A. C. Kingsley, and a host of others became itinerant evangelists. By 1840 the concept of large campaigns led by preachers without specific parishes was accepted by the church.

Despite the large number of evangelists and campaigns, the religious life of America was in decline from 1840 until 1857. Many causes were responsible: agitation over the slavery issue had reached fever pitch and many were disillusioned over spiritual things because of the extremes of the Millerites.[34] William Miller and his followers had proclaimed that Christ would return to earth between March 21, 1843, and March 21, 1844. Although there was no general abandonment of business, no preparation of ascension robes, and no gathering in cemeteries and on hilltops by the Millerites as has often been reported, multitudes were deceived into expecting the second coming. When nothing happened Miller then set the date at October 22, 1844, and again many who trusted were infuriated at being deceived. So widespread was the clamor that the churches generally were mocked, including those that had nothing to do with the Millerite delusion. In August 1857 a financial panic occurred, with banks failing, railroads going into bankruptcy, and fiscal chaos arising everywhere.

The Third Great Awakening began inconspicuously in Hamilton, Ontario in October 1857. Soon religious journals picked up the news and reported that three to four hundred conversions had occurred in a few days. Expectation of a great moving of the Spirit became general. On December 1, 1857, two hundred pastors gathered in Pittsburgh for the sole purpose of discussing the opportunities for and hindrances to an awakening. The meetings continued for three days in an anxious and solemn manner. In a short time a similar convention was brought together in Cincinnati, and hundreds of clergymen studied questions such as the need of the

---

34. For the best recent scholarship on the Adventists see Cross, *Burned-over District,* pp. 287-321.

churches and the possibilities of revival. Much prayer was offered and awakenings soon flamed in the churches of Ohio and the West. In downtown New York, a tall and quiet forty-eight-year-old business man named Jeremiah Lanphier began work as an urban missionary for the North Dutch Reformed Church in July 1857. On September 23, 1857, he instituted a noonday prayer meeting for laymen that began attracting great numbers. Within six months, as the financial panic of 1857 shattered complacency, a total of ten thousand men were gathering for daily prayer in many places. When the churches were packed out, the prayer meetings were moved to theaters. Although prominent pastors such as Henry Ward Beecher and Theodore Cuyler attended and lent their enthusiastic support, laymen provided the leadership. Said the *New York Herald* of March 6, 1858, "Satan is busy all the morning in Wall Street among the brokers, and all the afternoon and evening the churches are crowded with saints who gambled in the morning." There was no fanaticism or hysteria, but a melting and orderly impulse to pray among those multitudes. Little preaching was done. With the interest of the nation at first riveted upon New York City, awakenings were soon common throughout the nation. As J. Edwin Orr has said,

> The phenomenon of packed churches and startling conversions was noted everywhere. There seemed to be three streams of blessing flowing out from the Middle Atlantic States, one northwards to New England, another southwards as far as Texas, and a third westwards along the Ohio valley. An observer in a leading secular newspaper stated it well when he wrote: "The Revivals, or Great Awakening, continue to be the leading topic of the day . . . from Texas, in the South, to the extreme of our Western boundaries, and our Eastern limits; their influence is felt by every denomination." Newspapers from Maine to Louisiana reflected his view. . . .
>
> The influence of the awakening was felt everywhere in the nation. It first captured the great cities, but it also spread through every town and village and country hamlet. It swamped schools and colleges. It affected all classes without respect to condition. There was no fanaticism. There was a remarkable unanimity of approval among religious and secular observers alike, with scarcely a critical voice heard anywhere. It seemed to many that the fruits of Pentecost had been repeated a thousandfold. At any rate, the number of conversions reported soon reached the total of fifty thousand weekly, a figure borne out by

the fact that church statistics show an average of ten thousand additions to church membership weekly for the period of two years.[35]

Coming on the very eve of the Civil War, with the nation writhing in agitation over the slavery question and financial panic, the Third Great Awakening of 1858 was an astounding phenomenon. Calm and impressively orderly, with a massive emphasis on prayer, with no denominational rivalry, and led by dedicated laymen such as Lanphier, the movement added more than a million converts in two years to America's churches. Because of its lack of spectacular leaders or objectionable aspects, the Third Awakening has often been overlooked by historians. But its influence spread across the Atlantic and affected the British Isles greatly, and the men and women it enlisted for Christian service were powerful leaders in the years ahead.

---

35. J. Edwin Orr, *The Second Evangelical Awakening in America* (London: Marshall, Morgan & Scott, 1952), pp. 31, 33.

10

The Perfection of Urban Evangelism—Dwight L. Moody

As his first major endeavor for Christ, young Dwight L. Moody chose one of the toughest parts of Chicago, "the Sands," to establish a Sunday school. This was a notorious slum section, and Moody was convinced no one else cared for the souls of its impoverished inhabitants. It was the red-light district of the booming young city and was filled with tumbledown shanties, saloons, and gambling halls. It would have been difficult to argue with Moody's conviction that nobody cared. In the spring of 1859—Moody was twenty-two—he secured the use on Sundays of the North Market Hall, a city-owned market that had a large, dingy, and dilapidated hall on the second floor, hardly conducive to worship or study but large enough for Moody's vision.

It was superb training for him. Met with scorn when he announced the school's opening, Moody was undaunted and proceeded to fill the huge place with hundreds of children through his perseverance. Not knowing what were the conventional methods used to attract children, he simply used common sense and any method which worked, such as offering a squirrel in a cage as prize to the boy who could bring in the largest number of friends. Recruiting pupils was only the beginning. "I would have to be up by six o'clock to get the hall ready for Sunday school," he related. "Every Saturday night a German society held a dance there, and I had to roll out beer kegs, sweep up sawdust, clean up generally, and arrange the chairs."[1]

---

1. William R. Moody, *The Life of Dwight L. Moody* (New York: Revell, 1900), p. 57. This is the "official Authorized Edition" of the life of Moody by his son, published soon after Moody's death, and is filled with anecdotes, as is the revised edition of 1930. Another excellent work by a friend of Moody's is William H. Daniels, *D. L. Moody and His Work* (Hartford: American Publishing, 1876).

The urchins' initial scorn was soon replaced by curiosity, and then by eager attendance. By degrees the school increased to 500 children, and in time to 1,500, the largest attendance at a Sunday school in Chicago. President Abraham Lincoln's visit to the school when on his way to Washington to begin his first term of office gave it much favorable publicity and turned the tide of public acceptance. One teacher described a typical Sunday:

> The scholars were bubbling over with mischief and exuberance of vitality and sorely tried the patience of the teachers; but the singing was a vent for their spirits, and such singing I had never heard before. The boys who sold papers in the street had an indescribable lung power, and the rest seemed not far behind. . . . It was no easy task to govern such a boisterous crowd, but the teachers seemed to interest their classes, and the exercises passed off with great enthusiasm.
>
> At the close of the school Mr. Moody took his place at the door and seemed to know personally every boy and girl; he shook hands and had a smile and a cheery word for each. They crowded about him tumultuously, and his arm must have ached many a time after those meetings. It was easy to see the hold he had on those young lives, and why they were drawn to that place week after week. The institution was a veritable hive of activity—meetings almost every evening, with occasional picnics and sociables, and services on the Sabbath that occupied most of the day.[2]

Dwight L. Moody kept his pockets full of candy when he toured the Sands looking for prospective pupils, but such means (and even presidential visits) were not enough to secure the consent of some parents. Many fathers were indolent loafers with a great suspicion of slumming missionaries, and at one point Moody was greatly irritated by some Irish Catholics who were sent to cause disturbances in the all-too-successful school. Typically, Moody went to the top in rectifying the situation—to Bishop Duggan, the prelate of the diocese. The maid who answered the bishop's door doubted that Moody would be granted an audience, but he took the precaution of stepping over the threshold, and saying cheerfully that he would wait until the bishop was at leisure.

Eventually the bishop appeared in the hall, and Moody briefly stated his mission, asking if the bishop would use his influence to stop future interference. But, replied the bishop, it would be easier for Moody to work among those people if he were a Catholic. But

---

2. W. R. Moody, *Life of Moody,* pp. 56-57.

then, said Moody, he could no longer work among Protestants. Not at all, came the episcopal reply. Did the bishop mean then that he would let Moody pray with a Protestant if Moody became a Catholic, asked the missionary innocently. Oh, yes, that was indeed possible. Well, said Moody, that was very good, but would the bishop pray with a Protestant? Again the answer was affirmative. Then would the bishop kneel and pray with him then and there that Moody might be led aright in this matter?

Bishop Duggan must have been startled at that turn of events, but he did as Moody asked. The result of their conference was the cessation of all annoyance at the Sunday school. Moody accomplished his objective in the visit, and did not join the Bishop's fold, but the latter must have breathed a sigh of relief on ushering out the persistent young fellow, knowing that if the interview had continued he might have been persuaded to come and teach a class in the Sunday school.

Moody was well aware of his limitations in education, and he left the teaching to others better qualified. Recruitment, administration, and discipline were his forte. Before the lessons, he took control of a large roomful of toughs with names like Red Eye, Madden the Butcher, Darby the Cobbler, Black Stove Pipe, and Rag-Breeches Cadet.[3] On one occasion a young troublemaker was repeatedly warned to stop creating disturbances. Because grace had failed and because it was against Moody's rules to throw anyone out, he saw that recourse to law was inevitable. He turned to John V. Farwell, the wealthy businessman who was superintendent and patron of the school, and said, "If you see me go for him and take him to the anteroom, ask the school to rise and sing a *very loud hymn* until we return." The troublemaker was removed, and the sacred strains muffled the cacophony of loud combat. Soon master and disciple emerged, red-faced and sweating; the boy was thereafter an exemplary one.

Moody's concern extended to the oft-times illiterate and indigent parents of those children, and they too were invited to evening class meetings three nights a week "for instruction in the common English branches." By 1863 the school had outgrown the depressing slum surroundings, and with substantial gifts from Farwell and other concerned Christians, a lot was purchased at the corner of Wells and Illinois streets in Chicago. In the spring of 1864 a large

3. Ibid., p. 74.

brick building was finished, with an auditorium seating 1,500, numerous classrooms, and a chapel. This became known as the Illinois Street Church, with a clearly evangelical ministry of a nondenominational character, although at the first it was helped by the Congregationalists.

By any estimate, Dwight L. Moody was a very unusual fellow. As a budding businessman he was equally aggressive. In 1859, when he began the Sunday school, he was a shoe salesman making $5,000 in commissions above his salary, a huge sum in those days. But his beginnings in life had given no hint that he might turn out to be a wealthy business entrepreneur—or the greatest evangelist of his time.

Even the booming, bustling Chicago of 1860, so congenial to Moody's own agressiveness, was not his native place. He had been born on February 5, 1837, in Northfield, Massachusetts, where both his parents' families had lived for generations. His father, Edwin, had followed the family trade of stonemason, but his sudden death when Dwight was only four had left the family in desperate straits. Mrs. Moody had seven children to care for, and twins were born shortly after her husband's death. Creditors came and took everything movable from the home, including the firewood. But Betsey Moody was a courageous woman, and with help from the numerous relatives in the area she found ways to provide for her large family. For the next dozen years, every child had to contribute what he or she could to the bereft home, and Dwight and his brothers went to work as farmhands. That allowed little time for schooling, and Dwight was able to attend the local academy for what would be the equivalent of six grades. For the rest of his life his grammar would reflect that lack of schooling.

When he was seventeen Dwight decided he could help the family more if he left home and earned a salary in the city. He went to Boston, the closest big city, and sought employment. But he had to trudge the streets for days before getting a job. Two of his maternal uncles had a shoe business there, but Dwight was reluctant to ask them the favor of hiring him, and they were afraid he would soon try to run the store. After looking elsewhere without success, Dwight swallowed his pride and requested employment, but the uncles were wary of the temptations of the big city to an inexperienced youth and made him promise to attend church and Sunday school.

Figure 10.1 D. L. Moody, 1884 (from the painting by Edward Clifford; copyright Church Army)

This stipulation that he frequent church was the first time that Dwight had come under Christian influence in any marked degree. In Northfield after his father's death, Dwight had been baptized in the local Unitarian church. Although his mother was not irreligious, the boy was taught nothing of consequence regarding the faith.[4] Thus when he chose Boston's Mt. Vernon Congregational Church, at his uncle's stipulation, Dwight Moody came not only as one utterly untaught in the basics of Christianity, but also as one who was completely unacquainted with the Scriptures. Mt. Vernon Church was a dynamic, evangelical fellowship, and its pastor, Dr. Edward N. Kirk, had previously been an associate of Charles Grandison Finney and later an evangelist himself.

In addition to the preaching of Dr. Kirk, which probably had little effect on Dwight at first, he was fortunate to sit in the young men's Bible class taught by Edward Kimball. When Dwight first attended, Kimball announced that the students should turn to the gospel of John, from which the lesson was taken. Dwight began thumbing through Genesis, to the accompaniment of snickering from his classmates. He was rescued from embarrassment by the alert teacher who gave the boy his own Bible already opened to the text. Kimball took an increasing interest in Dwight and determined that he would lead him to Christ, as he related it:

> I determined to speak to him about Christ and about his soul, and started down to Holton's shoe store. When I was nearly there I began to wonder whether I ought to go in just then during business hours. I thought that possibly my call might embarrass the boy, and that when I went away the other clerks would ask who I was, and taunt him with my efforts in trying to make him a good boy. In the meantime I had passed the store, and, discovering this, I determined to make a dash for it and have it over at once. I found Moody in the back part of the building wrapping up shoes. I went up to him at once, and putting my hand on his shoulder, I made what afterwards I felt was a very weak plea for Christ. I don't know just what words I used, nor could Mr. Moody tell. I simply told him of Christ's love for him and the love Christ wanted in return. That was all there was. It seemed the young man was just ready for the light that then broke upon him, and there, in the back of that store in Boston, he gave himself and his life to Christ.[5]

---

4. Stanley N. Gundry, *Love Them In: The Proclamation Theology of D. L. Moody* (Chicago: Moody, 1976), p. 18. This is a superb scholarly work that corrects numerous mistakes of other recent authors on Moody.
5. Cited in W. R. Moody, *Life of Moody,* p. 41.

From the minute Dwight Moody received Christ, his entire life changed. However, his conversion was not a highly emotional experience, and that perhaps explains why in his later evangelistic campaigns he did not try to produce an overwhelming emotional response in his hearers. Rather, he was more concerned that the understanding of their new faith and commitment be firm, rather than that their emotions should be temporarily raised.

For Moody himself, with little religious teaching to fall back on, progress in doctrinal knowledge was slow. On May 16, 1855, hardly three weeks after his conversion, he presented himself before the church deacons for membership. The examination was a disaster. In answer to the question, "What has Christ done for you, and for us all, that especially entitles Him to our love and obedience?", Dwight replied, "I think He has done a great deal for us all, but I don't know of anything He has done in particular." Edward Kimball was present and was distressed at his pupil's lack of understanding. He agreed with the examining committee's flat rejection of Moody's candidacy. Moody tried for membership again on March 3, 1856, and that time was accepted.

But Moody was not happy in Boston. He decided there was no future for him there and, as many others at that time did, he went west to Chicago, then the most rapidly growing city in the nation.[6] Chicago hustled, he wrote. At Moody's arrival, what was to be a giant of a city was only beginning, but already it gave promise of tremendous potential. It was a mecca for immigrants, and more than half the city's population was foreign born, with the mushrooming factories and businesses needing all the help they could get. Even before the Civil War, Chicago had become a great railroad and steamship terminus, and by 1856 eleven major trunk lines sent their rails far out into the grain fields of the West, bringing back to the city vast amounts of livestock, corn, and wheat. Money was easy to make and Moody, not yet twenty, had decided that here he would make his fortune.

Despite all the opportunities in business, Moody was still jolted by the "wicked city" that he wrote home about, a city where "many of the folks keep the stores open on the holy Sabbath," a thing that was "enough to sicken anyone."[7] Obviously he had no intention of

---

6. James F. Findlay, Jr., *Dwight L. Moody, American Evangelist 1837-1899* (Chicago: U. of Chicago, 1969), p. 52, contains the various reasons for Moody's move to Chicago. Findlay's biography is the standard recent work on Moody; it is scholarly, well-written, fair, and thorough.

7. Findlay, *Dwight L. Moody,* p. 56.

leaving behind his newfound faith. On September 25, 1856, he wrote to his mother, "God is the same here as He is in Boston, and in Him I can find peace." And great things were happening. The Third Great Awakening of 1857-1858 was beginning (to be led almost entirely by dedicated laymen), which would bring into the churches across the land over one million new members. Moody was growing in grace and becoming alert to the movements of the Holy Spirit, as he wrote to his mother on January 6, 1857: "There is a great revival of religion in this city. I go to meeting every night. Oh, how I do enjoy it! It seems as if God was here Himself. Oh, mother, pray for us. Pray that this work may go on until every knee is bowed. I wish there could be a revival in Northfield."[8]

Moody plunged into the whirl of activities and began as a clerk for E. E. Wiswall Co., a retail shoe and boot outlet. The shoe and leather business in Chicago was enjoying huge expansion, with great promise for ambitious young men like Moody. "I can make more money here in a week than I could in Boston in a month," he wrote to his brother George. He also began to lend money to friends at high interest and confided to some that his ambition was to be worth $100,000 in time—a fortune then. But he was not allowing secular interests to overcome the spiritual; he transferred his membership to the Plymouth Congregational Church in May 1857, and shortly after that he became deeply involved in the YMCA work in Chicago.

After joining the Plymouth Church, Moody decided he was not content with mere membership; surely Christ required more of him. It was the day of rented pews, and out of his own pocket he rented four long pews. He began to go into local boardinghouses early on Sunday mornings to invite strangers to come to his pews for the services. He particularly singled out commercial travelers (salesmen) and invited them to be his guests. At this he became quite successful, and the four pews were usually filled. But it did not seem enough to do for his Lord, and he then found a far greater outlet in the YMCA. The first YMCA had been founded in Boston in 1852 as a strong evangelistic arm of the church. Moody's work with the YMCA began informally, much as with the rented pews, in encouraging other men to attend its prayer meetings. Soon he was the librarian of the Chicago YMCA and head of the visitation committee.

8. Ibid., p. 63.

His boundless energies had hardly been touched, so during business hours Moody formed the practice of going out on the sidewalk and asking prospective customers for shoes to come inside. Soon after he joined Wiswall's a jobbing department was added, and Moody found a new method for selling shoes and boots by watching the railroad depots and hotel registers for possible customers arriving. His success at that caused Wiswall to send him out as a salesman and collector of bills, but in 1857 Moody transferred to the shoe firm of C. N. Henderson where he became a close personal friend of the owner. When Henderson died late in 1858, his widow showed her confidence in Moody by asking him to settle up her husband's estate worth $150,000 (the equivalent of 2 million dollars today). He was overwhelmed by the trust shown in that request, but he declined and went to work for Buel, Hill, and Granger, another prominent shoe business. Already he had saved $7,000 toward his goal of becoming wealthy. But the allurements of the business world and great wealth were paling. He had begun the Sunday school in the North Market Hall in the spring of 1859, and it was thriving beyond all expectations. Perhaps he felt that he had proven himself in the intense competition of business, and that working for God in the salvation of souls was far more rewarding and challenging.

At any rate, Dwight Moody was certainly coming to believe that he could no longer do justice to both his business and spiritual interests. So, acting as decisively as he always did, he abruptly turned his back on the world of commerce and offered his energies to God in June 1860. In later years Moody often told the story of what prompted his decision—the visit of one of his Sunday school teachers to his shoe store. The young man appeared very pale and ill and told Moody he was hemorrhaging from the lungs and was under doctor's orders to return to New York. But the man was greatly distressed because his class of very frivolous girls was unsaved, and he asked Moody to accompany him on one last visit to their homes. "It was one of the best journeys I ever had on earth," Moody declared. They went to one after another of the girls' homes, and Moody watched as the dying teacher implored each of his class to accept Christ. Every one was won to the Savior.

> He had to leave the next night, so I called his class together that night for a prayer meeting, and there God kindled a fire in my soul that has never gone out. The height of my ambition had been to be a successful merchant, and if I had known that meeting was going to

take that ambition out of me, I might not have gone. But how many times I have thanked God since for that meeting![9]

The next seven years of Moody's life, until 1867, allowed him to prove his sincerity in serving Christ. Freed from the restraints of secular employment, he was able to devote himself entirely to spiritual enterprise after spiritual enterprise. Chief among them were the Sunday school and the YMCA, but with the outbreak of the Civil War in 1861 a great new opportunity appeared. The YMCA became, in a sense, the link between the evangelical churches and the Northern soldiers, and between the churches and captured troops of the Confederate army. Out of that emerged the United States Christian Commission, in which Moody played a leading role. Camp Douglas was built south of Chicago, and Moody spent much time there, especially after 9,000 Southern troops were imprisoned in the camp. During the war years he saw much pain and death, and he followed the Union armies in the battles of Shiloh, Murfreesboro, Pittsburg Landing, Chattanooga, and in the Richmond campaign.

During those years Moody also met Emma C. Revell, a very lovely girl of nineteen, and married her on August 28, 1862. Moody always marveled that he had won the love of a young lady from such a different background from his own, one seemingly so superior to his in every respect. He was brusque, impulsive, and outspoken, with little education, whereas Emma was well educated, conservative, retiring, and averse to publicity. Yet they complemented each other perfectly. He came to rely heavily upon her excellent judgment, and she was a great help to him in innumerable ways the rest of his life. They had three children: Emma, born in 1863; William, born in 1869; and Paul, born in 1879. It was a very happy family over the years.[10]

Moody was such an activist that even the great demands of the war years hardly drained his enormous energies. In addition to his work with the troops, he continued with the Illinois Street Church as its unordained leader, doing much of the preaching and occasionally inviting clergymen in to preach and administer the sacraments. It was probably just as well that there was no other leader than Moody, for few pastors could have kept up with his pace. One deacon of the church recounted an unforgettable New Year's Day on which Moody led several men on no fewer than *two hundred*

---

9. W. R. Moody, *Life of Moody,* p. 65.
10. Beginning on p. 96 Findlay has some excellent material on Moody's family life.

visitation calls. He would burst into a home and greet the astounded family with, "I am Moody; this is Deacon DeGolyer; this is Deacon Thane; this is Brother Hitchcock. Are you well? Do you all come to church and Sunday-school? Have you all the coal you need for the winter? Let us pray." He would fall to his knees, offer thirty words of prayer, and be out the door to the next call before the bewildered members of the family knew what had struck them.[11]

In 1866 Dwight Moody was elected president of the Chicago YMCA, a position he would hold for four years. As head of one of the most important local YMCAs, it became his responsibility to travel widely to meetings and conventions in Portland, Oregon; Baltimore; Albany, New York; and other places. Thus he greatly widened his contacts during that period. In addition to his work with the YMCA, he became involved in two new interdenominational movements of great power, the Sunday School Union and the Christian Convention. Both of those drew together leaders of churches throughout the Midwest, and Moody became a familiar speaker at their conventions. In such meetings he observed and tested for himself numerous techniques and ideas that he would incorporate into his later evangelistic campaigns. By 1870, when he was chosen to deliver one of the principle messages at the national YMCA convention in Indianapolis, he had become well known to Protestant leaders throughout the Midwest.

At the Indianapolis convention Moody met Ira D. Sankey, a delegate from New Castle, Pennsylvania. Sankey had a powerful yet mellow voice and was an accomplished singer and songleader. When Moody heard Sankey sing, he approached him, introduced himself, spent some minutes inquiring about Sankey's family ties and occupation, and then said, "Well, you'll have to give that up! You are the man I have been looking for, and I want you to come to Chicago and help me in my work."[12] Sankey soon gave in, resigned his business, went to Chicago, and from then on was the inseparable companion and colaborer in Moody's endeavors.

The beginnings of his partnership with Ira Sankey marked a new direction in Moody's life. In the spring of 1867 he made his first trip to Great Britain to observe, meet, and exchange ideas with British evangelicals regarding Sunday schools, YMCA work, prayer meetings, and evangelism. He remained there for four months and

---

11. J. Wilbur Chapman, *Dwight L. Moody* (Philadelphia: J. C. Winston, 1900), p. 102.

12. W. R. Moody, *Life of Moody,* p. 125.

became interested in the work of a lay group known as the Plymouth Brethren, which had been formed in the 1820s as a reaction to some of the tendencies of the Church of England. Under the leadership of J. N. Darby, the Plymouth Brethren preached the inerrancy of the Bible, premillennialism, and conversion through personal experience. Darby had visited America several times and probably spoke at the YMCA building in Chicago at Moody's invitation.[13] Another Brethren, Henry Moorhouse, became a very close friend of Moody's, and the latter gladly acknowledged Moorhouse's influence in several areas of his ministry. By the end of his visit, Moody had become friends with many of the leaders of the evangelical cause in the London area, and on the eve of his return to America a farewell reception was held, at which he was handed a substantial honorarium from his many friends.

That was a great testimony to the way Moody could quickly gather support for himself and his Christian projects. One other result of that first British trip was his hearing the words that affected him profoundly: "The world has yet to see what God will do with and for and through and in and by the man who is fully and wholly consecrated to Him." Moody responded, "I will try my utmost to be that man."

After he arrived back in Chicago in the fall of 1867, Moody saw the completion of his beloved YMCA building, Farwell Hall, which contained an auditorium seating three thousand and much else. To secure the necessary building funds, Moody had organized a stock company with twelve trustees chosen from Chicago's wealthy businessmen, including Cyrus McCormick, George Armour, John Farwell, and B. F. Jacobs. But despite his popularity, successes, and host of friends, Dwight Moody entered a period of spiritual crisis about that time. Even his energies were not forever equal to the speaking engagements and burdens he saddled himself with. The low point of his life came with the Chicago fire of October 1871. His home, personal belongings, the YMCA building, and the Illinois Street Church all were consumed in the fire. Although others rallied to provide leadership in rebuilding Farwell Hall, Moody alone had to shoulder the responsibility of raising the money for a new church. He stated later that the fire was the most important reason for his decision to leave Chicago.[14]

---

13. Findlay, *Dwight L. Moody*, p. 126.
14. Ibid., p. 130.

Moody's spiritual crisis lasted for at least four months, but it had been building up for some time. Suddenly, God broke through the gloom. Moody did not wish to speak too much of it, as it was "almost too sacred an experience to name." He was convinced "God revealed Himself to me, and I had such an experience of His love that I had to ask Him to stay His hand." Later he spoke of it as anointing, filling of the Spirit, unction, and empowerment for service. He began to preach that a similar experience was necessary for truly effective Christian service.[15] However it might affect him or other Christians, Moody emerged from that period a changed man, a preacher of much greater power than before.

Moody made another short trip to Britain in 1870, and after returning to Chicago he determined that he would make a third trip in June 1872. During both of those visits he renewed his friendships with major British leaders, and in July 1872 he delivered a major address at the annual Mildmay Conference in London. That address gave him exposure to hundreds of the most important Christians in Britain. At the same time, Moody's growing friendship with Henry Moorhouse made him reexamine his preaching and completely change its emphases. Moorhouse preached seven nights in Moody's Chicago church on the theme of the love of God, based on John 3:16. Moody was astounded. Before that, Moody had appealed to sinners to repent and flee the wrath to come, out of fear of judgment. Moorhouse completely reversed that emphasis, without suggesting that God would not judge. Moody saw the vast difference and began to teach that sinners should be drawn to God by love, for God wants sons, not slaves.[16]

With his new consecration, and the great power in his revitalized preaching based on God's love, plus his new association with Ira D. Sankey, Moody determined to set out on a completely different course of service. He made his final break with the burdens of Chicago in June 1873 and set sail for England with Sankey at his side. He had on the previous visits received numerous invitations to conduct extended preaching tours, especially from William Pennefather (the founder of Mildmay Conference), Cuthbert Bainbridge of Newcastle, and Henry Bewley of Dublin. The last two invitations bore the promise of funds to meet the expenses of Moody and Sankey.

---

15. For a full discussion of Moody's theological understanding of this, see the important material in Gundry, *Love Them In,* pp. 46, 153-55.
16. Gundry, *Love Them In,* p. 46.

When Moody and Sankey docked at Liverpool on June 17, 1873, they were greeted with the news that all three friends on whom they depended for moral and financial support had died. Moody turned to Sankey and said, "God seems to have closed the doors. We will not open any ourselves. If He opens the door we will go in; otherwise we will return to America."[17]

Then Moody found an unopened letter from the secretary of the YMCA in York, England containing an invitation to him to speak there. "This door is only ajar," he said. But with no other prospects he telegraphed to York that he would be there as soon as possible. Quickly the YMCA secretary, having expected nothing of the sort, scrambled to arrange for Moody to preach in various pulpits of the city. The meetings began slowly because Moody was unknown in York, but F. B. Meyer, the great preacher and writer, recalled,

> What an inspiration when this great and noble soul first broke into my life! I was a young pastor then, in the old city of York, and bound rather rigidly by the chains of conventionalism. Such had been my training, and such might have been my career. But here was a revelation of a new ideal. The first characteristic of Mr. Moody's that struck me was that he was so absolutely unconventional and natural. . . . But there was never the slightest approach to irreverence, fanaticism, or extravagance; everything was in perfect accord with a rare common sense, a directness of method, a simplicity and transparency of aim, which were as attractive as they were fruitful in result.[18]

After five weeks of meetings in York, which met with only modest success, the team of Moody and Sankey was invited to Sunderland to conduct a similar campaign. There Moody took the wise step of inviting his good friend Henry Moorhouse to share the preaching. The meetings went somewhat better than those at York, and evangelical groups began to hear of the dynamic American preacher and his singing companion. An invitation next came from the city of Newcastle, and meetings began there in September 1873. There the first large response to the team was met. Because of the numbers attending, the meetings were transferred from a church to the Music Hall, and the newspaper reviews became still more favorable.

One of the pastors of Leith, the port city of Edinburgh, heard of the unusual evangelistic work of the two Americans in Newcastle

17. W. R. Moody, *Life of Moody,* p. 155.
18. Ibid., p. 158.

and went to see for himself. He was so impressed that he extended an invitation on behalf of both the established and free churches in Edinburgh to hold meetings there. Moody examined the offer and became convinced that he would get widespread support from the churches and clergy. He accepted, and meetings began in the Edinburgh Music Hall, the largest in the city, on November 23, 1873.

Moody and Sankey knew that in strict Presbyterian Scotland, they would have to be very circumspect in every point to overcome some feelings against the kind of evangelism they practiced. Particularly was there some concern about Sankey's "singing the gospel." Scottish Presbyterians were just beginning to allow music as part of worship, with the exception of congregational singing of the psalter, and organs were first tolerated in the churches in the 1860s.[19] Sankey's use of a portable harmonium, and his singing of his own catchy, simple words and tunes came as quite a shock to Scottish nerves. Some began to speak of Sankey's "kist o' whistles" as an instrument liable to satanic uses.

For the most part the Scots were openminded and enthusiastic, and at the opening service the hall was "densely packed in every cranny, . . . and several thousand people went away, unable to obtain admission." Increasingly, as the days went by, greater and greater appreciation of the Americans' efforts was manifested, bringing increasing approval from all levels. Moody's simple message and call for unity among Christians was irresistible. He and Sankey were taken to the heart of the people of Edinburgh, and almost every minister voiced solid approval of the meetings. So deep was the spiritual awakening after a few weeks that the following letter was sent to every clergyman in Scotland.

Edinburgh is now enjoying signal manifestations of grace. Many of the Lord's people are not surprised at this. . . . They hoped that they might have a visit from Messrs. Moody and Sankey, of America, but they very earnestly besought the Lord that He would deliver them from depending upon them or any instrumentality, and that He Himself would come with them or come before them. He has graciously answered that prayer, and His own presence is now wonderfully manifested among them. God is so affecting the hearts of men that the Free Church Assembly Hall, the largest public building in Edinburgh, is crowded every evening with meetings for prayer, and both that build-

---

19. Findlay, *Dwight L. Moody*, p. 157, has a good discussion of the cross-cultural difficulties encountered by Sankey and Moody in the British Isles.

ing and the Established Church Assembly Hall overflow whenever the gospel is preached. But the numbers that attend are not the most remarkable feature. It is the presence and power of the Holy Ghost, the solemn awe, the prayerful, believing, expectant spirit, the anxious inquiry of unsaved souls, and the longing of believers to grow more like Christ—their hungering and thirsting after holiness.[20]

So completely did Moody and Sankey capture the affections of the Scots that even the initial concern over the little organ soon evaporated, as Professor Blaikie of New College, Moody's host during the campaign, reported, "It is amusing to observe how entirely the latent distrust of Mr. Sankey's 'kist o' whistles' has disappeared."

The other great city of Scotland, Glasgow, invited the Americans to conduct meetings there almost as soon as the Edinburgh campaign began, and after two months had been spent preaching the gospel in Edinburgh, a three month series was started in Glasgow. Here the attendance was as great as in Edinburgh, and the clergy as united in support. From February 8 through May 24 vast meetings were held, often two and three each day, and the crowds frequently reached 20,000. From Glasgow Moody and Sankey went to the north of Scotland. In Aberdeen, Dundee, Inverness, and every major town meetings were held, until most of Scotland had been reached. A year after the meetings in Glasgow, the famous preacher Dr. Andrew A. Bonar wrote, "We should like to testify to the permanence of the work among us, and any one who will come and see for himself will at once discover how extensive and sincere this work has been."[21]

From Scotland Moody and Sankey crossed over to Ireland, and held meetings in Belfast beginning on September 6 until October 8, 1874. They then moved to Dublin, where the entire Protestant population numbered only forty thousand, and met a very friendly welcome from all. The leading Roman Catholic paper of the city gave full coverage of the meetings and was extremely positive to them. Moody then returned to England, beginning meetings in Manchester in December, and moving to Sheffield and Birmingham in January 1875. Attendances were enormous. Nothing like it had been seen since George Whitefield drew twenty and thirty thousand to his outdoor messages in those cities more than one hundred years before, but Moody was able to pack comparable

20. W. R. Moody, *Life of Moody*, pp. 187-88.
21. Ibid., p. 202.

numbers inside the largest buildings the cities boasted. By the time the two Americans reached Liverpool, a flood of favorable newspaper reports had made every Englishman well aware of their ministry. Here another variation was introduced: none of Liverpool's buildings was deemed adequate for the anticipated crowds, so a huge temporary sheet iron tabernacle, called Victoria Hall, was erected.

In England it was not as easy to get the united support of the clergy, because of the number of different Protestant denominations. One pastor who was at first inclined to look with disfavor on Moody's work was the famous Congregationalist leader Dr. R. W. Dale. As the interest of the people increased, Dale decided to observe Moody, became more and more impressed, and eventually threw his wholehearted support behind the work, saying, "Of Mr. Moody's own power, I find it difficult to speak. It is so real and yet so unlike the power of ordinary preachers, that I hardly know how to analyze it. Its reality is indisputable. . . . On Tuesday I told Mr. Moody that the work was most plainly of God, for I could see no real relation between him and what he had done. He laughed cheerily, and said he should be very sorry if it were otherwise."[22]

Of course, there was some opposition and occasional attacks in the papers, mostly from jealous clergymen who made fun of Moody's Yankee pronunciations and his clipped "Dan'l" and "Sam'l" and so on. The *New York Times* could not believe that two fellow Americans had achieved such fame in the British Isles, and it stated it had reliable information that P. T. Barnum had sent them to England.[23] But by the time Moody and Sankey reached the climax of their British tour, the four months of meetings held in London from early March to early July 1875, such criticism could be laughed at or ignored.

All through January and February 1875 extensive preparations were made, house-to-house visitations conducted throughout much of the enormous city, hundreds of prayer meetings held, and Moody's methods of advance planning applied systematically. The committee directing the preparations divided London into four huge sections and rented or constructed large buildings as the central meeting halls for each of the four sections. Agricultural Hall, the largest hall ever occupied by Moody, was rented in Islington; the

22. *The Congregationalist,* no. 4 (March 1875): 138-39.
23. *New York Times,* 22 June 1875.

Royal Opera House in the fashionable West End; and two temporary structures were erected on Bow Road and in Camberwell
Green, the working-class areas of the city.

When the meetings began on March 9 much scurrilous material
had been printed in papers such as *Vanity Fair*, and Moody and
Sankey had been called "pernicious humbugs," "crack-brained Yankee evangelists," "abbots of unreason," and much worse. But immediately many of Britain's most important people began to attend,
and such epithets had to be tempered. The *Times* of London was
very positive, saying,

> Is any Christian church in this metropolis in a position to say that it
> can afford to dispense with any vigorous effort to rouse the mass of
> people to a more Christian life? The congregations which are to be
> seen in our churches and chapels are but a fraction of the hundreds
> and thousands around them, of whom multitudes are living but little
> better than a mere animal existence. If any considerable proportion of
> them can be aroused to the mere desire for something higher, an
> immense step is gained.[24]

For four months in the sprawling, difficult city of London the
two Americans faithfully presented the gospel, and when the time
was up Moody confided that four years would hardly be adequate
to reach the teeming population. While Moody's great love for
people might incline him to try to reach all of London, the attendance figures show that in reality a great multitude did hear him
during the four months. Obviously, the following attendance figures
include many repeaters: Agricultural Hall, 60 meetings attended by
720,000; Royal Opera House, 60 meetings attended by 330,000;
Bow Road Hall, 60 meetings attended by 600,000; Camberwell
Hall, 60 meetings attended by 480,000; and Victoria Hall, 45 meetings attended by 400,000. In all, 285 meetings attended by over *two
and one-half million people!*

After two years in the British Isles, Moody and Sankey returned
to America in June 1875 in the wake of a tidal wave of favorable
press reviews. Christian leaders in the United States, perhaps puz-
zled that Moody had risen to international stature and fame in a
foreign land, were quick to enlist his ministry at home. And Moody
was willing. After a rest from the gruelling pace of the previous two

---

24. *Times* (London), 22 April 1875.

years, Moody expressed his desire to conduct metropolitan campaigns in America: "Water runs down hill, and the highest hills in America are the great cities. If we can stir them we shall stir the whole country."[25]

Brooklyn was first. Already a city accustomed to great preaching from Beecher, Talmage, and Cuyler, Brooklyn prepared itself. The arrangements committee rented the Rink, which seated five thousand, and the trolleycar company laid extra tracks to the Rink's doors. On the opening day, October 24, 1875, 15,000 were lined up for blocks waiting to get in, and excellent meetings were held for a month. Moody might have remained much longer, but other cities were beseiging him and demanding campaigns. Philadelphia especially, under the leadership of the widely known and respected merchant John Wanamaker, was eager to begin an evangelistic work before the spirit of the American Centennial took over, and so the recently vacated Pennsylvania Railroad freight depot was refurbished to hold 13,000 seats. For two months Moody drove himself at his usual awesome speed, conducting two and three meetings a day as well as innumerable prayer services and inquiry sessions. Then it was New York City's turn, and the vast Hippodrome at Madison Avenue and 27th Street was used to accommodate over 14,000 each night for four months. Then Moody went back to Chicago in October 1876 for several months of meetings held in a specially constructed auditorium, and in the spring of 1877 it was Boston's turn to receive his ministry.

The five missions conducted in Brooklyn, Philadelphia, New York, Chicago, and Boston during the years 1875-1877 were the beginning of an evangelistic campaign in the United States that covered a period of more than twenty years. To recount the hundreds of cities visited until Moody's death in 1899, not only in the United States but also in Canada and in Mexico, in addition to a return mission to the British Isles in 1881, would take many pages. But certain things stand out clearly, and the *New York Times* changed its earlier negative tune in assessing Moody in later years: "Whatever the prejudiced may say against him, the honest-minded and just will remember the amazing work of this *plain man*."[26]

Moody shared his secret for success with all of the men previous-

25. W. R. Moody, *Life of Moody*, p. 263.
26. *New York Times*, 3 March 1889.

ly presented: (1) He was absolutely sincere, and even his worst critics immediately granted this; (2) He was on fire with love for Christ and for people, and this was very evident in all he did; and (3) He was unshakably sure of his own salvation and that God in His grace had gone to the uttermost limits to save all people, if they would only believe.

Conclusion

In the past two and a half centuries America has known some remarkable times of special visitation by the Spirit of God. Dozens of books and scholarly articles have dealt with the leaders of those revivals, the course of the awakenings, and every facet that historians could examine. Yet, for the general American Christian populace those outpourings of God's grace are little known.

The purpose of the preceding pages has been to address this lack of awareness and to show, through some of the outstanding leaders, that the influences of the awakenings have been beneficial, and that they affected the course of the nation and the lives of individual people for untold good. In the three Great Awakenings which have energized the churches and poured countless new converts into them, Christian people have felt the presence of God's Spirit and have gone to their knees, receiving transforming power from on high and pledging themselves to renewed holiness and service. In each of the three periods the church has poured its zeal for righteousness into the bloodstream of the nation. Although some secular historians have derided the awakenings, other scholars have found, to their surprise, that many of the finest impulses in modern life stem from the revivals. Renewed and empowered Christianity has been the single most important moral factor in making America great.

Regarding the impulse toward democracy, the history of American revivals shows that they have promoted equality and democratic ideals. Regarding the impulse toward education, of the nine colleges that existed in colonial America, six were born out of awakening. Regarding the humanitarian impulse, antislavery, prison reform, women's rights, temperance, concern for the poor and downtrodden, and philanthropy of a hundred different kinds has flowed in abundance from the awakenings.

The limitations of space have forced exclusion of the story of related awakenings in other parts of the world. It has been possible to describe Whitefield's and Wesley's international ministries and some of the global benefits of the Evangelical Awakening, but the reader must be informed that there is so much more.[1] And what of the twentieth century? Here, indeed, the scope must be broadened for any proper understanding of the situation, for the awakenings of this century have had international repercussions as never before.

The awakening that began in the United States in mid-1857 (called the Third Great Awakening) spread to Great Britain in early 1859 and remained effective for at least forty years. In Britain it began in Ulster, the most northerly province in Ireland. Approximately ten per cent of the population there professed conversion, and that was repeated in Wales and Scotland. In England the revival continued for years, a million members being added to the churches. Then, reverberations were felt in many European countries, in South Africa, India, and Australia, and those effects continued until the dawn of the new century.

To carry the story of awakenings briefly into the twentieth century, we may begin by describing the Welsh Revival with the effects it produced around much of the world: in India, China, Korea, Africa, the islands of the South Pacific, and Europe. It began as a local revival in early 1904 but had a shattering impact on the whole of Wales by the end of that year. Evan Roberts (1878-1951) left secular work to be accepted as a candidate for the ministry by the Calvinistic Methodist Church and underwent a profound experience of being anointed by the Spirit. Within a matter of weeks, under his preaching and conduct of prayer meetings, the revival had swept across Glamorganshire with tremendous power. It became a national phenomenon and led to more than 100,000 conversions.

---

1. For detailed accounts of the general awakenings, see the works of J. Edwin Orr, *The Eager Feet* (1790-1840), *The Fervent Prayer* (1858-1899), and *The Flaming Tongue* (1900-1920), all published by Moody Press, Chicago. For details of awakenings on the mission fields, see Robert H. Glover and J. Herbert Kane, *The Progress of World-Wide Missions* (New York: Harper, 1960).

Because it was followed in great detail by the press, it received worldwide publicity. The London *Daily Chronicle* reported that the spiritual enthusiasm in Wales during the revival was "as smokeless as its coal," because "all the paraphernalia of the got-up job are conspicuous by their absence." The newspaper went on to say,

> Tier above tier, from the crowded aisles to the loftiest gallery, sat or stood, as necessity dictated, eager hundreds of serious men and thoughtful women, their eyes riveted upon the platform or upon whatever other part of the building was the storm center of the meeting.
>
> There was absolutely nothing wild, violent, hysterical, unless it be hysterical for the laboring breast to heave with sobbing that cannot be repressed, and the throat to choke with emotion as a sense of the awful horror and shame of a wasted life bursts upon the soul. On all sides there was the solemn gladness of men and women upon whose eyes has dawned the splendor of a new day. . . .
>
> Employers tell me that the quality of the work the miners are putting in has improved. Waste is less; men go to their daily toil with a new spirit of gladness in their labor. In the long dim galleries of the mine, where once the hauliers swore at their ponies in Welshified English terms of blasphemy, there is now but to be heard the haunting melody of the revival music. The pit ponies, like the American mules, having been driven by oaths and curses since they first bore the yoke, are being retrained to do their work without the incentive of profanity.
>
> There is less drinking, less idleness, less gambling. Men record with almost incredulous amazement how one football player after another has forsworn cards and drink and the gladiatorial games, and is living a sober and godly life, putting his energy into the revival. . . . In this village I attended three meetings and in each case aisles were crowded, pulpit stairs were packed, and—*mirabile dictu!*—two-thirds of the congregation were men and at least one-half were young men, stalwart young miners, who gave the meetings all the fervor and swing and enthusiasm of youth. . . .
>
> They call it the Spirit of God. Those who have not witnessed it may call it what they will; I am inclined to agree with those on the spot.[2]

The records in the British Museum tell an amazing tale not only of crowded meetings and conversions, but of grudges healed, wrongs righted, and funds returned. A Pontypridd woman who had disowned a debt of twenty pounds for many years found that Christ had "got hold of her" during the meetings, and she immediately repaid the debt. Before a meeting of 1,500 people, three ministers

2. The *London Daily Chronicle,* 23 March 1905.

who had publicly quarreled about local politics became reconciled and ended their animosities by uniting in the work of the revival. Baptists and Quakers, Anglicans and Methodists, Congregationalists and Salvationists, found any separation banished by the powerful lever of prayer.

Shortly after the great movement of the Holy Spirit in Wales began to decline, it became apparent that the mission fields, many of them only recently evangelized, were enjoying visitations of grace. In particular we may briefly survey the Korean Revival of 1907, one of the most striking awakenings in areas where Christianity was still very young. The story has been retold often.[3] It is less well known that the Korean Revival came in three waves, in the years 1903, 1905, and the great year of ingathering, 1907. As Kenneth S. Latourette has described it,

> For the first few years the growth of the Protestant church membership was slow. In 1894 there were said to be only 236 baptized Protestant Christians in the entire country. They then began to multiply rapidly. In the years between the Russo-Japanese War (1904-1905) and the annexation of the country by Japan (1910) there was an especially marked rise. Between 1897 and 1909 the total of Protestant communicants sprang from 530 to 26,057. In 1906 a movement towards Christianity began, with striking emotional manifestations, repentance of sin, and moral reform. Eager to take advantage of the incoming tide, the various denominations united in 1910 in the Million Souls Movement, which had as its goal the presentation of the Christian message to every individual in the country and a million new converts. . . . The reasons for the rapid advance after 1895 and especially between 1906 and 1910 appear to have been mixed. They seem to have been associated with an accession of zeal on the part of the missionaries, with the inspiration of the news of religious revivals in other lands, . . . with the hope that Christianity might be a means of saving the nation, and with the bewilderment of many because of the changes and the desire for security and direction that the Christian faith and churches seemed to provide.[4]

---

3. See Charles A. Clark, *The Korean Church and the Nevius Methods* (New York: Revell, 1930); George H. Jones and W. Arthur Noble, *The Korean Revival* (New York: Foreign Missions Board of the Methodist Episcopal Church, 1910); George T. B. Davis, *Korea for Christ* (New York: Revell, 1910); William N. Blair, *The Korea Pentecost* (New York: Foreign Missions Board of the Presbyterian Church U.S.A., n.d.); and Alfred W. Wasson, *Church Growth in Korea* (New York: International Missionary Council, 1934).

4. Kenneth S. Latourette, *The Great Century in Northern Africa and Asia. A History of the Expansion of Christianity*, vol. 6 (New York: Harper & Row, 1944), p. 426.

Despite the harassment to the church that Japanese annexation brought after 1910 and the loss of all North Korea to organized Christianity in the Communist annexation after World War II, numerical growth continued in Korea. The number of Protestant adherents has almost doubled every ten years since 1940, and Protestants now number over four million, making the church in Korea one of the most dynamic in the world, thoroughly involved in evangelism.

Another great mission field begs for comment: China. As with Korea, China was the recipient of much prayer and financial giving by Christians in the mid-nineteenth and early twentieth centuries, and there again the Holy Spirit responded to the prayers of His people with great awakenings. Closed to missions for centuries, China finally opened in 1860, and J. Hudson Taylor and the China Inland Mission soon sent representatives into all the inland provinces. The decay of the Manchu dynasty hastened the Nationalist Revolution of 1911, and the new leaders, including the first president Sun Yat-sen, were for the most part the product of Christian schools. The 1900-1915 era was a time of unprecedented prosperity for missions, although warlordism continued to plague the infant church. Again in the years 1920 through 1927 great numbers of missionaries arrived, bringing mighty vitality to the native Christians. In 1927 there were 8,518 Protestant missionaries in China, and three million baptized Christians. During those years the famous revival campaigns of Jonathan Goforth (1859-1936) in Manchuria brought multitudes into the churches. His book *By My Spirit* told of those remarkable revivals and inspired much support for missions. The Communist takeover forced the Protestant missionaries to leave China, but even amid persecution it is estimated that more than a million still profess Christ, and a seminary at Nanjing is trying to supply pastors for the native churches.[5]

Volumes are needed to tell of the awakenings of the twentieth century, in many parts of the world. Since 1950 the power of the Holy Spirit has been felt in Korea, the islands of Indonesia, and across the southern half of Africa. With Communist nations closed

5. The *New York Times,* 19 November 1981, p. 2. The literature on Christian missions in China is vast, much of it centering on individual missionaries, denominational endeavors, or historical periods. For reliable surveys see Kenneth S. Latourette, *A History of Christian Missions in China* (New York: Macmillan, 1929) and *The Chinese Recorder* (Shanghai), the standard interdenominational Protestant missionary journal of China, published from 1867 until the Communist takeover.

to missions, the worldwide Christian church has wisely turned to concentrate on the evangelization of Africa. Not only is Africa's burgeoning population bringing it into the forefront of world events, but its future is seen by all analysts as crucial for world stability. Across the northern coast of Africa the Muslim populations fiercely hold to belief in Allah and vow to convert the rest of Africa to Islam. In many of the recently independent countries, competition among Christian and Muslim missionaries for converts is intense. Africans, some only a few years away from animism, have the beliefs of both these missionary religions thrust upon them, and entire countries are now in the balance, deciding whether to follow Christ or Mohammed. But in many areas of Africa, strong native churches are winning multitudes to the Christian faith, and the winds of awakening are blowing strongly.

And what of the future? Christians in the United States, Great Britain, and other places where God has greatly blessed with mighty awakenings in the past, look with gratitude upon revivals in other parts of the world. But they cannot help but ask, Will it happen here again? Or has the West become too cynical, too materialistic, secular, and humanistic, so that the church of Christ has been influenced by these trends and grown cold?

Today we live in a time of spiritual deadness throughout much of the nominally Christian West. In America and Europe, churches languish and die. At the same time the world seems to be coming apart. Some of the younger generation see little reason it should not descend into sexual obsession and perversions, addiction to alcohol and drugs, and a completely hedonistic society given to fads, cynicism, atheism, superficiality, and alienation. If God truly controls the universe, who but His Spirit could rouse the church from its stupor so that it may once again speak with authority and throw its potential into evangelizing the lost masses of mankind? To speak thus is to define a new awakening. Dr. Martyn Lloyd-Jones has said,

> I am profoundly convinced that the greatest need in the world today is revival in the Church of God. Yet alas! the whole idea of revival seems to have become strange to so many good Christian people. There are some who even seem to resent the very idea and actually speak and write against it. Such an attitude is due both to a serious misunderstanding of the Scriptures, and to a woeful ignorance of the

history of the Church. Anything therefore that can instruct God's people in this matter is very welcome.[6]

Should Christians, not only in the United States but around the world, look forward to more great movements of the Holy Spirit? Or will future awakenings be confined to the mission fields of the developing nations, the Third World? Has the West—the so-called Christian nations—grown so hardened in its secular humanism and hedonism that it is impervious to the movements of divine grace? Will no more great awakenings stir America and Britain?

Certainly no one can say. The church must never be deterred from praying toward the goal of revival, even if the days seem bleak, with little promise. It must have seemed to Martin Luther and other Christians before the Reformation began, that one thousand years of blind superstition and ignorant idolatry could hardly be reversed, even by mighty acts of God. But then came the mightiest revival since Pentecost, and biblical truth again triumphed.

Two portions of Scripture speak to our needs here. In citing these passages, no doctrinal, eschatological, or denominational position is taken. Millennial viewpoints need not be brought in. The passages are so plain that all Christians can unite in accepting their straightforward meaning. Spiritualizing or allegorizing have no place here.

The first passage is the words of our Lord Jesus Christ in the Olivet discourse, "And this gospel of the kingdom will be preached in the whole world as a testimony to all nations, and then the end will come" (Matt. 24:14, NIV).

Prior to the end of the age, according to these words of our Lord, the gospel must be preached to all nations. Has this yet happened? Has the Christian message yet reached to every part of this world? Clearly not!

Therefore, those who wonder if there may yet be other great revivals may perhaps draw the conclusion that energetic missionary advances are still to be made. And, because such advances have in the past two centuries involved sacrifices and determination on the part of many Christians in the sending lands, it may be inferred that at least some parts of Christ's church throughout the world will rise to the challenge and become embued with compassion for the

---

6. In William B. Sprague, *Lectures on Revivals of Religion* (Edinburgh: Banner of Truth, 1958), p. v.

lost—in other words, will become awakened. But as to whether these sending churches will be in the West or in the developing lands, that obviously has yet to be determined. Could the missionaries be from Korea, or Taiwan, or Zambia, or Sri Lanka (Ceylon)? Imagine the impact on America if Christian missionaries from Africa's Botswana came to evangelize darkest Manhattan!

The second portion of Scripture that speaks to our needs in considering the possibility of future awakenings is Romans 11, which deals with the final salvation of Israel. Here again no particular eschatological position need be taken. Paul says in Romans 11:11, concerning the salvation of the Jews, "Again I ask, Did they stumble so as to fall beyond recovery? Not at all!" (NIV). And in verses 24 through 26a (NIV), "After all, if you were cut out of an olive tree that is wild by nature, and contrary to nature were grafted into a cultivated olive tree, how much more readily will these, the natural branches, be grafted into their own olive tree? I do not want you to be ignorant of this mystery, brothers, so that you may not be conceited: Israel has experienced a hardening in part until the full number of the Gentiles has come in. And so all Israel will be saved."

Here the entire Christian church can agree on the general intention of Paul's argument, without quibbling over details and differences: *A great awakening shall come upon the Jews, and many of them shall be saved.* Although there are today an increasing number of "completed Jews" who worship Jesus as the Messiah of Israel, still no one can maintain that Romans 11 has as yet been fulfilled. It cannot mean less than that substantial numbers of Israelites will turn to God in Christ before the end of this present age. The scholarly and sober commentator Handley C. G. Moule says,

> This is a memorable passage. It is in the first place one of the most definitely predictive of all the prophetic utterances of the Epistles. Apart from all problems of explanation in detail, it gives us this as its message on the whole; that there lies hidden in the future, for the race of Israel, a critical period of overwhelming blessing. If anything is revealed as fixed in the eternal plan, which, never violating the creature's will yet is not subject to it, it is this. We have heard the Apostle speak fully, and without compromise, of the sin of Israel; the hardened or paralyzed spiritual perception, the refusal to submit to pure grace, and the restless quest for a valid self-righteousness, the deep exclusive arrogance. And thus the promise of coming mercy, such as shall surprise the world, sounds all the more sovereign and magnificent. . . . a

vast and comparatively sudden awakening of Israel, by the grace of God, however brought to bear. . . .

    That time of great and manifest grace shall be the occasion to Israel of the shock, as it were, of blessing; and from Israel's blessing shall date an unmeasured further access of divine good for the world. As we pass, let us observe the light thrown by these sentences on the duty of the Church in evangelizing the Gentiles for the Jews, as well as the Jews for the Gentiles. *Both* holy enterprises have a destined effect outside themselves. . . .

    We are not obliged to press the word "all" to a rigid literality. Nor are we obliged to limit the crisis of blessing to anything like a moment of time. But we may surely gather that the numbers blessed will be at least the vast majority, and that the work will not be chronic but critical. A transition, relatively swift and wonderful, shall show the world a nation penitent, faithful, holy, given to God.[7]

Think of it! There are approximately 15 million Jews throughout the world, according to the Jewish Statistical Bureau. If Dr. Moule is correct, then many of these, according to Paul, will turn to Christ in one vast movement which must yet be in the future.

Today's Jews are scattered around the world. North America has by far the largest concentration, about 6,000,000. Europe has about 4,000,000. Israel has about 3,200,000. Central and South America have about 800,000. Africa has about 250,000. New York, with approximately 1,840,000 Jews, is the city with the largest concentration of Jews in the world.[8] Which of the great enclaves of present-day Judaism will lead the way in this turning to the Messiah? Will it be soon, and if so will it be the Jews of the state of Israel who, perhaps because of the threat from their surrounding enemies, turn to Christ? Or will it be the Jews of America?

We cannot tell any more than Paul reveals. But just because the details are hidden from us in the eternal plan does not indicate there is any uncertainty about the outcome. At least one more great awakening shall shake the world, and possibly more, as all of God's elect are gathered in.

---

7. Handley C. G. Moule, *The Epistle to the Romans* (London: Pickering and Inglis, 1954), pp. 308-12.
8. S. V. McCasland, G. E. Cairns, and D. C. Yu, *Religions of the World* (New York: Random House, 1969), p. 215.

Selected Bibliography

There are an enormous number of works on American religious history that touch peripherally on awakenings. In addition there are a large number of biographies on significant individuals in past awakenings. But when we come to histories of the awakenings themselves, the list becomes considerably smaller. The bibliography that follows attempts to enumerate the strictly historical works of consequence.

This bibliography includes only a small fraction of the books consulted. Many others will be found listed in the chapter footnotes. This list usually repeats only recent secondary works that contain extensive and critical introductions to the primary and secondary literature of the subjects they treat.

The history of awakenings is—with no exaggeration whatsoever—an enormously exciting and inspiring story, one having worldwide influence to this day. When we consider the intimate connections between the Evangelical Awakening of the eighteenth century and the global missionary and evangelistic thrusts of the nineteenth and twentieth centuries, which spread the gospel into most of the world, we begin to understand the incredible influence (humanly speaking) of a relatively few individuals such as Whitefield, Edwards, the Wesleys, Dwight, Finney, Moody, and so on. To study their lives and activities is certainly to view what the Holy Spirit has led His church to do in recent years. My hope is that some of the excitement will be contagious, and that those who consult these works will find themselves ennobled and challenged anew.

Ahlstrom, Sydney E. *A Religious History of the American People.* New Haven, Conn.: Yale U., 1972.

Anderson, Courtney. *To the Golden Shore: The Life of Adoniram Judson.* Boston: Little, Brown, 1956.

Beardsley, Frank G. *A History of American Revivals.* New York: American Tract Society, 1912.

Beecher, Lyman. *Autobiography of Lyman Beecher.* Edited by Barbara Cross. 2 vols. Cambridge, Mass.: Harvard U., 1961.

Boles, John R. *The Great Revival.* Lexington, Ky.: U. of Kentucky, 1972.

Brandon, Owen. *Christianity from Within.* London: Hodder and Stoughton, 1965.

Bready, J. Wesley. *England Before and After Wesley.* London: Hodder and Stoughton, 1939.

Burns, James. *Revivals: Their Laws and Leaders.* London: Hodder and Stoughton, 1909.

Bushman, Richard L., ed. *The Great Awakening: Documents on the Revival of Religion, 1740-1745.* New York: Atheneum, 1970.

Cairns, Earle E. *Saints and Society: The Social Impact of Eighteenth Century English Revivals.* Chicago: Moody, 1960.

Cartwright, Peter. *Autobiography of Peter Cartwright.* Edited by Charles L. Wallis. Nashville, Tenn.: Abingdon, 1956.

Cleveland, Catherine C. *The Great Revival in the West, 1797-1805.* Chicago: U. of Chicago, 1916.

Cole, Charles C., Jr. *The Social Ideas of the Northern Evangelists, 1826-1860.* New York: Columbia U., 1954.

Cross, Whitney R. *The Burned-over District: The Social and Intellectual History of Enthusiastic Religion in Western New York, 1800-1850.* Ithaca, N.Y.: Cornell U., 1950.

Dallimore, Arnold. *George Whitefield: The Life and Times of the Great Evangelist of the Eighteenth-Century Revival.* 2 vols. Westchester, Ill.: Cornerstone, 1980.

Elsbree, Oliver W. *The Rise of the Missionary Spirit in America, 1790-1815.* Williamsport, Pa.: Williamsport Printing Co., 1928.

Findlay, James F., Jr. *Dwight L. Moody: American Evangelist, 1837-1899.* Chicago: U. of Chicago, 1969.

Finney, Charles G. *Revivals of Religion.* Westwood, N.J.: Revell, 1951.

Gaustad, Edwin Scott. *The Great Awakening in New England.* New York: Harper & Row, 1957.

Gewehr, Wesley M. *The Great Awakening in Virginia, 1740-1790.* Durham, N.C.: Duke U., 1930.

Gillett, E. H. *History of the Presbyterian Church in the United States of America.* 2 vols. Philadelphia: Presbyterian Board of Publication, 1864.

Glover, Robert H., and Kane, J. Herbert. *The Progress of World Wide Missions.* New York: Harper, 1960.

Goen, C. C. *Revivalism and Separatism in New England: Strict Congregationalists and Separate Baptists in the Great Awakening.* New Haven, Conn.: Yale U., 1962.

Gundry, Stanley N. *Love Them In: The Proclamation Theology of D. L. Moody.* Chicago: Moody, 1976.

Halévy, Elie. *The Birth of Methodism in England.* Edited by Bernard Semmel. Chicago: U. of Chicago, 1971.

———. *England in 1815.* New York: Peter Smith, 1949.

Handy, Robert T. *A Christian America: Protestant Hopes and Historical Realities.* New York: Oxford U., 1971.

Hardman, Keith J. *Jonathan Dickinson and the Course of American Presbyterianism, 1717-1747.* Ann Arbor, Mich.: University Microfilms, 1971.

Heimert, Alan, and Miller, Perry, eds. *The Great Awakening: Documents Illustrating the Crisis and Its Consequences.* Indianapolis: Bobbs-Merrill, 1967.

Henry, Stuart C. *George Whitefield: Wayfaring Witness.* New York: Abingdon, 1957.

Hudson, Winthrop S. *Religion in America.* New York: Scribner's, 1981.

Johnson, Charles A. *The Frontier Camp Meeting: Religion's Harvest Time.* Dallas: Southern Methodist U., 1955.

Johnson, James E. *The Life of Charles Grandison Finney.* Ann Arbor, Mich.: University Microfilms, 1959.

Keller, Charles Roy. *The Second Great Awakening in Connecticut.* New Haven, Conn.: Yale U., 1942.

Latourette, Kenneth Scott. *Missions and the American Mind.* Indianapolis: Nat'l. Foundation Press, 1949.

Loetscher, Lefferts A. *The Broadening Church: A Study of Theological Issues in the Presbyterian Church Since 1869.* Philadelphia: U. of Pennsylvania, 1954.

Loud, Grover C. *Evangelized America.* Freeport, N.Y.: Books for Libraries Press, 1971.

McLoughlin, William G., Jr. *The American Evangelicals, 1800-1900: An Anthology.* New York: Harper & Row, 1968.

———. *Billy Graham: Revivalist in a Secular Age.* New York: Ronald Press, 1960.

———. *Modern Revivalism: Charles Grandison Finney to Billy Graham.* New York: Ronald Press, 1959.

———. *Revivals, Awakenings, and Reform.* Chicago: U. of Chicago, 1978.

Marsden, George M. *The Evangelical Mind and the New School Presbyterian Experience.* New Haven, Conn.: Yale U., 1970.

Marty, Martin E. *Righteous Empire: The Protestant Experience in America.* New York: Dial, 1970.

Maxson, Charles H. *The Great Awakening in the Middle Colonies.* Chicago: U. of Chicago, 1920.

Miller, Perry. *Jonathan Edwards.* New York: William Sloan Assoc., 1949.

Murray, Iain H. *The Puritan Hope: A Study in Revival and the Interpretation of Prophecy.* London: Banner of Truth, 1971.

Niebuhr, H. Richard. *The Kingdom of God in America.* New York: Harper & Brothers, 1937.

Orr, J. Edwin. *The Eager Feet.* Chicago: Moody, 1975.

———. *The Fervent Prayer.* Chicago: Moody, 1974.

———. *The Flaming Tongue.* Chicago: Moody, 1973.

———. *The Second Evangelical Awakening in America.* London: Marshall, Morgan & Scott, 1952.

Rosell, Garth. *Charles G. Finney and the Rise of the Benevolence Empire.* Ann Arbor, Mich.: University Microfilms, 1971.

Smith, H. Shelton; Handy, Robert T.; and Loetscher, Lefferts A. *American Christianity: An Historical Interpretation with Representative Documents.* 2 vols. New York: Scribner's, 1960-1963.

Smith, Timothy L. *Revivalism and Social Reform in Mid-Nineteenth-Century America.* Nashville: Abingdon, 1957.

Sprague, William B. *Lectures on Revivals of Religion.* Edinburgh: Banner of Truth, 1958.

Sweet, William W., ed. Religion on the American Frontier series. Vol. 1: *The Baptists.* New York: Holt, 1931. Vol. 2: *The Presbyterians.* New York: Harper & Brothers, 1936. Vol. 3: *The Congregationalists.* Chicago: U. of Chicago, 1939. Vol. 4: *The Methodists.* Chicago: U. of Chicago, 1946.

_____. *Revivalism in America: Its Origin, Growth, and Decline.* New York: Scribner's, 1944.

Tanis, James R. *Dutch Calvinistic Pietism in the Middle Colonies: A Study in the Life of Theodorus Jacobus Frelinghuysen.* The Hague: Martinus Nijhof, 1967.

Tracy, Joseph. *The Great Awakening: A History of the Revival of Religion in the Time of Edwards and Whitefield.* Boston: Tappan and Dennet, 1842.

Trinterud, Leonard J. *The Forming of an American Tradition: A Re-examination of Colonial Presbyterianism.* Philadelphia: Westminster, 1949.

Tyerman, Luke. *The Life of the Rev. George Whitefield, B.A., of Pembroke College, Oxford.* 2 vols. New York: Harper and Brothers, 1877.

Weisberger, Bernard A. *They Gathered at the River: The Story of the Great Revivalists and Their Impact upon Religion in America.* Boston: Little, Brown, 1958.

Whitefield, George. *Journals (1737-1741), to Which Is Prefixed His "Short Account" (1746) and "Further Account" (1747).* Gainesville, Fla.: Scholars' Facsimilies and Reprints, 1969.

Woodbridge, John D.; Noll, Mark A.; and Hatch, Nathan O. *The Gospel in America: Themes in the Story of America's Evangelicals.* Grand Rapids, Mich.: Zondervan, 1979.

Wright, Conrad. *The Beginnings of Unitarianism.* Boston: Beacon, 1955.

Index